RATIONAL CHOICE AND DEMOCRATIC GOVERNMENT

Drawing on a range of data from across disciplines, this book explores a series of fundamental questions surrounding the nature, working and effects of democracy, considering the reasons for the emergence and spread of democratic government, the conditions under which it endures or collapses – and the role of wealth in this process – and the peaceful nature of dealings between democracies. With emphasis on the 'ordinary' voter, the author employs rational choice theory to examine the motivations of voters and their levels of political knowledge and rationality, as well as the special interests, incentives and corruption of politicians. A theoretically informed and empirically illustrated study of the birth and downfall of democracies, the extent of voters' political knowledge and ignorance, the logic of political behaviour in both open and closed regimes, and the international effects of democratic rule, *Rational Choice and Democratic Government: A Sociological Approach* will appeal to scholars with interests in political sociology, political psychology, economics and political science.

Tibor Rutar is Assistant Professor in the Department of Sociology at the University of Maribor, Slovenia.

ROUTLEDGE STUDIES IN POLITICAL SOCIOLOGY

Brains, Media and Politics
Generating Neoliberal Subjects
Rodolfo Leyva

The New Demagogues
Religion, Masculinity and the Populist Epoch
Joshua Roose

The Political Attitudes of Divided European Citizens
Public Opinion and Social Inequalities in Comparative and Relational Perspective
Christian Lahusen

The Contentious Politics of Expertise
Experts, Activism and Grassroots Environmentalism
Riccardo Emilio Chesta

Comparing and Contrasting the Impact of the COVID-19 Pandemic in the European Union
Linda Hantrais and Marie-Thérèse Letablier

Masochistic Nationalism
Multicultural Self-Hatred and the Infatuation with the Exotic
Goran Adamson

Rational Choice and Democratic Government
A Sociological Approach
Tibor Rutar

For a full list of titles in this series, please visit: https://www.routledge.com/sociology/series/RSPS

RATIONAL CHOICE AND DEMOCRATIC GOVERNMENT

A Sociological Approach

Tibor Rutar

First published 2022
by Routledge
2 Park Square, Milton Park, Abingdon, Oxon OX14 4RN

and by Routledge
605 Third Avenue, New York, NY 10158

Routledge is an imprint of the Taylor & Francis Group, an informa business

© 2022 Tibor Rutar

The right of Tibor Rutar to be identified as author of this work has been asserted by him in accordance with sections 77 and 78 of the Copyright, Designs and Patents Act 1988.

All rights reserved. No part of this book may be reprinted or reproduced or utilised in any form or by any electronic, mechanical, or other means, now known or hereafter invented, including photocopying and recording, or in any information storage or retrieval system, without permission in writing from the publishers.

Trademark notice: Product or corporate names may be trademarks or registered trademarks, and are used only for identification and explanation without intent to infringe.

British Library Cataloguing-in-Publication Data
A catalogue record for this book is available from the British Library

Library of Congress Cataloging-in-Publication Data
Names: Rutar, Tibor, 1989- author.
Title: Rational choice and democratic government : a sociological approach / Tibor Rutar.
Description: Milton Park, Abingdon, Oxon ; New York, NY : Routledge, 2021. | Includes bibliographical references and index.
Identifiers: LCCN 2021013575 (print) | LCCN 2021013576 (ebook) | ISBN 9781032000657 (hardback) | ISBN 9781032000688 (paperback) | ISBN 9781003172574 (ebook)
Subjects: LCSH: Democracy--Social aspects.
Classification: LCC JC423 .R88 2021 (print) | LCC JC423 (ebook) | DDC 306.2--dc23
LC record available at https://lccn.loc.gov/2021013575
LC ebook record available at https://lccn.loc.gov/2021013576

ISBN: 978-1-032-00065-7 (hbk)
ISBN: 978-1-032-00068-8 (pbk)
ISBN: 978-1-003-17257-4 (ebk)

DOI: 10.4324/9781003172574

Typeset in Bembo
by Taylor & Francis Books

CONTENTS

List of figures   *vi*

1 Against romanticizing democracy   1
2 Wealth – the path to freedom?   21
3 Voters are not dumb, but we do not know much   57
4 Politicians are people, not angels   84
5 For and against democratic peace   108
6 Conclusion: Fukuyama's 'The End of History?' in social scientific retrospective   130

Bibliography   *137*
Index   *149*

FIGURES

1.1	The number of electoral and liberal democracies in the world, 1900–2000	2
1.2	Share of democratic ('free') countries in the world, 2006–2019	3
1.3	Average rate of freedom in the world, 2006–2019	4
1.4	Democracy score in the US, 2010–2018	4
1.5	Share of democratic ('free') countries in the world, 1980–2019	5
1.6	Average rate of freedom in the world, 1985–2019	6

1
AGAINST ROMANTICIZING DEMOCRACY

Introduction: the historical peculiarity of mass democracy

Life in a stable, cushy liberal democracy is taken more or less for granted by many people in the West. Not only that, we tend to assume without questioning the moral superiority of democracy over other political regimes.

Our obliviousness to how weird and uncommon democracy in general, and liberal democracy in particular, has actually been in human civilization is in one sense not very surprising, as most Western countries have simply not experienced any other form of government in decades. Multiple generations have grown up in consolidated democracies. Likewise, the moral status we ascribe to this system is, on the face of it, quite deserved. Liberal democracies provide the most expansive and robust political and civil rights in the world. The former include such seemingly obvious amenities as free and fair elections, the right to assembly, and a realistic chance of opposition winning in electoral competitions. The latter encompass fundamental rights of free and independent media, of freely practising one's religion (or nonreligious beliefs), of free expression in general, the rule of law, and so on. However, when stepping back a bit and taking a more historical perspective, we immediately and quite painfully come to recognize that none of this is as obvious, self-evident, or secure as it might at first seem.

The first observation about the obviousness of democracy is, as I have already intimated, the quickest to collapse. Even though it is true that today many parts of the world (not relegated solely to the West) are filled almost to the brim with democracies, these regimes nevertheless represent less than 50% of all countries and less than 40% of the world's population.[1] Most people, even today, still live in non-liberal and simply non-democratic, i.e. autocratic, regimes. Furthermore, mass democracy appears as an even scarcer and more fragile phenomenon if we look back in time. Since the emergence of first pockets of human civilization around 5,000 years ago and right up until the late 19th century, illiberal autocracy was

DOI: 10.4324/9781003172574-1

practically the only ubiquitous way in which states were governed. So, both spatially and temporally liberal democracy is the opposite of being obvious or given. It is a great, massive exception.

Of course, the fact that until very recently almost all *states* were authoritarian does not mean that all *societies* for the past few thousand years had also suffered the same fate. There existed quite a few 'early democracies', as David Stasavage has called them.[3] These were almost without exception relegated to small-scale tribal societies, such as the Iroquois and Huron Indians, or the Germanic tribes in Europe. Moreover, they were very different from the more familiar mass representative, rights-protected democratic regimes of the modern era. To take just one important difference, there were no formal elections of leaders and universal adult suffrage was absent. What usually happened is that the leaders had to consult with, and thus yield some decision-making power to, local councils or assemblies. Even the most well-known case of early democracy, that of Ancient Athens, which was truly exceptional in the extent to which power was shared with, and ordinary people participated in, the assemblies, nevertheless remained small-scale compared to neighbouring regions. We should also not forget that it was not even a question whether women and slaves could enjoy the same civil and political right that men did.

To anticipate a major theme of the book, these exceptions to the general rule of historical authoritarianism in state societies might seem to some to invalidate one of my central claims, which is that rulers primarily do what benefits them and that they are reluctant to share power with others. In fact, they do not invalidate it. It is precisely the small-scale nature of previous examples, or the leader's need to create a popular army (Athens), or the necessity of gathering local-level economic information for purposes of taxation – information that can only be reliably provided by community councils –, that are responsible for the leaders' *reluctant* decision to relinquish some of their power to the people.[4] In sum, democratic states are not the natural form of large-scale human civilization.

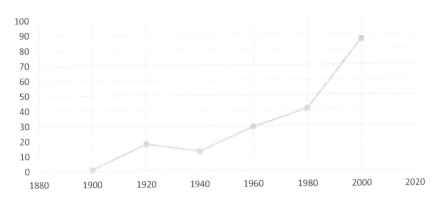

FIGURE 1.1 The number of electoral and liberal democracies in the world, 1900–2000
Source: OurWorldInData[2]

But what if we limit our gaze to the 21st century? Surely today, as we have already seen, things are different than in the past. State-mandated bondage is much less common than it once was. Political freedom is much more widespread. Mass democracies are finally flowering all over the world. Even here, however, there is no automaticity and obviousness.

In the last 14 years, since 2006, the world's democratic share has actually declined. In 2006, Freedom House counted almost 47% of all existing countries as 'free'. By 2018 this had dropped to 44%. And we are not only talking about one peculiar year here but a larger trend. A trend which, if we take account of the latest data, has turned for the worse and became somewhat worrying. In 2019, the share of 'free' countries dipped a further one-and-a-half percentage points to 42.5%. Freedom House classifies all countries as fitting one of their three master categories: 'free', 'partly free', and 'unfree'. The 'free' include all liberal democracies and a few non-liberal, electoral democracies that are nevertheless close to being liberal. The remaining two categories capture all other weaker non-liberal, electoral democracies, and all non-democratic, straightforwardly autocratic systems.

This 'democratic recession', as Larry Diamond has termed the phenomenon, does not only mean that democracies in the 21st century are vanishing but also touches upon the degree of freedom in the world more generally (see Figure 1.3; higher score denotes lower quality of freedom and fewer rights).[6] In the past decade and a half, political and civil rights have been diminishing all over the world and in *all sorts of regimes*. Freedom has been on a downward slide both in older, consolidated democracies, such as the United States of America, as well as in autocratic states the likes of Russia and China.

Even if we only focus, laser-like, solely on the *West in the 21st century*, liberal democracy is still not wholly obvious. Two trends are most important in this regard. The first concerns the degree of political and civil rights in long-standing democracies, which has taken a hit in the past few years. Of the 41 states that

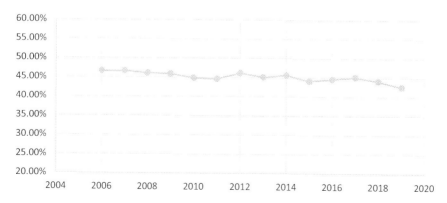

FIGURE 1.2 Share of democratic ('free') countries in the world, 2006–2019
Source: Freedom House[5]

4 Against romanticizing democracy

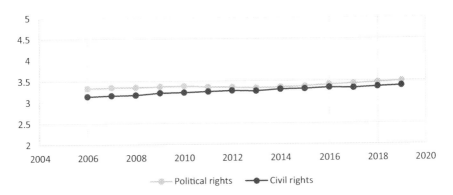

FIGURE 1.3 Average rate of freedom in the world, 2006–2019
Source: Freedom House (higher score means less freedom)

Freedom House consistently tagged as 'free' between 1985 and 2005, 22 have seen their democracy score go down in the mid 2010s. The most salient case is the United States, the oldest liberal democracy in the world. In 2010, the US scored 94 (out of 100), while today it hovers around 86 (see Figure 1.4).

The second trend has to do with the shift in beliefs of ordinary people in the West regarding how pleased they are with living in a democracy as well as how important such a regime is for them. In 12 Western countries, younger generations of people – those born in the 1970s and 1980s – have lower approval rates of living in a democracy than older generations. In 18 Western countries, youth thinks of democracy as less important than older people – those born in 1930s, 1940s, and 1950s. Both trends are in effect in, for example, Slovenia, Australia, Canada, Cyprus, Japan, the US, Britain, and Norway.[7]

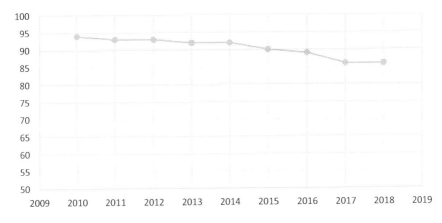

FIGURE 1.4 Democracy score in the US, 2010–2018
Source: Freedom House

Even so, we should be careful with how we think about this. Some researchers who study the democratic recession and wax apocalyptic about it tend to exaggerate its extent.[8] I think they are wont to forget at least three important empirical facts and one theoretical, or methodological, point. The facts are that, first, even though today there are fewer democracies in the world than 14 years ago – and not just one or two fewer – it might still be too early to say that the drop was extremely dramatic (see Figure 1.2). In fact, putting the year 2019 aside for a moment, the share of democracies had quite consistently hovered around 46 % and 44 % since 2006. We shall see what the years 2020 and 2021 bring. A further deepening of the recession, stalling, or perhaps a reverse?

Second, and more importantly, if we compare the number of contemporary democracies with that of the late 1980s or even the early 1990s, we clearly see that the state of democracy today is still happier than it was then – even including the year 2019 (see Figure 1.5). The same goes for the average rate of freedom in the world (see Figure 1.6).

Third, the decline in attitudinal approval and importance of democracy among the youth is statistically significant only in some countries and not others. For example, the approval of democracy is down only in *half* of the Western countries considered by that study.[9] Furthermore, we need to remind ourselves that the current generations of young people have, on average, much more liberal attitudes compared to the youth from previous periods.[10] According to a recent study of policy ideology among European mass publics, attitudes regarding homosexuality, abortion, women's emancipation, immigration, etc., have been shifting in a more liberal direction since the 1980s – most markedly in young people.[11] I gather from this that even though today's youth is, in some countries, less thrilled about democracy – what is at least partially a function of them not experiencing anything else and taking it for granted – their other attitudes about human rights are shifting *away* from those of would-be authoritarian leaders or their supporters.

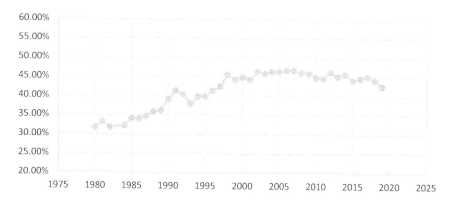

FIGURE 1.5 Share of democratic ('free') countries in the world, 1980–2019
Source: Freedom House

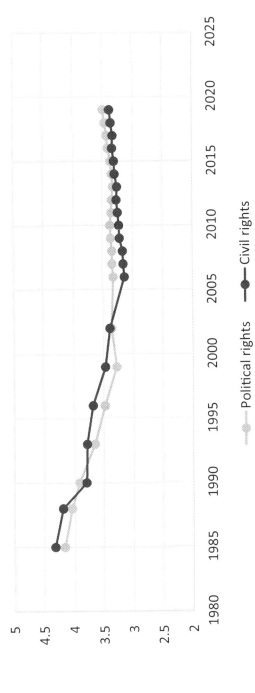

FIGURE 1.6 Average rate of freedom in the world, 1985–2019
Source: Freedom House (higher score means less freedom)

But to my mind the most important point is theoretical – one that will act as a guiding thread for the next chapter and the book as a whole. The democratic recession can be seen as catastrophic, inexplicable, and fundamentally disconcerting primarily by those who either knowingly or not subscribe to a particular, naïve theory of democratization which turns out on closer inspection to be fatally flawed. There are at least two general forms this theory can take.

According to one telling, the forward march of democracy throughout the world in the 20th century has been something almost akin to a natural force, all but inexorably bearing down on everything in its path. With the rise of Reason and Enlightenment in the previous centuries, so the story goes, democracy as an idea has finally had the chance to germinate and spread first in Europe and then elsewhere, being adopted by political elites, intellectuals, merchants, city-dwellers and so on. Now it is expected, sooner rather than later, that it should take hold virtually across the world and, once established in practice, put to rest other bad political ideas and experiments. Democratic government was only a matter of humans reaching their intellectual maturity.

The other story has it that the period between 1989 and 1991 was somehow a historical turning point which, after we had crossed it, should – again – sooner rather than later lead to the triumphant democratic dismantling of dictatorships across the world. This variant of the theory similarly holds that, once established, democracies should be virtually impregnable, held up as they are by the progressive sweep of history. In consolidated democracies, a variety of 'democratic norms' quickly becomes ingrained, through cultural socialization, in people's minds, practically guaranteeing that major democratic recessions do not occur.

Those who at least implicitly believe in stories like this (and not many would defend them explicitly today) are likely to be shocked, disappointed, and deeply concerned about the future. 'The theory is plausible,' they think to themselves – or, rather, feel. 'How, then, is it possible that this calamity happened? There must be some mistake, a weird anomaly throwing a right-wing populist wrench into our democratic gears. If only, say, populism had been prevented, then the recession would not have happened.' To the contrary. The democratic recession is surprising or anomalous only if we subscribe to a particularly optimistic theory that does not come close to capturing the truth. It is neither unusual, nor necessarily deeply worrying, that the growth of democracy across the world came to a halt and even reversed somewhat. And even though populists definitely contribute their fair share to the phenomenon, the recession would have been likely and unsurprising even without them. There are other, more run-of-the-mill social-structural reasons, and even ones having to do with certain natural, spontaneous tendencies of human nature, for why democracies are so stubborn to appear, spread, and consolidate.

Romanticists, Utopians, and activists

Both when lay people as well as intellectuals talk about democracy and democratic institutions – or politics in general – there are at least three general, prevailing modes of reasoning in which they tend to engage and against which the tone of this book is set.

First up are the *romanticists*. They implicitly, unwittingly romanticize politics in their heads and are, therefore, often surprised and indignant by its boorish real-world dynamic. The basic logic underlying their reasoning can be illustrated as follows. 'How is it possible – or, what is wrong with us – that our country constantly experiences corruption and houses selfish politicians who do not primarily care about the public good? How is this possible, when we all know that *real politicians* are not like that but are instead well and morally educated and have unflinching personalities due to which they are concerned with the welfare of others, not themselves, and thus *real democracy* is the embodiment of the public good?' The problem here is not that romanticists possess no theory of democracy. Rather, it is that they have a bad and usually only half worked-out, implicit theory the assumptions of which they are not even fully aware. This theory misconstrues the actual behaviour of politicians (and voters) to such an extent that the real world which we all experience almost always turns out to be quite different from the theory, producing seeming anomalies, surprises, and shocking events. That is why romanticists, some of whom are close to me personally and others that I regularly come to know through the classroom, are time and again honestly shocked when listening to the news, hearing about either voter irrationality (Trump, Bolsonaro, Orbán, Brexit, etc.) or political misdeeds (corruption, lies, selfishness, clientelism, etc.).

Then, secondly, we have *utopians*. They intentionally avoid dealing with how the real world works and instead come up with ways of thinking how an ideal world, one without institutional or human-nature constraints, might look like. The logic underlying their reasoning looks a bit like this, 'It is not all that important how currently existing institutions work or why they have been formed, nor is it truly important how we might be able to reform them in a reasonable amount of time with a realistic assessment of the situation. Further, it does not concern us what is likely to happen with our current institutions in circumstances A, B, or C, and which institutions are likely to replace them in conditions X, Y, or Z. What interests us are all the ways we might creatively dream up an ideal situation far off in the future. For example, just imagine how good democratic institutions might be if voters were wholly informed and responsible, while politicians renounced their self-seeking at the same time.'

Lastly, we come to the *activists*. They have firm political ideals – like many of us do – that they are ready to defend at all costs. When thinking about how politics works, they do not actively strive, not even for a moment, to step back from their ideals and come to an assessment somewhat impartially. The logic underlying their reasoning is notably different from the one employed by utopians, even though both are motivated by a similar, *evaluative* (not so much a descriptive social-scientific) goal. The difference is that utopians do not even make contact with the empirical reality, which is after all not the task they have set up themselves with, while activists definitely do mobilize facts (or ostensible facts) when reasoning but not in a way we would expect a social scientist to do. Drawing on my own experience as a (hopefully former) activist and thinking of some not all that pleasant exchanges with a few of my peers, a brief illustration would look as follows. 'I cannot stand these liberal-democratic institutions, tainted as they are by their bourgeois, capitalist, and Western-imperialist origins, which is why I will *a priori* dispute theories – not really examining their arguments and purported evidence – that show democracies tend not to fight wars among each other in virtue of their underlying structure. I do not really want this to be true, so it cannot be true.' The disapproval of democratic institutions in this illustration can, of course, be swapped out with the rejection of authoritarian institutions, or whatever else. 'Because I hate illiberal, non-democratic authoritarian regimes I simply cannot believe that they are able to economically develop – perhaps even faster or more robustly than democracies – which is why I will reject such theories out of hand, paying no attention to arguments and data.'

A fundamental assumption I make in the book is that all three ways of reasoning which I have stylized are wrong, if our goal is to get at how democratic countries really work in the here and now. That is why I will strive to avoid them and will, hopefully, pursue a fourth and more realistic way that might be simply called *democracy without the romance*. Of course, I do not mean to suggest that I am free from biases, errors, or (unwitting) romanticism. What, then, do I mean?

First, even though I myself live, and am very happy to be living, in a liberal democracy, some of my conclusions regarding the emergence, operation, and effects of this system are less rosy and triumphant than is common for people steeped in a democratic culture. For example, in contrast to social scientists like Steven Pinker, I will argue in chapter 2 that democracy does not simply emerge after the political elite has been properly enlightened and its members have recognized the gross error of their former dictatorial ways.[12] From the elite point of view, democracy is typically not the rational way of governing. That is why, as we shall see, democracies usually had to be, and still have to be, fought for by the common people from below and *against* the 'better judgement' of the elite classes. Moreover, although I conclude in chapter 5 that the democratic peace thesis holds, I will find – again in contrast to Pinker and other liberal institutionalists – the proposed theoretical mechanisms for the fact that democracies do not fight each other to be less than firm.[13] Additionally, we shall see in chapter 3 that the democratic system erects a perverse incentive structure which makes it irrational for voters to deeply educate themselves on political matters before casting a vote. Political ignorance is thus a pervasive phenomenon in developed democracies and there is precious little hope of this changing in the future. There will be still more talk about less than optimal incentive structures when, in chapter 4, we analyse how government officials, and politicians in general, act in democracies.

Second, I claim to examine democratic politics without romanticism because my explanations are based on those behavioural (or better yet, *motivational*) assumptions about politicians and other relevant actors that I take to be both consistent and approximately realistic. That is to say, I do not suppose political actors are primarily motivated by vastly different concerns than are those we all very well know motivate economic actors in market affairs. Instead of implausibly assuming most politicians are primarily driven by altruism and the public interest in their political pursuits, I take them to be primarily, although for sure not exclusively, concerned with their own welfare (in the form of power, money, and status) and with that of people close to them, be it family or close friends.[14] Note that this does not mean politicians are expected to generate solely results that go against the public interest. There is an important difference between what *motivates* them and how they *behave* in the end. Selfish motivations that are properly institutionally constrained can produce the public good, as Adam Smith famously (or infamously, depending on the political perspective) captured with his metaphor of the invisible hand. Sometimes the most self-interested thing to do is to cater to other people that you do not know and do not personally care about, but on whose goodwill you still somehow depend, be they customers or the electorate.

In employing these basic assumptions, and seeing where they lead, I follow an important although retrospectively quite obvious strain of economic and political-science thinking called *public choice theory*, or simply *political economy*. James Buchanan, who in 1986 received the Nobel Memorial Prize in Economics for his contribution to this body of theory, his collaborator Gordon Tullock, Anthony Downs, and Duncan Black are perhaps the most well-known founders of political economy.[15] Just as important, however, is Mancur Olson's contribution whose claim to fame is his theory of collective action problems.[16] Another winner of the Nobel Prize is the economist Kenneth Arrow who has also indirectly contributed to public choice.[17]

I am a sociologist, and it might seem from what you just read that I have sadly succumbed to the dreaded 'economics imperialism', the odious notion – especially in the eyes of sociologists and anthropologists – that all social sciences should be based on the 'economic way of thinking', or rational choice theory. In fact, as will be seen, I do not wholly subscribe to rational choice analysis, and I am aware of, and have even written quite extensively on, its limitations. I will address them in the next section. Consider first, however, that sociologists are substantively no strangers to the motivational assumption of public choice, or the so-called 'economic way of thinking' in general, notwithstanding the usual ritualistic song and dance we perform denouncing it. Here is one of the most important historical sociologists of the second half of the 20th century, Charles Tilly:

> At least for the European experience of the past few centuries, a portrait of war makers and state makers as coercive and self-seeking entrepreneurs bears a far greater resemblance to the facts than do its chief alternatives: the idea of a social contract, the idea of an open market in which operators of armies and states offer services to willing consumers, the idea of a society whose shared norms and expectations call forth a certain kind of government.[18]

Another great historical sociologist in this period, Michael Mann, based his whole widely used four-volume magnum opus *The Sources of Social Power* on the rationality assumption: 'human beings are restless, purposive, and rational, striving to increase their enjoyment of the good things in life and capable of choosing and pursuing appropriate means for doing so.'[19] The classics, Karl Marx and Max

Weber, were no strangers to it either, with Marx perhaps independently discovering the game-theoretic logic of 'social dilemmas', where the rational actions of individuals lead to irrational collective outcomes, and Weber – a firm methodological individualist – employing what he called 'instrumental rationality' as the major explanatory resource in his scholarly exploits.[20] The list of path-breaking sociological works (implicitly) undergirded by the rationality assumption, not even including other luminary rational choice sociologists such as James Coleman, John Goldthorpe, Diego Gambetta, or Raymond Boudon, could get quite boringly long.[21]

Theoretical framework

I can summarize the basic building blocks of the book's theoretical approach through four simple points.

> 1 *Complete explanations of social phenomena and their change require that we provide microfoundations for them.*

The purpose of social-scientific theories is to explain how one social phenomenon leads to a second one. And there is only one way anything social happens – through the actions taken by people. Stipulating a causal connection between two macrosocial phenomena, for example, economic development and democratization, is therefore not an explanation in itself, but rather the very thing that needs to be explained. It screams out for microfoundations or, what is the same, for an underlying behavioural mechanism upholding the macrosocial connection. The question is, *how precisely* economic development unleashes democracy. How do people act when experiencing economic development, and why do they act that way? Why and how does that set of actions, influenced as it was by the surrounding social environment, produce a democratic transition? To answer these questions, we need a microtheory of human behaviour. Mind you, this requirement of microfounded explanations is synonymous with methodological *individualism*, not methodological *atomism*. I do not think people should be theoretically treated as isolated monads who are oblivious to the influence of other people and the broader social environment. Quite the opposite.

> 2 *The average person is responsive to incentives, and the way in which they respond to them, especially when a lot is at stake, is primarily (but not exclusively) self-interested.*

If a certain choice A – say, being submissive to a ruler – is more beneficial to a person than choice B – resisting the ruler – the person will likely opt for A over B. If a course of action X – say, fleeing the country – hurts the person less than the opposite course of action Y – staying put – they will more likely choose X. Put slightly differently, when people are materially or psychologically rewarded for a behaviour and draw benefits from it, they are likely to pursue it. If they are punished and suffer costs, they will tend to avoid it.

I experience how powerfully incentives shape human behaviour every year in my classes. When I suggest extra homework to my students without also stipulating that their final grades will suffer or improve accordingly, all those who are not intrinsically motivated by the prospect of extra school work (and the number of such students is much higher than I would hope) invariably fail to follow my request. Of course, those who simply love reading and writing will tend to do it without any external nudges and incentives. However, when I decide to sanction good and bad homework behaviour, the papers of all of the students are virtually always turned in, regardless of how personally fond they are of my task.

As we shall see in more detail in the following chapters, 'rewards' and 'punishments' – incentives – in the social world need not be, though they often are, explicit sanctions that are actively created and distributed by a person or a group of people. Instead, they can be the effects of various particular distributions of resources, social institutions, and the more general social environment in which people act.

3   *Institutions (and social circumstances in general) determine the incentives which people face.*[22]

Institutions or other circumstances due to which people have a harder time achieving their goals, or that make it costlier for them to pursue those goals, discourage action by creating disincentives. Those that work the other way around are encouraging behaviour by generating positive incentives. But what, exactly, are institutions? They are both formal and informal rules – so, laws and norms – that regulate the functioning of a given social situation. The key feature of institutions is that they reliably work only if someone is enforcing them. Without that, they usually lose their power over behaviour. In sum, institutions are the rules of the game that enable, prevent, encourage, and discourage how people act. The rules on my class syllabus are a mini-institution which, if I enforce it, students take into account when strategizing how they will behave in my class.

A classic historical-sociological example of how institutions determine incentives is capitalism. Before the emergence of modern economic institutions, such as secure property rights and market competition, most economic actors did not have the incentives to invest their wealth into production and thus generate more wealth, because they knew their newly found riches were likely to be expropriated away by powerful landlords or kings. Even on the eve of the French Revolution property rights and other modern economic institutions were so sorely lacking in France that the state of its economy was, by a variety of measures, similar to how it had been three centuries prior.[23]

4.   *When explaining cases of socially pernicious behaviour, we should not assume right away that people are evil, ideologically blinded, or stupid. Rather, the initial assumption is that people simply want more of the good life, and that the perniciousness of their behaviour is the unintended consequence of their actual goal.*

Bad social outcomes tend to result from the actions of *ordinary* people with *ordinary* motivations – say, protecting and improving your own position and that of your family and close friends – who unfortunately are facing *bad* incentives. Good institutions are those that align, as much as possible, the private interests of individuals with the social interest, thus generating good incentives. Bad institutions decouple the public good from the personal good, creating bad incentives and (perhaps unintendedly) encouraging bad behaviour that makes a given person better-off, while others are left out to dry.

This problem is especially acute in situations that are structured as an 'n-person social dilemma'. Sometimes the circumstances people find themselves in are such that any one person has the chance to improve their own position without (individually) hurting anyone else, even though all will suffer if *everyone* acts self-interestedly. An individual is very much tempted to act this way, the more so because he knows that *whatever he personally* decides will not help or hurt anyone, but it can benefit him. The standard model of such a social dilemma is the *tragedy of the commons*.[24] Real-world examples abound. To take just one, overfishing is a bad outcome resulting from the fact that each individual fisherman has an incentive to take as many fish as possible for himself, not really hurting anyone else's catch due to the ocean's vastness, but because *every* fisherman has that same incentive and acts accordingly, the individually marginal effects collectively add up. Over time, the stock of fish collapses, fish being unable to reproduce fast enough, and everyone is made worse-off than if people had just restricted somewhat their collective use of the resource. Individual rationality produced collective irrationality.

The preceding four theoretical principles constitute rational choice theory as I see it. This theory is a standard approach in economics, political science, and international relations, but much maligned in my home discipline of sociology. There exists, even in sociology, a vast specialist literature insightfully expounding on the intricacies, the twists and turns, of the theory.[25] I, myself, have contributed to the literature.[26] For present purposes, though, I will focus solely on rebutting a few popular, but wrongheaded, criticisms of the rational choice approach, and on some of its actual important limitations. The theory is definitely limited, because, as is the case with every useful social science framework, it intentionally abstracts away many details of the real world. After all, simplification – through mental abstraction – of the immensely complex social reality is the key purpose and quality of any theory. There is simply too much stuff to mentally get any grip on how the world works otherwise. Moreover, many factors and characteristics are not even relevant for understanding a given phenomenon.

For example, the hair colour, or sex or language, of Bolshevik revolutionaries in 1917 has no place in a robust explanation of the October Revolution, and neither does Russia's early 20th century architecture, its geographic location, or cuisine. These characteristics are simply causally irrelevant for explaining an event such as the October Revolution. Social science theories are like maps. If they completely coincide with the real world, not strongly abstracting away many of its less relevant features, they are not very useful tools for (explanatory or predictive) navigation through the world. Of course, if we abstract away *too much*, or ignore precisely those parts that matter crucially, that is a problem. The theoretical explanation will be misleading and even false. Every theory, not just rational choice, faces this issue. Even the best theories will generate false explanations or will be unable to provide proper explanations for some phenomena. The only question is how many phenomena like this a theory encounters, and how important they are.

With that out of the way, here are three popular critiques of the rational choice approach:

i   the theory wrongly ignores how the social context, i.e. social structures, institutions, and interactions between people, affect behaviour;
ii the theory wrongly bases itself on the outdated positivist philosophy of science;
iii the theory wrongly recommends greed and normative individualism.

The first critique is quite obviously false as social structures are precisely the factor that generates the incentives to which, according to the theory, people respond. Without institutional incentives the theory would become explanatorily toothless. Moreover, not only does rational choice analysis not ignore the fact that people interact, but rather this fact is a core premise on which one of its more technical tools, *game theory*, depends. The original inventors of game theory, John von Neumann and Oscar Morgenstern, created it with the sole intention of analysing people's strategic choices which – being strategic – could not happen without the presence and interaction of other people.

The second critique can, in principle, hold water. Like any theory, rational choice can be grounded in virtually any philosophy of science. Positivism is certainly one possibility. But other examples are quite plausible as well. Today, many adherents of rational choice in sociology hold to a realist, not positivist, philosophy of science.[27] What is the difference? In contrast to positivism, realism does not commit one to believing in the existence of universal, exception-less covering laws that are, as critics rightly allege, nowhere to be found in the social world, and perhaps not even in the natural domain.[28] A general, vanilla commitment to the existence of causality is all that is demanded. Furthermore, realism does not abide by what is sometimes called 'instrumentalism'. This is a positivist belief holding that, when testing theoretical proposals, one only needs to concern oneself with examining whether the prediction turned out to be correct, paying no mind to how correct the underlying assumptions of the theory are.[29] Realist philosophy of science demands of us that we empirically justify both our assumptions and testable implications flowing from our assumptions.

The third critique wrongly elides the distinction between the descriptive and the normative, between describing something and valuing it. Rational choice theory is a *descriptive* theory purporting how the social world works. It has no necessary logical link to *normative* prescriptions about how the world should work, what political ideology a researcher should adopt, whether she should be more altruistic, etc. What there is, or what we think there is, does not allow us to deduce what there should be, or what we think there should be.

Now, how about the real limitations of the theory? Its first important shortcoming is that people sometimes behave without thinking, simply unconsciously executing a habit or following a norm. This means that individuals are not always responsive to incentives, not paying attention to the costs and benefits of different possible courses of action. A simple example is a guy going to the same store he is used to, year after year, even though right beside it a new store has opened up whose staff are just as friendly and welcoming but the goods they sell are even cheaper and of higher quality. To make the example clearer, let us assume that the guy has no special attachment to the old store, which might otherwise incentivize him to keep visiting it. No, over time he has simply formed a strong unconscious habit of going to the old store without thinking about it, and so now when a new and better option appears he is not taking it. Note, however, that this limitation of the theory is not as all-encompassing as it might seem. People's obliviousness to incentives varies with certain conditions. Unthinking habits are more likely controlling behaviour when not much is at stake. I will say more on that in chapters 3 and 4.

A second limitation of the theory is that not *all* people are self-interested, nor are they *always* or *completely* selfish. Here, we should be wary of pressing this point too much. Looking only at the most giving nations in the world, we see that people, on average, contribute only about 2–3% of their annual income to charity. Moreover, in the US, which is one of the most volunteering nations in the world, only a quarter of the population engages in regular volunteer work. The average time spent volunteering by this minority group is roughly an hour per week, while the average time working for oneself amounts to around 40–50 hours per week.[30] Still, it is certainly correct that self-interest is far from the only guiding thread of human life. That means that rational choice analysis, as I apply it, will be unable to cover all cases of human behaviour.

Another limitation stems from the fact that, even when responsive to incentives, people are not always informed about all the incentives they face. Sometimes a person does not *know* that, given all the circumstances in which they have found themselves, a different decision would be more appropriate in pursuing their given goal. This can happen either due to human fallibility or due to only partially gathering information, as information-seeking itself carries with it costs and benefits that one strives to balance.

The last limitation I shall mention here is that human decision-making is sometimes strongly influenced by various psychological heuristics and biases.[31] Such mental shortcuts and innate propensities, the function of which is to allow us to take action when information is scarce (or when there is too much of it), can distort calculations of costs and benefits, thus short-circuiting the logic of rational choice analysis. In these cases, other theories of human behaviour must be applied, such as prospect theory or the various explanations propounded by evolutionary psychology and cultural evolution.

Why, despite all these limitations, will I use rational choice theory? There are at least three key commonly overlooked reasons for doing so. First, even though the theory can sometimes lack descriptive realism as it does not always capture all the relevant factors and characteristics of a phenomenon, it is explanatorily incredibly powerful. With this I mean two things.

On the one hand, rational choice is easy to use. There are not a lot of moving parts to the theory whose precise interactions and mutual implications might elude us when applying the theory to the real world. In contrast to many other social science, especially sociological, theories (think of Parsonian structural functionalism, Habermasian critical theory, or symbolic interactionism), rational choice is quite easy to understand and handle, and is therefore readily applicable.

On the other hand, and relatedly, rational choice theory enables us to posit precise hypotheses. Its stringency, i.e. the assumption of self-interested responsiveness to incentives, allows us to extract from the theory only a small set of plausible hypotheses about people's likely behaviour in a given social situation. The theory is not so wide and vague as to predict dozens upon dozens of possible, or even plausible, results for given circumstances. This quality of the theory stems from how narrow it is. Because it does not assume, at least not at the very start of an analysis, that people are sometimes informed and other times uninformed, sometimes self-interested and other times unconditionally altruistic, sometimes responsive to incentives and other times not, it provides us with clear theoretical guidance when handling empirical evidence. We are in the dark, theoretically, if in the name of total descriptive realism our theory proclaims that the world is immensely complex and variegated, unpredictably changing from one situation to the next. I do not, of course, deny that the world sometimes tends to be something like that, but such descriptive truisms do not a theory make.

The second reason for using rational choice is that I do not know of a better alternative. Critics sometimes allege that one should instead turn to more culturalist or irrationalist theories which explain human behaviour with reference to sheer ideology, ideas, and social norms (norms, that is, that are not to be thought of as institutions underpinned by sanctions and working through the logic of incentives). I think the key difficulty with this exhortation is that such theories usually turn out to consist basically of the claim that a phenomenon X occurred due to an ideology A or a norm B somehow forcing people to behave in the stipulated manner. To my mind, this is not even a *theory*, let alone a useable one, but is instead a claim that is in need of a theory, an unexplained black box that calls out for an explanation. The question is precisely: *why* did people cause phenomenon X under the influence of ideology A or norm B (and why exactly did they embrace a certain idea now, but not before)? Was it because of the underlying incentive structure they were faced with? Was it due to a certain psychological mechanism that is more likely triggered in a given social situation? Did the social environment suddenly change such that circumstantial incentives shifted and thus a certain otherwise unappealing idea suddenly became more attractive to people?

A 'theory' which claims that a large proportion of the German population voted for the Nazis in 1932 or 1933 simply *due to Nazi ideology* is not a theory but an interesting beginning of a research problem. How is it possible that Germans' support for the Nazis was paltry before the year 1930, amounting to only a few percent compared to approximately 40% a few years later, just before Hitler rose to power? Nazi ideology existed and was known in Germany even before 1930 but ostensibly did not 'work'. Why is this? And how come it suddenly started 'working' from then on, putting a swathe of Germans under its sway? Merely pointing to an ideology or a norm, not invoking any underlying theoretical logic, or any mechanism that might underpin it and explain how it works, is no explanation.

My third and final reason for using rational choice is the counter-intuitive fact that it can provide explanatory insight even in cases when rationality starts breaking down. For example, in chapter 2 we shall see that the theory is useful in explaining elite mistakes during the liberalization of autocratic regimes. Moreover, in chapter 3 rational choice will help us understand why voters are uninformed, and even irrational in the sense of not basing their beliefs in empirical evidence. It does, of course, not follow from this that the theory can carry us all the way, as I shall also show in the second part of chapter 3.

Outline of the book

In chapter 2, I take up the task of constructing an easy to understand but at the same time quite exhaustive theory of democratic transitions. I start off with the modernization correlation which shows how strongly wealth and democratic rule seem to be causally tied together. To understand why this might be, i.e. what are the precise causal mechanisms that probabilistically transform wealth into democracy, I present what I call the 'puzzle of democracy'. The puzzle is simple: how is it possible that any mass democratic regime has ever emerged when we know ruling political elites do not have an interest in such a regime and will not rationally choose it? I then combine my answer to the puzzle with the modernization correlation. I summarize some of the more well-known, and propose a few less recognized, causal mechanisms which account for the connection between development and democracy. I also consider how more surface-level, short-term exogenous shocks, such as economic crises, can affect prospects for democratization.

However, because democratic transitions do not happen solely for developmental reasons and pressure from below, the next section takes up elite interactions and reasons for (limited) democratization. I summarize a variety of international, informational and other mechanisms through which elites, in certain circumstances, come to produce democracy. Although wealth and popular forces have no role here, I explain elite transitions by the same general logic of rational decision-making and strategic thinking that underlies the discussion from the first section. In the third part of the chapter, I take up democratic consolidations and downfalls. This section summarizes the reasons why more developed and richer democracies tend to survive while their poorer counterparts are prone to collapse. To illustrate the theoretical discussion, I consider the rocky Latin American experience of democratic openings and breakdowns. In the last part, I discuss what conclusions one should, and should not, draw from modernization theory about the prospects of future Chinese democracy, given the empirical data we have on the current and historic state of the Chinese economy, its surveillance technology, and its unprecedented regime of social control.

In chapter 3, I first describe how much the average studied voter knows about politics, democracy, and social facts on the basis of which she or he is expected to decide whom to vote for. I find, as is well known in the literature, that the average voter is not very informed at all. I then take up the seemingly paradoxical task of explaining, using rational choice theory, why this is so. I present four plausible explanations: (1) cognitive insufficiency, (2) inability to access correct political information, (3) rational ignorance, (4) rational irrationality. I find the first two to be empirically lacking, while I present a few reasons why the last two are, in line with previous literature, powerful and realistic explanations for voter ignorance and irrationality.

In the second part of the chapter, I put rational choice aside and review the psychological literature on political behaviour. On the one hand, I take up evolutionary psychology and specifically discuss possible evolutionary roots of human tribal psychology that is on display in modern politics. On the other hand, I summarize the basic psychological findings of the rough division of human cognition to system 1 and system 2, and the various cognitive biases that make us prone to not recognizing our tribal behaviour, such as confirmation bias, the Dunning-Kruger effect etc. I also draw lessons from recent psychological experiments conducted, for example, by Dan Kahan and his colleagues regarding the counter-intuitive interaction between political bias, intelligence, and curiosity. It seems that when engaging in politics the typical person is not to be thought of as a judge, impartially deciding on the truth, but more as a defence attorney who tries to get the client off the hook no matter the evidence. And the more educated the attorney, the easier the task. I also summarize the latest findings of public opinion surveys that looked at how political partisans perceive each other. There is an interesting, and worrying, 'perception gap' in how Democrats see Republicans, and vice-versa. I suggest a few explanations regarding its emergence and amplification in recent years, focusing primarily on news media and social media.

In the last part of the chapter, I focus on what voters do seem to know more about. Here I take up the issue of retrospective voting and discuss how biased it is and what sources of knowledge about the economy voters rely on. I present empirical evidence, primarily flowing from recent studies on immigration and trade shocks (e.g. Brexit), that the average voter is most likely sociotropic, not ego-centric, and explain how this fits into my overarching rational choice framework.

In chapter 4, I begin by introducing public choice analysis and the notion of government failure. I briefly outline what market failure is and why it occurs, and then move on to defining and explaining the parallel failure that tends to occur in politics. I argue that government failure should not be seen as anomalous and that therefore it should not shock or surprise us when politicians are not acting in the public interest. In the next part of the chapter, I focus on a particular type of government failure – regulatory capture. Following the empirical literature, I distinguish between weak and strong capture and outline two mechanisms that produce regulatory capture. The first is simply standard rent-seeking behaviour or the fact that both economic and political actors have, on average, self-regarding preferences. The second can be described with the principle of concentrated benefits and diffused costs.

In the next part, I present the most prominent sociological critiques of public choice analysis and show both theoretically and empirically why they mostly miss their mark. However, in doing this I also point out a few real limitations of public choice that need to either be acknowledged or addressed. In the last part of the chapter, I turn to selectorate theory and use it to explain why government failure is much more common in non-democracies compared to democratic regimes. Specifically, I use it to detail why democracies are, in general, less prone to corruption and why, more specifically, rich democracies are the least prone to it.

In chapter 5, I take up the ostensible international effects democratic regimes have, at least on each other. My starting point is the notion of democratic peace which is a strong statistical correlation between democratic dyads on the one hand and international peace on the other. Drawing on international relations (IR) theory, I present three contending theories that strive to explain this statistical association: (1) democratic peace theory, (2) capitalist peace theory, (3) and hegemonic/bipolar peace theory. In the chapter, I briefly explain the main differences (as well as similarities) between liberal IR theory on the one hand and realist IR theory on the other. I do this because democratic and capitalist peace theories fit under the liberal IR paradigm, while hegemonic/bipolar peace theory flows from the realist IR paradigm. I then consider each of the three theories in-depth, exploring both their theoretical, causal logic as well as quantitative and qualitative empirical evidence associated with all of them. In the end, I find that although statistical studies reveal a robust correlation between democratic dyads and peace, with capitalism also playing an important supporting role, the theory underpinning and explaining the correlation has been at least moderately, if not strongly, undermined by realist IR scholars and is in need of being patched up. In sum, we can be fairly certain that democracy helps cause peace (between democracies), but we do not know precisely why it does so.

In the concluding chapter, I bring together and summarize the most important points of the previous five chapters. I also present the unfairly maligned and misinterpreted essay by Francis Fukuyama, 'The End of History?', and consider how well his thesis holds up three decades hence and given a more empirically minded social scientific outlook. I argue there are at least four general sets of reasons that suggest liberal-democratic capitalist societies will tend to emerge victorious, or simply outlast, authoritarian state-capitalist societies like Russia or China.

Notes

1 If we do not restrict our tally solely to liberal democracies and also include all of the weaker, electoral ones, both shares jump up markedly above 50%. See Diamond 2015, 143.
2 Roser 2013. See also Roser's source: Coppedge et al. 2019.
3 Stasavage 2020.
4 Ibid., chapter 2.

5 Freedom House 2021. All subsequent figures in this chapter are compiled with data from this source.
6 Diamond 2008.
7 Norris 2017.
8 Foa and Mounk 2016; Foa and Mounk 2017.
9 Norris 2017.
10 Alexander and Welzel 2017.
11 Caughey et al. 2019.
12 Pinker 2018.
13 Pinker 2012.
14 I do not claim that politicians are *never* altruistic or sincerely interested in the public good, only that as far as the typical politician goes these goals are of secondary or tertiary importance.
15 Buchanan and Tullock, 1962; Downs, 1957; Black, 1986. In some political circles, Buchanan's name evokes profoundly negative feelings. This is partly so due to the recently published and controversial book by MacLean 2017. In drawing on public choice *theory*, I take no stand on Buchanan's *personal politics*, whatever they are. I do, however, find Henry Farrell's and Steven M. Teles' critical review of MacLean's book instructive, see Farrell and Teles 2017. Furthermore, for what it is worth, my political ideology is not libertarianism.
16 Olson 1965.
17 Arrow 1963.
18 Tilly 1985, 169.
19 Mann 1986, 4.
20 See Singer 1996; Kiser 2006.
21 See Rutar 2019.
22 North 1990; North et al. 2009.
23 Acemoglu et al. 2005; Acemoglu and Robinson 2012.
24 Hardin 1968.
25 Goldthorpe 2007; Goldthorpe 2016. See also Chong 2000.
26 Rutar 2019; Rutar 2020.
27 Kiser and Hechter 1998; Hedström 2005.
28 Cartwright 1983.
29 Friedman 1953.
30 NCCS 2015; BLS 2015.
31 Kahneman 2011.

2
WEALTH – THE PATH TO FREEDOM?

Introduction: economic development and popular rule

There exists a striking social-scientific fact. The richer a country, the more likely it is for that country to also be a democracy. To be more precise, knowing only the figures for GDP (gross domestic product) per capita, we are able to predict the political regime of 91% of countries before World War I, 85% of countries in the interwar period, and 76% of countries after World War II.[1] Wealth and democracy go hand in hand.

Although the details of this statistical association are still controversial, during the 20th century it has become one of the most famous sociological and political science findings, and the basis for one of the more prominent social theories – *modernization theory*.[2] In its classic (and not wholly adequate) form the theory had emerged already in the first decade after the end of World War II when Martin Seymour Lipset, using very simple statistical methods, noticed the intriguing connection between wealth and democracy.[3] Despite its fame and surface attraction, however, the statistical association cannot be taken for granted as it poses many theoretical questions that have not yet been fully satisfactorily answered. Moreover, as any undergraduate student knows, one should never directly infer causation from mere correlation. The simple correlation Lipset uncovered cannot be taken to imply that a country's wealth *causes* democracy. There are at least two general sets of issues here.

The first problem is that Lipset could not have known whether there is actually a hidden third variable present which causes, at the same time, both rising wealth and the transition to democracy. For example, what if unbeknownst to us tucked into that correlation is a third phenomenon such as the Protestant ethic that explains both? If this is the case, the original statistical association is not really robust and can be dissolved into this further phenomenon. To give a simpler, more intuitive example which reveals the problem at hand, consider the strong

DOI: 10.4324/9781003172574-2

association between nicotine smudges on people's fingers and lung cancer. We know that although these two phenomena are statistically connected, the first variable (nicotine smudges) does not produce the second variable (lung cancer). In fact, there is a hidden third variable present – tobacco smoking – which really accounts for both former variables and their *seemingly causal* connection. Tobacco smoking sharply increases one's chances of getting lung cancer (due to inhaling carcinogens) and of having nicotine smudges appear on one's fingers (due to regularly holding cigarettes). Moreover, even if there are no third variables present, simple correlations do not reveal to us which way the arrow of causality is pointing. Is it wealth that causes democracy? Or is it democracy that causes wealth? Absent more complicated statistical methods and a powerful, plausible theory, we simply cannot say.

The second issue with statistics is that even if all of the above were resolved it still does not offer us a deep explanation of *why* or *how* wealth produces democracy. Associations are not the theory that tells us how things work. Associations are in need of a theory. They are a black box whose internal workings are opaque to us. We know what goes in (GDP per capita or tobacco smoking) and what comes out (democracy or lung cancer). But we do not know how the former resolves or translates into the latter. What is it about tobacco smoking that makes the human organism develop cancer tissue on the lungs? What is it about wealth that makes human societies more likely to transition to democracy? How does wealth impact individuals, such that they are more likely to move their political regime in a democratic direction? What are the *causal mechanisms*, the processes that lead from A to B?

These concerns with more primitive varieties of modernization theory, but also other accounts of democratization, have recently been pithily expressed by Daron Acemoglu and James Robinson. As they say, 'why anybody believes any particular causal claim is usually unclear, as are the causal mechanisms linking particular putative causes to outcomes … In our terms, a general proposition about democratization would be an empirical claim, derived from a model with microfoundations, about what forces tend to lead to democratization.'[4] In his literature review, Adaner Usmani expresses similar concerns. He claims that modernization theory 'has underdeveloped microfoundations. Staple accounts do not give much thought to the actors who actually fashion or obstruct the democratic transition.'[5] Following these critiques, I strive to present theoretical accounts of democratization that are especially careful to specify the underlying microfoundations, i.e. the happenings at the level of human individuals that can account for phenomena at the level of societies.

Since Lipset's early investigations, the association between wealth and democracy has been thoroughly empirically examined and has, surprisingly, received only mixed support.[6] Furthermore, the relationship has recently been challenged in a more systematic way by a meta-study that looked at 33 econometric papers published in the last two decades. Aggregating the results of all the papers, it found no statistically significant effect of wealth on democracy.[7]

However, this conundrum seems to be resolvable. As has long been theoretically speculated and as an important study has empirically just demonstrated, wealth is probably only a very rough proxy for the real cause of democratization.[8] The real cause is *industrial economic development*. This would explain both the strong surface relationship between GDP and democracy, and the mixed support found in statistical estimations. It would also make more understandable the fact that although the association is found to hold both in the time period of earlier waves of democratization (in 19th and early 20th century) as well as later democratic transitions (during the second half of the 20th century), it does get weaker in the post-war period. If GDP per capita is only a rough proxy for economic development, which is the real cause of democratization, all this would be a matter of course. It would mean that if a country achieves high-income status *without* significantly modernizing its economy, it is rich but will not likely become democratic. Growing rich without modernizing became possible precisely in the second half of the 20th century as some countries started discovering vast amounts of oil and other natural resources.

Moreover, and to foreshadow my later discussion, economic development is only a latent structural cause of democracy. This means that, as we shall see, the democracy-inducing powers of economic development need to be triggered or activated by some unexpected event to actually produce a democratic transition. Long-term structural social changes cannot, after all, replace dictators. *People* replace dictators. And although they are more likely to do so in modern social circumstances, they have to first experience a propitious moment for collective action that is brought about by, for example, an economic crisis or a similar kind of external shock. This can take years after a country has already developed. Therefore, it is not surprising that some statistical studies do not find an effect of GDP on democracy, as they do not look at the *lagged* relationship between both variables. Studies employing such lagged measures do find robust evidence for modernization theory.[9]

How democracies come to be

I pointed out in the introduction that we can, for the majority of cases (76–91%), successfully predict whether a country is democratic or not just by looking at its GDP per capita. This statistical connection can be presented in other ways as well. For example, between 1950 and 1990 the likelihood of a poor regime (GDP per capita of around $2,400 in today's terms and adjusted for purchasing power differences) becoming democratic was 18-times smaller than the likelihood of it being a dictatorship. Similarly, although less dramatically, a less poor country (GDP per capita of around $9,500) was only 2-times less likely to democratize compared to the likelihood of suffering a dictatorship. However, middle and higher-income countries (GDP per capita of $14,300 and $19,050 respectively) were 6-times more likely to transition to a democracy than to sustain a dictatorship.[10]

These are the facts. But why are they the way they are? What explains them? What kinds of mechanisms might be in place in wealthier countries that, with some exceptions, helped them achieve democracy faster?

The basic logic of democracy from below

First, we need to take a step back from modernization. Let us forget, for a moment, about the association between wealth and democracy and simply ask ourselves: how could democratic regimes have emerged at all? In fact, this is precisely the fundamental puzzle of democracy. How is it possible, in general, for such popular, non-elite regimes to ever have come into being? Democracy takes power away from political elites and diffuses it throughout the populace, but every currently existing liberal democratic regime had its own non-democratic predecessor over which a powerful non-democratic elite presided. Why would such an elite entity, which has no interest in giving away its power and thus losing its privileged social position that affords its members a comfortable, rich life, ever acquiesce to popular rule? In a non-democratic regime, the elite can do almost whatever it wants without the bothersome meddling of its subjects. It can change laws, extract economic resources from ordinary citizens (or even from elite groupings that are below the ruling elite in the hierarchy, such as merchants or businessmen), enforce its own ideology and beliefs on the people, ensure itself a leisurely life, etc. Why would powerful individuals ever relinquish their power willingly – and, as the premise of this book has it, rationally?

At first, the answer to this riddle seems rather simple. Democratic change happens when, or if, ordinary citizens who are exploited and subjugated by the ruling political elite stage a rebellion. Indeed, many classical and contemporary scholars thus quite reasonably posit that popular protest is precisely the main cause (or even the only cause) of democratic transitions. Marxist sociologists, such as Göran Therborn and Dietrich Rueschemeyer, on the one hand, and prominent mainstream economists and political scientists, such as Daron Acemoglu, James Robinson, and Carles Boix, on the other, all build their theories on the assumption that democracies emerge due to the struggle of popular classes against the elites.[11]

This idea is quite convincing, although as we shall see it has important explanatory limitations, especially in more recent history. The ruling elite is, by definition, a small group while ordinary people include everyone else in the country. If the latter form a cohesive collective and act against the elite, they can, due to the power afforded to them by their sheer numbers, do the following. First, they can get rid of the ruling elite directly by a revolutionary overthrow, i.e. they can kill the rulers, jail them, marginalize or banish them from the country, and set up a democratic regime on the ruins of the former autocracy. This is rarely feasible and rarely successful.[12] But secondly and more likely, ordinary citizens can inflict, through more peaceful and protracted collective action, major costs upon the elite and its most important supporters, its 'pillars of support', e.g. the police, the military, the business elite, etc. At some point, if costs start to mount, either the elite or its main supporters reflect on whether ceding some power to the people might be more beneficial (or, better put, less costly) for them than continuing to stubbornly maintain the non-democratic *status quo*. Assenting to protesters' demands would calm them down and thus diminish the costly effects of popular collective action on the regime.

But what kinds of costs can non-violent, non-revolutionary collective action even muster? Perhaps most importantly, general strikes, mass protests, demonstrations, and other forms of large, drawn-out tactics of dissent and civil disobedience can shrink economic activity and thus affect the state budget upon which the elite draws for its own and its supporters' resources. Furthermore, a shrinking economy directly hurts the profits of businessmen on whose political support the ruling elite usually counts and which it might quickly lose under conditions of mass dissent. Collective action might also lead to the destruction of important and valuable private or state property, which is another way for pro-democracy protesters to inflict costs on the elite as long as it sticks to maintaining the current autocratic *status quo*. Popular disobedience might provoke a sympathetic response from the international democratic community which is able to impose economic sanctions on the regime, or promise rewards to either the elite or its pillars of support if the regime abstains from repression and enacts political reforms.

At this point, however, another complication arises in the puzzle of democracy. Why would the ruling elite ever cater to the protesters' demands, or succumb to internal pressure coming from its pillars of support, when it has alternative means of removing the source of rebellion – violence? The answer is that repression itself is a costly action. And not just from the obvious popular point of view, but from the elite's as well. In certain circumstances, repression and its inevitable social consequences imply great pains for the elite and its close supporters. Violently crushing protesters sometimes pays off, but not always. Moreover, it is not just that repression sometimes simply is not the rational strategy, given the elite's circumstances, but also that elite's *capacity* to wield repression is not always high. On those occasions, the elite cannot, even though it might want to, use violence to re-establish order and business as usual.

Thus we come to our first general thesis regarding the emergence of democracy. Democratic regimes come to be when the ruling political elite accepts the popular demand for democracy. The elite does so when (1) it is facing pressure from below (as well as, due to it, further lateral pressure from its own pillars of support), and (2) when it reasons that acquiescing to the protesters' demands is more beneficial (or less costly) than mobilizing repression against them. On its own, this thesis sounds somewhat tautological or at least as lacking precise empirical content. In order to know when these two general conditions are more likely to be satisfied, we need to examine two sets of causes. First, we need to understand what the long-term, structural causes of both (1) and (2) are. Second, more short-term, surface-level triggers of both (1) and (2) need to be considered as well.

Modernization and freedom

This is where we turn our attention back to the modernization correlation. I take modernization to account for, or embody, the long-term, structural causes of democratic transitions. It is not a coincidence that, almost without exception, mass democratic regimes first started cropping up in human history only in the 19th and 20th century – the period just after the industrial capitalist revolution. Modern economic development brings forth a variety of (unintended) social structural changes that radically transform the *opportunities* as well as the *incentives* of ordinary people who have an interest in fighting for democracy, and of the political elite which has an interest in fighting against democracy. The changes are such that ordinary citizens, due to their transformed social position, are more motivated and capable of collectively struggling for democracy, while the elite is less motivated and less likely to succeed in struggling against the impending democratic tide. The proposed causal chain looks, schematically, like this: capitalist (or modern) economic development → structural social changes → changes in the opportunities and incentives for pro-democratic or anti-democratic collective action → greater likelihood of (successful) pressure from below → greater likelihood of democratic transition.

Researchers have proposed many causal mechanisms as processes leading from economic development to democracy, but here I will focus only on those that have, with one exception, been empirically most corroborated and that cohere with rational choice theory.

1 The separation of politics from the economy

Modern economic development is the result of modern economic institutions.[13] In general terms, the latter include secure private property rights and the replacement of pre-modern monopolies, guilds, and similar politically sanctioned market privileges, with market competition and free access to the market by potential new entrants. I take these conditions and changes to represent the separation of politics from the economy. Put differently, in the context of modern economic institutions surplus wealth is no longer necessarily or even primarily generated by the use of political force. In the pre-modern world, kings, princes, and landlords maintained and increased their riches only by relying on their political clout and, more proximally, by using their own armed forces to extort the immediate producers, mostly peasants, to relinquish resources to them. Similarly 'taxed' were the merchants for whom the political elite had, in return for the 'tax', generated market privileges and crown-sanctioned monopolies.

This all slowly begins to change with the emergence of capitalism. Landlords are no longer facing and extorting peasants, who possess their own plots of land and use them to provide for their families. Instead, capitalist industrialists seek dispossessed workers who cannot provide for themselves and must thus, themselves, find an employer willing to pay them for their labour. The nature of the modern economy is such that, even in the absence of force or political pressures, workers are willing to offer their services to capitalists, and capitalists are willing to employ them. Small peasants could have lived without their overlords, but dispossessed workers cannot live without their employers That is why they (but not the peasants) are willing to work for them (and even generate profit for them) even if the employers are not threatening them with knights and swords.

Because in the modern world politics and the economy are separated in the described manner, *political freedom* does not entail that elites lose their wealth. Even if the political regime is democratic, workers still line up in front of factories and offices, and capitalists still receive their profits. Thus democratization is not as frightening a project in the minds of the elites as it once was. Worker emancipation does not undermine the wealth creation process upon which modern elites sit, but it would have undermined it in the cases of pre-modern elites, dependent as they were on political oppression for wealth extraction. In contrast to pre-modern elites, modern ones have a less intense interest against democracy.

2 The emergence of the middle class

In countries where modern economic institutions spring up and unleash development, a middling stratum of semi-rich citizens is soon to follow. The removal of barriers to market entry and the creation of open competition, free movement of labour across professions and sectors, and secure property rights enable an increasing share of the populace to either become small entrepreneurs, or to simply earn enough through the sale of their labour, which further enables them to accumulate some private property. Due to their social position, this middling group has interests that are in certain respects aligned with the interests of the social elite. Although members of the middle class are not themselves an elite, they own much more property than the ordinary worker and therefore have a larger stake in its preservation.

The middle classes were classically thought of as being a boon for democracy due to being more enlightened and freedom-loving than the ordinary citizen. Researchers expected them to be leading the fight for democracy. As the historical sociologist Barrington Moore famously put it, 'no bourgeois, no democracy'.[14] However, no such heroic assumptions need to be made to understand why a country with a large middle class was more likely to democratize than the one which lacks it. Indeed, the middle class has an ambiguous historical preference regarding democracy.[15] Its members did want, and bravely fought for, political freedom for themselves but not necessarily for people below them.[16]

Instead, what makes the presence of a middle class conducive for wholesale democratization is the fact that it soothes elite anxieties. Elites generally worry about the prospects of large-scale wealth redistribution under democracy away from them and toward the citizenry. In politically free regimes ordinary citizens are able, through elections, to steer political decision-making toward more progressive taxation schemes that are beneficial for them and less beneficial for the rich elite. Now, in the presence of a large, semi-rich, property-owning middle class, the rich elite knows that it has a potential partial political ally in the middle class when it comes to fears of redistribution. The elite reasons that if, in the new democratic regime, ordinary citizens were to electorally demand the abolition of property or insist on a radical programme of wealth redistribution, the elite could mount a political fight against them with the aid of the middle classes who want to protect their (albeit smaller) property just as much as the elite does. So, holding all else constant, the presence of a large middle class should increase prospects for democratization by making elites less inclined to fight, tooth-and-nail, the demands for democracy coming from below.

3 Middling levels of wealth inequality

Historically, economic development first raises existing inequalities but then, as the middle class starts enlarging, somewhat lowers them. Wealth inequality in most developed countries stabilizes around the middle to lower-middle levels. In contrast to very low or very high levels of inequality, such a situation seems to be most conducive to democratization for the following reasons.[17]

First, very low levels of inequality make democracy an economically less attractive development for ordinary citizens. In such a society people know that, if a democratic transition happens, they will still not be able to redistribute much wealth away from the elite – simply because the rich are not all that much richer compared to the ordinary person. Of course, they might still press for democracy due to key non-economic considerations such as freedom. But they have a lesser economic incentive for initiating the struggle for democracy.

Second and at the other extreme, very high levels of inequality imply that ordinary citizens have a very strong incentive to demand redistribution as the rich elite possess so much wealth. The incentive might be so strong that they do not merely struggle for democracy but instead mount a wholesale revolution against the elite. After all, they have (almost) nothing to lose and everything to gain, economically speaking. If this holds, the elite will do everything it can to repress them and stop a devastating revolution. Too much is at stake. There will be no democratic concessions, liberalization openings, or negotiations. Only repression.

Third and in contrast to both previous situations, middling levels of inequality seem to offer the most propitious conditions for democratization. On the one hand, ordinary citizens have at least a weak economic incentive to press for democracy, and on the other, the elite is not greatly worried about radical redistribution or even a revolutionary overthrow of the whole system. Thus, pressure from below is more likely to emerge, while the elite is more likely to make at least limited democratic concessions.

4 The replacement of pre-capitalist landed elites with industrial or post-industrial capitalists

The next mechanism has to do with the appearance of industrial (and later post-industrial) capitalists, which is usually caused by modern economic institutions and economic development. Comparatively speaking, the former elites, i.e. the landed gentry, have both more to worry about from the introduction of democracy and less to lose by trying to violently repress movements for change. This doubly undermines the likelihood of democratization or, when they are replaced by modern elites, doubly increases its chances.[18] Let us briefly explore the logic behind these incentives.

First, the wealth landlords possess – land – is much easier to measure, tax, and redistribute among the ordinary citizenry than the wealth industrial or post-industrial capitalists possess – physical, financial, and human capital. Machines, tools, financial instruments, ideas, and even factories are much easier to either completely or partially hide, or move abroad, than land, which cannot be hidden nor moved around. This explains why modern elites have less to fear from democracy in which ordinary people electorally impose redistribution on them than pre-modern ones.

Second, long-lasting, drawn-out social conflicts that might linger on when the elite decides to repress its democracy-demanding populace hurt capitalists more than landed elites. Mass protests, strikes, and violent clashes cannot really destroy land, but they can definitely damage physical and human capital. Furthermore, in times of conflict or mass repression capitalist trade is less efficient or even stagnant. This implies lesser profits. In both cases, the opportunity cost of repression (instead of conceding democracy or initiating partial reforms) is higher for modern elites and lower for pre-modern elites, which is why the latter are more inclined to use violence than the former.

5 The replacement of rural peasantry with urban workers

With the transition to a modern, capitalist economy, peasants were largely transformed into urban industrial workers. Because both peasants and workers are a non-elite class that would greatly benefit under democracy, they have similar economic and non-economic interests in political freedom. There are no large asymmetries of incentives here. However, the *capacities* of both classes in struggling for democracy are very different. It is easier for industrial workers to undertake collective action than peasants. This is so for at least two general sets of reasons.

First, urban workers live in large, densely populated cities and perform their labour in large, overcrowded factories. Such geographic and employment concentration makes it – in comparison with dispersed smallholding peasantry – both likelier and easier for them to communicate with each other and coordinate potential collective action.

Second, workers are able to strike, to withdraw their labour, shut down production, and thus endanger the profits and economic viability of their employers. Moreover, a well-coordinated strike might, in short order, paralyze a country's power supply, transportation, and public services or, taking a longer perspective, even bring down the whole economy. In short, the bargaining power of workers is usually much higher than that of peasants.

In sum, even though both peasants and workers have the same general interest in living in a democracy, workers have a much larger structural capacity of actually initiating large-scale collective action, which is costly to elites and their supporters and is thus an important catalyst of democratic transitions.[19]

With these theoretical considerations in mind I now turn, for purposes of illustration, to the classic case of modernization and democracy from below, Britain. Before 1832, British politics was pronouncedly non-democratic and oligarchic. The right to influence political decision-making through elections was, not surprisingly, restricted to the wealthy, a category that amounted to about 8% of adult males.[20] With the Reform Act of 1832 this share increased to around 14%. Acemoglu and Robinson report that there is virtual consensus among historians that the primary motive for enacting this liberalizing reform was, indeed, to calm social unrest that had slowly been brewing since the coming of the industrial revolution. Similarly, according to *Encyclopaedia Britannica*, 'The first Reform Bill primarily served to transfer voting privileges from the small boroughs controlled by the nobility and gentry to the heavily populated industrial towns.'[21] Despite this, the reform was actually incredibly limited in its scope, as it stopped with the middle classes and did not address concerns of the ordinary citizens.

One immediate consequence of the bill's conservative nature was the forming of the Chartist movement a few years later (1838). The movement was made up primarily of workers who strove for actual extension of the franchise and other democratic rights with no property requirements. In the following years, waves of strikes and other forms of social conflict swept over Britain, fanned on by inequality, lack of political freedom, and economic crises. In the 1860s, another Reform Act was passed and in 1884 a third one. After this, voting rights were enjoyed by around 60% of adult males. A few decades later, when World War I ended in 1918, all adult British males had the right to vote. That same year women got the right to vote but it was limited to only those that fit certain property requirements. Ten years later, all adult women could vote.

Elites in Britain were thus gradually incorporating ordinary citizens into their political system for almost a century. They did so not because they were enlightened and noble at heart, but because they feared revolution was upon them otherwise. As Acemoglu and Robinson point out in their summary of the events: 'The concessions were gradual because, in 1832, social peace could be purchased by buying off the middle classes.'[22] Britain was the first European society that underwent modern economic development already in the first half of the 19th century, with its roots stretching back through the 18th century, at the start of the industrial revolution, and all the way to the 17th century when strong capitalist institutions first emerged and were entrenched in the broader society.

When capitalism replaced the pre-modern, feudal economy, politics separated out from the economy, the middle class emerged and began spreading, the landed elites were replaced by industrial capitalists, and rural peasantry transformed into urban workers. With this, Britain was turning more and more to democracy. Due to major social structural changes, the capacities and incentives for collective action on the part of ordinary citizens started increasing, while elites recognized that in these new circumstances democracy is not as dangerous as it had been for their pre-modern ancestors.

Exogenous shocks and regime breakdowns

This brief sketch of the British transition to democracy illustrates the deep, long-term, structural mechanisms of democratization that I have been discussing up until now. But what about the more surface-level, short-term causes that trigger the democratization process precisely, for example, in the middle, not the beginning or end, of a particular decade? A theory that can enumerate only structural causes and does not pay attention to surface triggers is unsatisfactory.

Here, the most intuitive suggestion, which is also in line with decades of social scientific research, as to where to begin would be to consider a variety of unpredictable, but impactful, events that can happen suddenly and profoundly shake up the social terrain. Devastating interstate wars, international or domestic economic crises, and the military defeat of a foreign ally or oppressor have been the most important triggers of largescale social conflicts that can bring down a dictatorial (or oligarchic) regime.[23] These sudden phenomena can, in short order, radically transform both the anticipated costs and benefits of fighting for (or against) democracy on the part of popular (and elite) classes. They can also importantly impact the capacities of both classes, and thus raise or lower the likelihood of democratization. That is why democracies often emerge – if they do at all – after the structural mechanisms considered in the previous section have been operating for a while *and* after an interstate war or a shocking economic crisis has also happened in the meantime.

Exogenous shocks can be thought of as acting in three general ways:

i   They can weaken the repressive apparatus of the state.
ii They can reduce the means used to pacify the populace.
iii They can have a 'demonstration effect'.

Let us consider each in turn.

(i) Weakened capacities of repression

A demoralizing interstate war or a budget-destroying economic crisis can cause the army, which is otherwise used by the dictator to threaten or repress insurgent citizens, to decide not to whole-heartedly support their leader anymore. Such a dissident decision has two important effects. First, elite capacity to quell a protest or an uprising is immediately reduced, thereby increasing the protesters' chances of succeeding in bringing down the non-democratic regime. Second and relatedly, protesters can find out that the military (or police) is no longer completely loyal to the leader, which motivates them to enact what would otherwise be costlier collective action against him.

A recent illustrative case is the Arab Spring, particularly the Egyptian case. Egyptian dictator Hosni Mubarak bought the army's loyalty by granting officers control of parts of Egypt's economy. Estimates vary, but the army under Mubarak was in control of between 5% to 45% of the domestic economy. Furthermore, due to geopolitical reasons having to do with Israel, since 1979 Egypt had been receiving US foreign aid to the annual tune of $2 billion, and the army, in particular, was one of the actual recipients.[24] When the global recession hit in 2008 it, unsurprisingly, also damaged the Egyptian economy, and when the United States almost simultaneously threatened to stop the flow of aid funds, the army distanced itself from the leader. It is not hard to understand, then, why in early 2011 the disgruntled military decided not to fire upon crowds of protestors storming the president. Similar losses of dictatorial control over the repressive apparatus of the state have caused the downfall of many authoritarian regimes in history, ranging from Russian Tsarism in 1917 and Shah's Iranian rule in 1979, to the Philippines in 1986, Romania in 1989, and Liberia a year later.[25]

Exogenous military shocks can, of course, topple dictatorships in a more direct way that has less to do with either popular protests or a weakened repressive apparatus.[26] Saddam Hussein's brutal regime ended in 2003 simply due to the invasion and the occupation of Iraq by the United States. Similarly, the eccentric dictatorship of Jean-Bédel Bokassa in Central Africa was toppled by the French, while Idi Amin's Ugandan autocracy collapsed due to Tanzanian military forces. Although dictators fall, in such cases the likelihood of democracy, let alone a consolidated democracy, emerging in their stead is slim.

(ii) Reduced means of acquiescence

The second way in which exogenous shocks increase the chances of popular resistance likewise flows from economic crises. Downturns generate two sets of harmful effects for dictatorial survival.

First, economic crises imply higher rates of unemployment and lower wages. When this happens, ordinary citizens are obviously less satisfied than in times of business as usual. Furthermore, in times of economic downturn people have, due to economic losses, less to lose when resisting the regime. This means that the opportunity cost of popular protest is lower and so the likelihood of collective action is higher. On the other hand, as long as median incomes are rising, and unemployment is kept down, we should expect a lesser willingness of ordinary citizens to risk it all in an open rebellion. To take an obvious example, the remarkable economic stability and constant economic improvements of the Chinese regime since 1978 have importantly contributed to its *political* stability. As a recent survey of Chinese public opinion finds: 'individuals who have seen their incomes rise in recent years and believe they will continue to grow in the years ahead are more likely to support the regime.'[27]

Second, think back for a moment to the previous discussion on capacities for repression. I claimed that an economic crisis reduces monetary resources (i.e. the state budget) that are used by the elite to buy the army's loyalty. When this happens, the elite loses an important pillar of support. But let us take this line of reasoning further. A crisis does not only weaken the elite's capacities for repression, nor does it only directly undermine the economic situation or ordinary citizens, but it also weakens the elite's capacity to actively buy the loyalty of other important, non-military social groups. When the economy is strong, the elite has no problem in developing and maintaining clientelist networks into which it strives to incorporate parts of the opposition, ordinary citizenry, and its own bureaucrats and other immediate elite supporters.

This fact tends to be missed in lay discussions of authoritarian regimes, and it is sometimes obscured even in certain sociological analyses where, besides repression, only ideology (not material rewards) is considered to be an important means of generating popular consent. It is usually recognized that popular resistance is rare in authoritarian regimes because of both the threat and actuality of repression. However, what tends to be underemphasized is that in non-democratic regimes rebellion is also forestalled because of the targeted elite buying of loyalty among the potentially most disruptive sectors of society.[28] In contrast to the widespread common-sense belief, ideology is not the main reason – besides repression – why ordinary people in dictatorships acquiesce to their unenviable situation. The classic Marxist thesis of 'false consciousness' of the exploited classes or 'the dominant ideology' that blinds the masses and passivizes them might have a surface theoretical attraction but is, in fact, empirically only weakly corroborated.[29] As the cognitive scientist Hugo Mercier has concluded in his recent book-length review of empirical evidence from various disciplines, 'the successes of mass persuasion are, more often than not, a figment of the popular imagination'.[30]

Especially richer authoritarian regimes build the amount of stability they have with a mixture of repression *and* 'by distributing benefits to ordinary citizens, providing good economic policy, and making opportunities for education and upward mobility available to people whose futures looked bleak before.'[31] Of course, this should not be overstated as even in richer dictatorships there exist real limits to this, especially to offering 'good economic policy' as we shall see later in the chapter. However, benefits in the form of monetary transfers, pensions schemes, and even apartments or jobs can be doled out to certain sections of the populace in return for assent.

The loyalty of more immediate supporters of the leader or the ruling party is bought in a similar way. This is the case not just in richer regimes but is also necessary in poorer ones, simply because immediate regime supporters and regime insiders potentially represent a much greater threat to the dictatorship. Usually, when a dictator, or his regime, falls it is because of the actions of his inner circle.[32] It is, therefore, essential for the survival of the leader and the regime that these groups are paid off. As Barbara Geddes and colleagues describe in a recent study:

> Party officials and activists often draw salaries. They have preferential access to jobs in the state bureaucracy and schooling for their children. They have insider opportunities to form businesses subsidized by the government and to manage or even take ownership of expropriated businesses and land. Their connections help them to get lucrative government contracts and profit from restrictions on trade. They have the possibility of rising in the party to achieve the political power and, usually, wealth associated with high office.[33]

Just before Arab Spring came to Syria, the Syrian dictator Bashar al-Assad had quickly started rewarding groups of ordinary citizens and closer supporters of the regime so that they would be less eager to join the protest movement. For example, he had 'frozen rising electricity prices, increased heating-oil subsidies, and raised salaries for public workers – anticipating that the wave of uprisings emerging across the Middle East may spread to Syria.'[34] (In his case material rewards were not enough and the velvet glove was quick to be replaced by an iron fist, meaning activists were arrested, jailed, and even shot at.)

When rewards such as these dry up or are distributed in smaller proportions due to an economic crisis, resistance becomes, at least in part, a more attractive strategy. Multiple mechanisms can spring to action. For example, a decreased amount of state rents and other types of elite income can trigger intra-elite bickering and splits which can spill over to larger conflicts. If this happens, intra-elite solidarity is greatly reduced which, in turn, increases its vulnerability to outside forces as it leads to both lesser group stability and less efficient communication, two factors that are otherwise crucial for quick and decisive repression. If the elite is actually hit, in this propitious moment, by popular pressure from below, then the likelihood of regime failure is greater. Moreover, if citizens become aware of intra-elite instability, they are more willing to mobilize against it as they now know that chances of repression are lower, and thus collective action is less costly than would otherwise be the case. This means that resistance is not only more likely to succeed but also more likely to even happen in the first place.

Embodying all the social processes discussed above is the impactful global economic crisis from the 1970s that hit authoritarian regimes in Latin America, as well as Africa and Eastern Europe. In the decade following the crisis 'regime stalwarts were losing their government jobs and facing wage cuts in many developing countries ... benefits to regime supporters [were reduced] at the same time that the crisis itself reduced acquiescence among ordinary citizens.'[35] Regimes began to break down. 'As long as economies functioned well enough for personalist leaders to provide supporters with access to opportunities and resources, the supporters remained committed to the regime. ... Without these material inducements, allies and supporters deserted their leaders.'[36] The main two causes of these sudden changes were the economic crisis as well as economic pressure from the international community. Similar events unfolded after the 2008 global recession that helped trigger the Arab Spring in 2011.

(iii) 'The demonstration effect'

The third general way in which exogenous shocks help pressure from below to emerge and spread concerns the military defeat of a regime's foreign ally, or simply any downfall of neighbouring authoritarian regimes. When this happens, the country is faced with two dangerous consequences: it loses outside military support that could otherwise be used to help suppress domestic insubordination, and its citizens become more aware of how quick seemingly rock-solid dictatorships can actually unravel. In the latter case it is not only that ordinary citizens become more aware of the possibility of bringing the regime down but also that, encouraged by successful external events, they tend to think of their own collective action as less costly than before and thus are more likely to initiate it.

The Arab Spring is again a good example. In January 2011, Ben Ali's dictatorship in Tunisia came crashing down and was quickly followed in the next couple of months by Egypt and Libya, and then even Syria, Yemen, and Bahrain. Eastern Europe experienced something similar in 1989 when communist dictatorships started falling like dominoes. The downfall began with waves of strikes in Poland and the victory of the Solidarity movement, it continued with encouraged Hungarians, and progressed even further with the fall of the Berlin wall. In the latter case, Gorbachev's announcement that the Soviets are not willing to militarily intervene and prop up communist rule in Eastern Europe also helped. These anecdotes, used to illustrate the demonstration effect, have been much more systematically confirmed by quantitative statistical analyses.[37]

In sum, I have shown that running alongside the long-term modernization causal chain is another more short-term process that helps explain, more concretely, when pressure from below and with it possible democratic transitions are more likely to appear. This second causal chain has little to do with economic development but is nevertheless important. Schematically it looks as follows: exogenous shocks → changes in the opportunities and incentives for pro-democratic or anti-democratic collective action → greater likelihood of (successful) pressure from below → greater likelihood of democratic transition.

Those of us who tend to romanticize politics are wont to ponder why there are, relatively speaking, so few instances of massive popular resistance in authoritarian regimes. It seems obvious that if people are oppressed, they should rebel – if not, we think to ourselves, they must be duped. However, as we have just seen there is a plethora of good reasons as to why resistance from below is not more common. To take just the cost of rebelling, for example, and put a rough number on it, between 1989 and 2011 when struggles for democracy were particularly successful only a quarter of them actually succeeded.[38] Simply put, resisting autocracy is from the point of view of an ordinary individual an exceedingly costly, risky, and unattractive course of action, except in rare special circumstances.

The resource curse

Let us return to modernization theory. As I have already said, critics of the claim that wealth is in some way importantly explanatorily related to democracy sometimes sceptically point out that there exists a series of awkward exceptions to the rule. Especially those countries, the critics charge, that have come to be exceedingly rich by exporting oil but are nonetheless dictatorships and have never been anything else pose a problem for modernization theory. In fact, studies show that oil-wealth *strongly reduces* the chances of democratic transition.[39]

As should be clear by now, this fact is completely consistent with the theory. First, the central claim of contemporary modernization theory is not that *wealth* (GDP per capita) causally produces democracy but that *economic development*, of which wealth is merely a rough proxy, does so. Oil-rich countries are usually very rich *without being economically the most developed*. That is why it should come as no surprise that they remain dictatorships. They simply do not embody the theory's causal logic. GDP is not a perfect measure of economic development.

Second, there exists a wide variety of mechanisms that are wholly consistent with what I expounded on previous pages and that explain why oil-rich countries are unlikely to become democratic anytime soon. The first such mechanism is the fact that oil regimes have an abundance of monetary resources that are not dependent on the health of the domestic economy and which can be used to buy off the military. As Michael Ross summarizes:

> Iranian president Mahmoud Ahmadinejad ... has given billions of dollars in no-bid contracts to businesses associated with the elite Revolutionary Guards ... Some of the world's biggest oil producers, including Oman, Saudi Arabia, and the United Arab Emirates, are also some of the biggest military spenders. When the citizens of Oman and Saudi Arabia took to the streets, their armies proved relatively willing and able to suppress the protests.[40]

The second mechanism has to do with all these monetary resources being distributed to ordinary citizens in exchange for their acquiescence. Moreover, oil regimes have a lesser need for taxing the populace and extracting wealth from them in order to fill the state budget. And lower taxes quite obviously translate to lower dissatisfaction with the regime. As Ross again reports on both counts, during the Arab Spring 'Algeria announced plans to invest $56 billion in new infrastructure and to cut taxes on sugar; Saudi Arabia directed $130 billion toward increasing wages in the public sector, unemployment benefits, and housing subsidies; Kuwait offered each of its citizens a cash gift of 1,000 dinars (about $3,600) and free food staples for fourteen months.'[41]

There is a third mechanism tied to the relatively 'tax-lax' environment of oil regimes. It has to do with the fact that, because the regime is to a much lesser degree dependent on the domestic economy, the majority of citizens comes to find out that, had they been willing to resist, their bargaining power would have been largely undermined. Because the elite cannot be financially threatened by the ordinary worker, strikes are not nearly as effective a bargaining tool in social conflicts as they are otherwise.

Summing up the first part of the chapter, we have seen that modern economic development (more than wealth itself) helps explain an important part of the puzzle of democracy. It explains why, with only a few special cases, democracy has almost exclusively been absent from human history up until the 19th and 20th century. It also happens to explain why even today robust democracy has scarcely come to the lesser and least developed parts of the world. Although not quite sufficient on its own (exogenous shocks play an important non-modernization role), it should form the starting point of any investigation into the social origins of modern democratic regimes.

Democracy from above

Empirical investigations confirm that, indeed, many democracies both in the 19th and 20th, as well as the 21st, centuries were born through struggle of ordinary citizens against the ruling elite, with this struggle from below being made more likely (and more likely being successful) due to modernization and exogenous shocks. According to one study that spans from 1950 to 2012 popular resistance was a more important cause of democratization than anything else, e.g. civil war, the end of a mandate, elite coup, or the dictator's death.[42] Among those dictatorships that fell due to popular struggle, almost every other regime breakdown resulted in democracy. According to a different study, which focused on the period after 1972, dictatorships fell in 67 countries, and in more than 70% of them civil resistance in the form of strikes, boycotts, civil disobedience, and mass protests had, among other causes, a strong influence on regime breakdown.[43] Even according to the recent empirical investigation done by Haggard and Kaufman, two researchers who are otherwise sceptical of modernization theory, more than half of democratic transitions between 1980 and 2008 happened 'from below'.[44] Collective action is an important cause of democracy.[45]

Nevertheless, pressure from below is simply not the whole story. Therborn, Reuschemeyer, Acemoglu and other 'conflict' analysts of democratic transitions miss out on important cases which do not embody the popular path to democracy. Quite a few transitions, especially in recent decades, occur in large part 'from above' and are triggered more by autonomous elite action than by ordinary citizens. Given the puzzle of democracy that we explored in the first part of the chapter, how is this possible? Why would elites ever consider at least limited liberalizing reforms and experiment with at least minimal democracy if they are not pressured to do so by the oppressed people who would benefit from such a freeing arrangement?

There are actually a few theoretical possibilities (and empirical realities), and none involve implausible assumptions of elite enlightenment or sudden bouts of altruism. All of the following scenarios can be understood through the same fundamental logic that was expounded on in the previous part, although the details are different. That is to say that elite calculation of costs and benefits of (a partial) democratization still form the heart of the analysis.

Power needs to be shared

The first reason for partial, minimal democratization that is caused by the elite itself concerns the issues of power-sharing.[46] In contrast to the common-sense image of dictatorships as regimes where one person has absolute power, the reality of authoritarian regimes is much more complicated. As we shall see in greater detail in chapter 4, no person can rule without the support of at least a small number of other people, and no group can hold onto power without the support of at least a small number of other groups. Democracies, by definition, embody a dispersed form of rule but the fact that power cannot but be at least somewhat dispersed holds (to a profoundly more limited extent) in dictatorships as well. In fact, social scientific research shows that *the most important threat* to an authoritarian leader is not posed by ordinary people but by the members of his own inner elite or other pillars of support. Elite coups are the main cause of a dictator's ouster and even wider regime breakdown.[47]

It goes without saying that elite members are not the biggest *democratic* threat to a dictatorship. Ordinary citizens, as we have already seen, assume this role. The likelihood of a dictatorship being replaced with democracy following a successful coup is lower than 10%, while the chances that popular struggle brings political freedom are higher than 40%.[48] Despite this profound asymmetry, elite or military coups rightly remain the main worry of authoritarian leaders. The latter are, after all, not worried about the likelihood of their regime being replaced specifically with *democracy* but of being *replaced* in whatever way.

Now, what is a dictator to do about this? How can he stave off elite attack? Obviously, he can distribute more benefits to his closest supporters and allies. He can, as already discussed, dole out money, political positions, tax privileges, company ownership titles, monopoly privileges etc. But this might not be enough for at least two reasons. First, perhaps a dictator running a poor regime does not have, and will not have, sufficient benefits with which to buy elite loyalty. Second, perhaps some of his supporters are seeking something greater that cannot, even in principle, be divided and physically distributed, namely the role of the dictator itself or a few leading political positions below that of the leader. These benefits are sometimes called 'ego rents' to distinguish them from the previously mentioned, run-of-the-mill, 'material rents'. Third, there is always a chance that elite supporters happily accept the rewards and acquiesce to dictator's rule, but then later on decide to use precisely the economic and political resources they got in exchange for loyalty, and rebel against the leader to take his place. After all, it is better to be directly in control of the sources of benefits and dispose of them freely than to have a person standing between yourself and the sources. In sum, the dictator should not be, and often is not, worried solely about popular pressure from below. There is also – and more importantly – elite pressure from within.

Although it seems counterintuitive at first, the way in which these concerns can be addressed, if they become pressing enough, is with the help of one of the fundamental institutions we usually associate with democratic rule: multiparty elections. The existence of elections, however exclusive with regard to ordinary citizens, signals to elite supporters that there exists a non-negligible likelihood of them coming to power and replacing the current leader or the political positions just below his, at least for a few years. Such semi-competitive elections affect elite strategic decision-making because this political institution reduces the anticipated benefits of a coup, thus making it less attractive as now there exists an alternative, less costly method of achieving power – one not involving violence, conflicts, destruction, and even civil war.

This is one possible elite-initiated path to democracy, albeit a very limited, electoral, non-liberal form of democracy that is more aptly termed a 'mixed' or a 'hybrid regime', as other attributes of robust democracy like the separation of branches of government, rule of law, media freedom, human rights and so on are of course going to be lacking. Furthermore, for understandable reasons having to do with both the dictator's and the broader elite's preferences to avoid popular rule, political candidates are often handpicked by the leader or at least the electoral terrain is strongly tilted in the regime's favour. This means that such elite-initiated 'democracies' have a homogenous media landscape, the existing political opposition – if permitted – is structurally weakened, some voters are bought off while others can face intimidation, and election results might be tampered with. But precisely this contradictory amalgamation and the hybrid nature of the system is one of the main interesting characteristics of many political regimes in the 21st century. Note that here, again, no assumptions of elite enlightenment were made to explain how a somewhat freer regime can emerge out of a closed dictatorship. Even if we take the leader and his supporters to be solely self-regarding and concerned just with their own material welfare and power, and even if ordinary citizens are left out of the picture, liberalizing change is still theoretically possible due to power-sharing issues confronted by the leader.

The dictator's dilemma

A second way in which we can understand how elites can initiate, by themselves, at least limited political reforms is to turn to endemic information problems with which the ruling elite is faced. Rulers in authoritarian regimes tend to be trapped in what can be termed the 'dictator's dilemma'. Two inescapable facts form the two horns of the dilemma. On the one hand, in order to rule, the elite needs an iron fist with which it is able to threaten the people so that they do not resist the regime and with which it is also able to actually repress them if they do resist. On the other hand, the elite usually wants to have at least a general, but if at all possible a much more detailed, grasp on how unpopular its actions are among the populace. This is so not in order for the elite to be able to genuinely help the people but so that it can initiate certain cosmetic corrections which, in turn, forestall popular discontent or prevent it from escalating.

So what, precisely, is the dilemma? *If* the elite threatens and uses repression, it cannot be sure what the people really think about it and how disgruntled they are. Ordinary citizens are not willing to disclose the truth about their private opinions on the regime, due to obvious fear of sanctions.[49] However, *if* the elite wants to gather authentic information on the private thoughts of citizens, it has to, in large part, relinquish its arbitrary use of repression and threats of using it. People would then be willing to disclose what they really think. So, either the elite uses repression but is in the dark informationally, or it succeeds in informing itself but cannot use repression. Neither situation is attractive to the dictator. What can he do?

He can opt to allow elections to happen and, although limited in scope, to not be a complete sham. This seems counterproductive at first as dictators and elections do not mix well. Elections, if not completely rigged, imply sharing power with the people and that can spell quick disaster for the ruling elite. However, a secure elite can afford to allow limited elections, especially on more local and regional levels, without a real fear of losing power through them. This is so because political opposition is excluded or structurally weakened through, for example, media destruction, and so the real contest is held only among various candidates of the ruling party. And if all else fails and voting patterns become worrying, the elite can still suspend elections in the future or simply does not report the correct results. Even if it came to that, elections have still fulfilled their role, as I shall explain now.

So why bother with elections at all? How can this democratic institution work to resolve, at least partly, the dictator's dilemma? It can because elections are an information-gathering device.[50] If secret ballot is guaranteed, even if elections are only somewhat fair and free, ordinary citizens have the opportunity to anonymously reveal their true private preferences regarding the regime without fearing for their life. In this way the elite can come to know how unpopular the regime, its leaders, mayors, local chiefs and so on, are either in general or in particular districts. True, the elite does not possess knowledge of specific people that are disgruntled, but it still gets access to information about what is happening on the ground, i.e. it finds out in which regions dissent is most concentrated. With this newly acquired knowledge three possibilities open up for the elite.

First, it can engage in cosmetic corrections and thus almost without cost pacify the populace. For example, the elite can replace the most excessive, corrupt, and mindlessly brutal low-level officials, the indiscretions of which it has just learned through local elections, courtesy of local citizens. This possibility, once it opens up, also works as an incentive for all the future local officials not to abuse their power too much as they will otherwise be sanctioned. In technical terms, elections are an ingenious way to solve *principal-agent problems* where, in the case of dictatorships, the principal is the dictator and the agents are his local officials whom we cannot directly supervise and are thus prone to more than their allotted share of resources, theft, and other forms of both regime and citizen abuse.

Second, and putting principal-agent problems aside for a moment, information gathered through elections is also helpful in a different way. That is, the elite can now engage in a strategy of more targeted repression or co-optation so as to nip the brewing subterranean conflict in the bud without the costs associated with more universal forms of repression or co-optation. Put more specifically, the elite can mobilize or reallocate troops to those regions where dissatisfaction seems highest, and it can also, more benignly, funnel extra resources to those same regions, hoping it can buy its way out of potential conflict.

Third, even if none of the above happens, the elite can still, using elections as an information-gathering device, find out if citizens are becoming increasingly hostile to the regime. Even if it is too late and so serious social conflict can no longer actually be contained in a targeted way, at least the elite is not going to be surprised by rebellion and can prepare for the fight in advance.

Whatever the concrete details in each case, elections – especially the more limited, localized events – can be a rationally chosen device, from the point of view of a dictatorial elite, for revealing private information where it would otherwise remain hidden. We can again see how some liberalization reforms can occur 'from above' and how a movement to a more hybrid, less closed regime can commence without significant popular struggle.

International inconveniences

Low-quality democratic or hybrid regimes can also spring up due to international pressures experienced by the ruling elite. These pressures can be more or less explicit. Usually they come in the form of economic sanctions against an autocratic regime, decided upon by individual countries or the larger international community wishing to change it. If the elite thinks a partial democratization is more beneficial (or, better, less costly) to its standing in new international circumstances than sticking to the increasingly costly *status quo*, then it will decide to liberalize even without pressure from below. Autocratic countries in which business elites are strongly dependent on foreign trade and free trade agreements with democratic countries can experience something similar. If businesspeople in a non-democracy have reduced, or even no, access to international markets due to democratic regimes deciding to end their agreements with the non-democracy, domestic business elite can put internal pressure on the ruling elite and thus incentivize it to open up the regime at least partially.

Withdrawal of foreign aid or military support on which the regime has come to depend is another example of a more explicit costly pressure on non-democratic elites that can motivate them, out of pure self-interest, to liberalize. A series of recent studies corroborates that during the third wave of democratization, stretching from the mid-1970s onward, offering conditional foreign aid to dictatorships, where the condition is the introduction of at least semi-competitive multiparty elections, incentivized dictators to open up their regimes.[51] Various African countries, such as Benin and Zambia, introduced elections in part due to such international pressure.[52]

However, why would democratic countries decide to react to abuse occurring in autocratic states and pressure them, in a way that is also costly to democracies, to change? Put simply, why would democracies spring to action in the first place? Putting cases of aid withdrawal aside, as this is not a costly thing to do for a Western country, why would self-regarding democratic leaders care about what goes on in the unfree world? After all, think of the behaviour of democratic United States in the Cold War era. The US had no misgivings about *supporting* a variety of dictatorships around the world simply because geopolitical struggle against communism and the Soviet Union was seen to be much more important than the moral fight for punishing any and all dictators, or of upholding democratic norms. In cases where dictatorships had taken a staunchly anti-communist outlook, the Americans overlooked and even encouraged, indirectly and non-intendedly, their dictatorial nature and disregard for fundamental human rights. The idea that rich, developed democracies will strive to spread democratic institutions throughout the world out of the goodness of their hearts is not very plausible. As a recent study found, 'the West assists democratic movements only when that assistance coincides with its material interests'.[53]

Reasons for costly pro-democratic international intervention become clearer if we keep in mind three important facts. First, the Cold War ended 30 years ago and so the fight against communism as the number one priority is not on the agenda anymore. Second, some democracies are spatially close to unstable non-democratic regimes, and the former are quite obviously but self-interestedly not fond of being so close to regional instability. They can change this by (selectively) pressuring foreign authoritarian leaders. As Steven Levitsky and Lucan Way report:

> For the United States and EU members, the potential social, political, and economic effects of instability in the Caribbean Basin and Eastern Europe are greater than those of instability in sub-Saharan Africa or most of the former Soviet Union. For example, threats of regional instability and refugee flows caused by Serbia's proximity to Western Europe explains why the North Atlantic Treaty Organization (NATO) opted for a military response in Kosovo but took little action in response to similar or worse crises (in terms of refugees and internal displacement) in Afghanistan, Angola, and Sudan.[54]

Third and as we shall see in chapter 5, democracies tend not to fight each other, which is why at least some of them could want, simply for security reasons, to pressure neighbouring non-democratic regimes to change.

In sum, where, due to their unpropitious international circumstances, autocratic elites find maintaining their regime more and more costly, they may decide to reduce these costs by succumbing to pressure and partly opening up their political system. The same logic holds if elites are offered conditional foreign aid. We are not necessarily talking here about authentic democratic transitions because the usual structural conditions are absent. These are no economically developed democracies from below. It, therefore, should not surprise us that, after the Cold War had ended and the US (with European help) had gained geopolitical superiority, weak electoral democracies started springing up across the world but never really consolidated and – as soon as international pressure waned – reverted back to ordinary authoritarianism.

Hard and soft authoritarians, and faulty impressions

Up until now I have explained the possible reasons that are behind elite-induced transitions to (weak) democracy, which can happen even without significant pressure from below. There exist, however, still other more middling cases of transition, such as Poland in 1989, where popular pressure acts as an important background condition but is not the most important cause. These are sometimes grouped under elite-led transitions but can also be seen as instances of democracy from below. However we decide to label them, we have a general political science model that helps us understand them.

Let us imagine an authoritarian society with three political groups, hard-line authoritarians, soft-line authoritarians and an excluded democratic opposition.[55] Hard-liners are in power and want to stick to their current system of closed autocracy. If soft-liners came to power, they would want to open the system up somewhat so as to absorb the democratic opposition and incorporate it into the regime. The excluded opposition cannot, but would want to, fundamentally transform the system and move it from autocracy (either closed or open) to democracy.

Let us further imagine that neither hard- nor soft-liners want democracy and can use repression to prevent this possibility from happening. Only the democratic opposition is willing to organize and mobilize in order to achieve a democratic transition. The opposition can be either weak or strong. If it is weak, it is not able to successfully mobilize and will thus be defeated. If it is strong, it can successfully mobilize and achieve democracy, but only provided it acts at the right time. The right time would be if soft-liners came to power and enacted liberalizing reforms such as implementing semi-competitive multiparty elections. The last assumption we make is that if, for whatever reason, soft-liners are facing a mobilized strong opposition they are not willing, even though they could in principle, to use repression against it. It seems plausible to assume this because even though soft-liners prefer dictatorship to democracy, they also see democracy as a lesser evil compared to a drawn-out social conflict that would ensue if they tried repressing the strong opposition when it has already mobilized.

It logically follows from such a model that a transition to democracy 'from above' is impossible if hard-liners are in power. It also follows that if due to an exogenous shock or for other reasons soft-liners manage to come out on top, two possibilities open up. First, they face a weak opposition that is incapable of successfully mobilizing. Soft-liners thus go ahead with liberalizing reforms that are intended to broaden the dictatorship and incorporate a weak opposition into it. A more open dictatorship, but not democracy, results. Second, soft-liners might be facing strong opposition. In this case they do not want to enact liberalizing reforms because they know that would provide the strong opposition with the opportunity to mobilize and topple the whole dictatorship. Thus soft-liners do not get what they most prefer, i.e. broadened dictatorship, but they also avoid what to them is an even greater cost, i.e. transition to democracy. This means that in both cases (weak opposition, strong opposition) soft-liner rule will not result in a democracy.

However, up until now I have tacitly assumed that all three groups are fully informed. Soft-liners know whether the opposition is weak or strong, and they know where liberalization leads in both cases, thus they tailor their actions accordingly. But in reality where people make mistakes and information-gathering is costly, as we have already seen, things are not so clear. So if soft-liners wrongly think that the democratic opposition is weak when it is, in fact, strong they will start opening up the regime and unknowingly give the opposition precisely the propitious moment it needs. The opposition will mobilize and soft-liners are suddenly faced with the fact that if they clamp down on it they risk perhaps even civil war, or if they do nothing democratization will ensue. They prefer the latter to the former and democracy from above is born.

This theoretical analysis comports quite nicely with the actual sequence of historical events in Poland from the late 1970s up until the fall of the regime in 1989.[56] In the 1970s, the Polish economy was in the grip of serious economic crisis. The ruling elite tried to stave off popular resistance in these dire circumstances by indebting itself. In six years, Polish foreign debt increased from less than $1 billion to $23 billion. It was only a matter of time before waves of strikes and protests hit.

In 1980, the famous independent trade union Solidarity was formed. Workers went on strike after strike, but life for the ordinary worker did not improve. The ruling elite decided on repression and violently quashed unrest.

Years later, at the end of the 1980s, the elite upended its strategy and decided, instead, on liberalizing reforms intended not to fundamentally change the system but to absorb the opposition and defuse dissent. The Solidarity trade union was legalized and could participate in semi-competitive multiparty elections. The ruling elite were not worried that anything serious might happen on election day for two reasons. First, the electoral contest was not completely open. The ruling party was virtually guaranteed to name the prime minister because the majority of seats were not up for democratic contestation, rather they were reserved for the ruling party and its allies. Second, the elite was convinced that, in any case, there was simply not enough society-wide support for the Solidarity democratic opposition. They were relying on opinion polls which did not indicate mass dislike of the ruling party, or support of the opposition.

The elite was badly mistaken on both counts.[57] Solidarity achieved spectacular success because it enjoyed much wider private popular support than was publicly demonstrated. It won all seats but one, and, even though they were barred from getting the majority, a few elite-allied parties broke their loyalty and joined with Solidarity giving it more than 50% of seats. The cat was out of the bag now and suspension of election results would spell social disaster for the ruling party, especially given Gorbachev's announcement that Eastern European regimes could no longer count on Soviet military intervention to prop them up. Such elite informational blunders and electoral missteps are quite important. They contributed to democratization not only in Poland but also, for example, in Pinochet's Chile, Sandinistas' Nicaragua and Diouf's Senegal.[58]

We have now seen that focusing solely on popular resistance (and economic development) to solve the riddle of democracy, although both intuitively attractive as well as scientifically apt, is not nearly enough to paint the complete picture. Democratic transition, particularly if we count transitions to mere electoral democratic rule or even hybrid regimes among them, can also occur 'from above'.

Consolidation – Or breakdown

Even though we tend to take living in a democracy for granted, by now it should be clear that there really are no guarantees for democratic regimes, especially robust liberal ones, to ever emerge. From a historical point of view, democracies are exceedingly rare affairs, even if we take note of the 20th and the 21st century when political freedom became more widespread. It should by now also be theoretically clear why democracy is sparse. However, even when politically inclusive regimes manage to emerge the story does not simply end. As with their birth, there are, again, no guarantees of democratic *stability*. Once a democracy rises, it may either suddenly or protractedly collapse back into dictatorship. Particularly those democratic regimes which are poor or, despite all odds, have sprung up in economically less modernized societies are understandably weak and vulnerable. Countries that achieved freedom during the third wave of democratization which swept the world in the last decades of the 20th century are, sadly, the most obvious examples.

I noted at the beginning of this chapter that a consensus has formed among democracy scholars that increasing wealth (as a proxy for economic development) really does correlate with democratic openings. However, there is an even greater, less controversial consensus that, whatever the effects of modernization on democratic transition, wealth is strongly and robustly associated with democratic *survival*. As Adam Przeworski and Fernando Limongi famously discovered, between 1950 and 1990 no democracy with a GDP per capita higher than that of Argentina in 1975 ($6,050 in 1985 dollars, adjusted for purchasing power parity) had fallen.[59] For easier comparison, in today's terms (2019) that comes out to around $14,500 or higher. Poorer democracies were more likely to fall and the poorest the most likely.

Indeed, more than two decades later we can test whether their discovery still holds by examining the great number of democratic breakdowns since 1990. We find out that Przeworski and Limongi's observation still holds after the end of Cold War.[60] The majority of democracies that emerged but then failed to survive and consolidate between 1990 and 2015 have a non-oil GDP per capita of less than $2,000 (in 1985 dollars, PPP). Only two democracies were outliers. The island nation of Antigua and Barbuda fell in 1992 with a GDP per capita of $8,304. The Russian experiment with electoral democracy ended in 2004 when its non-oil GDP per capita was slightly above the $6,050 mark.

None of this should be surprising if we take modernization theory on board. It is true that the theory predicts democracy is less likely to emerge in poorer and less developed conditions. However, the theory is probabilistic – not deterministic – so it does not completely rule out such a scenario. It takes it to be less likely (and it is, statistically speaking, less likely), but still possible in principle. Furthermore, as we have seen, limited political freedom can, indeed, come to poor countries due to the effects of, for example, strong exogenous shocks, certain elite dynamics and a favourable international environment. Now, *if* democracy appears in a poor country and *if* we accept modernization theory, it follows that this newly founded freedom will be precarious. That is so because, absent economic modernization, a stable balance of various social forces with just the right structural capacities and incentives for or against democracy is missing. The less modernized elite will have a stronger temptation to dismantle democracy, and the less modernized popular forces will have a lesser capacity to resist.

That modernization, not just wealth, is the crucial factor here seems to be the case for two reasons. First, statistical studies show that, even when GDP is controlled for, a strong correlation between modern economic institutions and democratic survival still persists. If we take Fraser Institute's Economic Freedom of the World index (EFW) as a proxy measure of economic modernity, the following striking image forms:

for countries in the top 25% by EFW score, more than 90% remain democratic, whereas the bottom line shows that for those in the bottom 25%, reversals into dictatorship come rapidly so that after four years, half can be expected to have reverted into dictatorship, and that less than 10% remain democratic after 20 years.[61]

More modern democracies have a lower likelihood of reverting to their pre-democratic states. Second, qualitative historical case studies reveal that modernization mechanisms are contributing to democratic survival, while their comparative absence is harmful. Twentieth-century Latin America offers a clear illustration.

Chaotic democratization in Latin America

Most Latin American countries moved to democracy later, and more precariously, than early, classic modernizers such as Britain and the United States or even France. This is completely understandable as Britain and the US underwent economic modernization much earlier and to a greater extent. Capitalism and the industrial revolution, much like democracy itself, are not automatic, predetermined processes and thus did not appear all over the world simultaneously.[62] Britain and the US were there first, already in the 18th century, then France, Germany, Italy and Japan followed in the second half of the 19th century. The rest of the world started experiencing sustained economic development only in the 20th century, particularly in its second half. Delayed modernization explains delayed democratization.

Moreover, later developers did not always undergo the same kind of modernization compared to the pioneers. For example, multiple Latin American countries imported already existing technology from abroad instead of developing it themselves, and thus partly missed out on the chance to incubate a large industrial domestic working class. Their working class was comparatively smaller than the one that 'had emerged at comparable stages of development in the advanced capitalist countries.'[63] The strategy of state-led industrialization, based on export substitution, in time enlarged the working class but not as much as in the classic developers.[64] Latin American development relied much more on export agriculture than on industrialization and on building a strong domestic economy. That is why the old landed classes were able to hold onto power for longer and to a greater extent, the urban industrial working class was weaker and smaller, and the extent of the middle class very limited. Furthermore, historically – i.e. at the end of the 19th and beginning of the 20th century – levels of wealth inequality were higher in Latin American than in Western Europe. This trend continued through the 20th century.[65] Even in 1988, average inequality in Latin America was 65% higher than in the rest of the industrialized world.[66]

We should not, therefore, be surprised to find out that when Latin America was eventually swept over with a wave of democratization this wave soon crashed on the rocks. Calls for democracy were met with violent repression. There were some successful pro-democratic attempts that actually achieved a democratic transition but these successes were soon reversed by military coups. In certain cases, the key reason for democratic failure seems to have been precisely the limited extent of the middle class and the humble size of the working class. In comparison to El Salvador and Guatemala, Costa Rica enjoys a much more stable, consolidated democracy, and it has a comparatively larger middle class as it was able to develop relatively early.[67] This contributed to Costa Rica being able to partially democratize as early as the middle of the 19th century and then finishing the transition in the first part of the 20th century. Less economically developed El Salvador and Guatemala were dictatorships in the 19th century and then tried democratizing, unsuccessfully, in the first part of the 20th century.[68]

The Latin American path to democracy was also, in many instances, troubled by its pre-modern agrarian economy and the old landed classes. Brazil, Guatemala and Venezuela were still largely agrarian, rural societies even in the middle of the 20th century. When democratic openings appeared, the poor citizenry demanded land redistribution, a dangerous call unlikely to be heeded by the landed elites. Predictably, the 'response to demands for radical land redistribution in Brazil in 1964, Guatemala in 1954, Venezuela in 1948, and Chile in 1973 was a coup.'[69] Transition to democracy is less likely to succeed in the presence of landed elites because they, more so than industrial or post-industrial capitalists, are fearful of popular demands for wealth taxation and redistribution. If democracy does somehow manage to succeed in such circumstances it likely will not survive for long nor consolidate.

Democracy came to Argentina, which had already experienced a long agricultural export boom in the 1880s, in 1912 and survived all the way to 1930 when the military decided to step in and topple it in order to protect traditional elite interest from radical redistribution policies. Argentina experimented with democracy again in 1946 but in less than a decade the experiment came to a close, due to popular reforms seen as too dangerous by the elite. In the following decades periods of coup and dictatorship, on the one hand, and popular resistance and democracy, on the other, volatilely superseded each other.[70] Argentinian democracy finally became entrenched after 1983 when it experienced exogenous shock in the form of military defeat and a surge of pressure from below.

> The political history of Argentina is one of incessant instability and conflict. Economic development, changes in the class structure, and rapidly widening inequality, which occurred as a result of the export boom from the 1880s, coincided with pressure on the traditional political elite to open the system. But, the nature of Argentine society meant that democracy was not stable. Traditional interests were too threatened by the rise to power of the Radicals and continuously worked to undermine democracy.[71]

Democratic regimes that are not able to consolidate and do not survive are usually those that have not taken root in an economically developed society. It is true that Argentina more than doubled its GDP per capita between 1880 and 1912, and that its wealth was comparable to that of Britain or the US.[72] Moreover, in this period Argentina saw the expansion of both the middle and working classes.

And it is precisely due to the partial industrialization it underwent at the time that early transition to democracy was even possible and remained in place for as long as it did. However, because industrialization was only partial and based on a sudden agricultural export boom, the landed elites were still present and powerful. Inequality was high and rising. When the export boom inevitably ended, economic development slowed down. Industrialization stagnated and traditional interests were firmly entrenched. Around 1930 Argentina was hit by the Great Depression which made the landed elites uneasy and thus ended the first period of Argentinian democracy.

Wealth, not just modernity, aids consolidation

Economic development is an important, but not the only, reason why rich democracies are usually much more stable, and have a much lower likelihood of regressing to autocracy than poorer ones. The mere fact that rich democracies are *rich* helps them survive. There are two general theoretical sets of reasons to think so.

First, *the opportunity costs of reversion to dictatorship* are higher for the elite in a rich democracy and lower for the elite in a poor democracy. The opportunity cost of doing something, like mounting a coup or otherwise dismantling democracy, is represented by the potential value that the actor loses or cannot capture because she does this instead of something else she could have done. The higher the opportunity cost of an action, the less likely it is going to be undertaken. High opportunity costs demotivate us from acting. Now, for simplicity's sake let us suppose that, at least in principle, the elite in both rich and poor democracies would be better off, holding all else constant, if the political system they presided over was a dictatorship. After all, if this was the case, they would not have to bother with being accountable to the people and being constrained by them. To know how interested the elite would be in reversion, we must also ask what are the alternative actions it can undertake in either a rich or poor democracy to benefit itself, instead of trying to subvert democracy and transition back to dictatorship. In other words, what is its opportunity cost in both scenarios?

The answer is that there is much that the elite in a rich democracy can do, and must forego, if planning and executing a coup. Instead of risking it all and trying to capture state power, it could instead simply run its business as usual, i.e. trading, investing, rent-seeking, enriching itself. A democratic *status quo* is, for the elite in a rich democracy, quite a lucrative alternative. The situation is different for the elite in a poor democracy. The elite does not risk foregoing a lucrative *status quo* deal when considering illegally taking state power. Because it finds itself in a poor democracy, where prospects for business as usual are not as attractive as for the elite in a rich democracy, the former's opportunity cost of mounting a coup are lower and the action is therefore more likely to take place.

Second, *the potential benefits of reversion to dictatorship* are higher for the elite in a poor democracy. If it manages to dismantle democratic rule, it gets rid of the necessity of spending a very limited state budget on public goods and ordinary citizens. Because the country is poor, state budget is meagre, and because the country is a democracy, only a small fraction of the overall budget can find its way into the elite's hands. Transitioning to a dictatorship does not do much for the wealth of the society and the absolute extent of state budget. However, it does make it possible for the elite not to bother as much with ordinary citizens and their public goods demands. If the elite fails to deliver as much to the ordinary person as under democratic rule, citizens now cannot as easily 'throw the rascals out' as before. This means that, although the budget is the same as before the transition, the elite can now take a much larger percentage of it for its own spending needs.

If the elite in a rich democracy does the same, it also no longer has to bother with providing public goods and can now, if it wants to, capture a larger percentage of the state budget for itself. However, because the budget is enormous in a rich country, even the small fraction that the elite can take for itself (under democracy) is, in absolute terms, quite hefty. That means that although we can plausibly posit that the elite in both rich and poor democracies would like to dispose of the budget as unconstrained as possible, this opportunity is much more pressing for democratic rulers with tiny budgets, where a small fraction of the sum represents a low absolute number, than for those who control large budgets where even a same small fraction comes out as a large absolute number.

When will modern China democratize?

When communist dictator Mao Zedong died in 1976, China was one of the least developed and poorest countries in the world. In the following four decades, however, China underwent such profound economic change that it has almost universally come to be hailed as perhaps the greatest economic miracle in human history. Chinese economic progress should, of course, not be exaggerated. In 2019, its GDP per capita (in PPP terms) was comparable to that of Serbia and more than two times smaller than that of, for example, Slovenia. But the mere fact that China increased its wealth more than 20-fold in only four decades does make it truly extraordinary. The Chinese succeeded both because they profoundly reformed their economic institutions and also because their country was so underdeveloped in the 1970s and had an enormous pool of unproductively employed rural labourers just waiting to be tapped into. Without the former, China would not have achieved sustained economic development, while without the latter its development would not have been as impressive and sudden.

Modernizing reforms of the Chinese economy can roughly be divided into two periods or steps. First, peasant property was decollectivized in the 1970s and 1980s so as to dismantle the bad incentive structure that collectivization produces. Collective property tends to produce a tragedy of the commons, which in the Chinese case presented as a series of unimaginable famines.[73] With the introduction of the so-called 'Household responsibility system', in which each household was responsible for the fate of their own land, agricultural productivity started rising. In turn, the price of basic goods such as rice, wheat, and corn started dropping (up to 50% in two decades) while family incomes started rising.[74] In the same period, China started opening up for foreign investment, it introduced aspects of business freedom and replaced its planned system of prices with a dual-track system which allowed markets to set prices along those determined by the planners. The next step came in the 1990s with privatization reforms and more aggressive dismantling of tariffs on imported goods (the end of protectionism). In the years that followed, the private sector was greatly expanded (in 2005 it accounted for more than two thirds of total GDP) and the average tariff rate fell from more than 40% at the beginning of 1990s to only 10% in 2003, where it remained at least up until 2010.[75]

In sum, China's economy underwent quite substantial modernization. Therefore, unsurprisingly, the middle class has expanded and nowadays represents around 20% of the population.[76] Hundreds of millions of Chinese peasants stopped farming and moved over to the industrial and service sectors. When Mao died, almost 80% of the population was employed in agriculture, while today the share has dropped to less than 30%.[77] Income inequality also rose from an extremely low Gini coefficient of 0.16 under Mao to a middling-high of 0.55. Expectedly, labour and social unrest is increasing. Between 1993 and 2003 the annual number of protests rose from 10,000 to 58,000.[78] With time, the numbers continued to increase. A commonly cited figure is 180,000 cases of mass unrest in 2010, calculated by professor Sun Liping at Tsinghua University. A year later, in 2011, the Arab Spring strongly influenced Chinese citizens, and a country-wide pro-democratic protest was ongoing for a whole month.

So, when will China democratize, given its several modernizing steps? The answer to this question is complicated. Although there have been, without a doubt, important structural changes which have unleashed certain democratizing social forces, there are also forces pushing in the opposite direction. It is not at all clear, as is usually the case in social science, what the likely sum of these vector forces actually is. One of the more important reasons for scepticism about the prospects of Chinese democratization concerns its behemoth system of social surveillance.

Contemporary China can much more easily and effectively monitor and repress its citizens than was possible in classic cases of democracy through modernization such as Britain. There are more than 200 million CCTV cameras all over China, constantly watching and recording. Moreover, sophisticated software runs on this vast camera network, enabling computer recognition of people's faces and even their gait. On this basis, individuals can be identified and their activities logged in personalized profiles.

The infamous Social Credit System (SCS), inspiring Black Mirror episodes and evoking images of Orwellian dystopia outside China, is a part of this network. The SCS is an additional factor that strongly incentivizes conformist behaviour and demotivates citizens from dissent and subversive activities. It does so because the system actively rewards the former and punishes the latter. For example, 'deviants' who have repeatedly been spotted acting against government prescriptions are disallowed from buying plane tickets or boarding fast trains.[79] Moreover, there also exist non-governmental, commercial versions of the system which, although not strictly mandatory, work similarly. Citizens who are awarded a high score due to their proper behaviour have easier access to credit loans, enjoy vehicle discounts, and can even be granted prioritized access to health care.[80]

Now, the fact that the Chinese government has an easier time repressing popular dissent, because it can easily identify dissenters, implies at least two negative consequences for democratization. First, it is easier for protests to be nipped in the bud, defused before they even properly begin. The originating perpetrators can be identified and a targeted response from the government ensues. This was much harder in 19th century Britain, lacking street cameras and computer recognition software. Second, if protests somehow do manage to take off and spread, the government still has an easier time putting them down. This means that chances of successful resistance are doubly undercut. Furthermore, the fact that China also possesses social scoring systems means that individuals are more easily dissuaded from participating in unruly activities such as popular protests. This is so because if they do participate, their social score will be lowered, and with it access to social amenities reduced. If they do not participate, and instead show off how only government sanctioned activities interest them, they will be rewarded.

As we have just seen, even though China is modernizing and is thus structurally increasing its chances for democratization, there are also other, novel factors that work against this trend and thus, at the same time, reduce prospects for Chinese democratization. We cannot predict how these pull and push dynamics will work out in the end.

However, what is easier to predict, at least in rough and conditional terms, is that the Chinese political elite might soon be faced with an important dilemma.[81] The first scenario in the dilemma goes like this. *If the ruling elite does not allow its political regime to be opened up and sticks to dictatorship, long-term economic growth and development will be seriously endangered.* The problem with this is that in such conditions popular protest that is for now kept at bay will take off.

Institutional economics tells us that there are both direct and indirect mechanisms at work here. The direct mechanism is simply that dictatorships, if they want to survive, need to strongly restrict the freedom of speech and, relatedly, free information flows between the country and the outside world, as well as among the citizenry. Internet access, mass media, and other forms of communication have to be limited in scope, and their content carefully censured, as Beijing is well aware. This, however, has an enormous cost. Restricting information flows and suffocating free speech hurts the economy in the long run.

Once a country reaches a certain level of development – i.e. the point up until which growth is relatively easy to achieve as the labour supply from the countryside seems endless, a lot of physical infrastructure was built (roads, bridges, streets, apartment buildings etc.) and the starting point was so low that even small increases in development were cached out in huge growth rates – further sustained growth is not as easy to come by. High growth rates become less and less likely, and amassing physical capital and simply laying down infrastructure do not cut it anymore. From that point on, sustained, long-term economic growth and development is achieved primarily by technological innovations and revolutionary ideas about what to produce in an already saturated market, or how to organize production in as of yet unthinkable ways, so as to further increase productivity that is already high. However, authentic technological innovation and revolutionary new ideas are usually, correctly, not thought of as the main selling points of free-speech-crushing, secretive, punitive, and censorious closed autocracies such as China.[82]

The indirect mechanism does not directly concern restricted flows of information and the consequences of those restrictions for innovation in technology and ideas, but it does tie in to that as well. In order for economies to sustain long-term growth, there have to exist certain robust institutions, such as secure property rights, market competition, the absence of barriers to market entry etc. Without those, economic actors tend not to have strong and sustained incentives to invest in new entrepreneurial projects, as they know this task to be futile or undermined by the government. For example, in the absence of secure property rights, a successful businessperson might get expropriated (partially or wholly) by the dictator for his own personal enrichment or that of his cronies. A business might get taken over by the government or a large proportion of its profits might be taxed away. Or, to take a different example, the absence of market competition means that the government provides special privileges for favoured companies (those run by the dictator's cronies and pillars of support) and perhaps even explicitly punishes other, new economic actors who might be more efficient or have revolutionary products, thus undermining the economic position of the regime's close supporters. This all makes complete political sense for the dictator and his elite, but it discourages precisely those economic activities that are vital for the long-term economic growth and development of a country. And, indeed, today's Chinese entrepreneurs are very worried about expropriation. A majority (51%) report that they have already experienced it.[83]

The dictator cannot rule alone. He retains power by keeping his elite supporters happy. But the very means used to maintain elite stability, i.e. corruption, business expropriation, awarding monopoly privileges, preventing new, disruptive entrants to the market, undermine the country's ability to grow in the long run. On the one hand, absence of secure property rights discourages bottom-up – i.e. spontaneous, non-governmental – innovation and investment. This is precisely the type of innovation that aids in long-term economic development, because creativity and revolutionary ideas are unpredictable and thus hard to plan for, while the capacities for producing new ideas are dispersed through the populace across the whole country. On the other hand, barriers to entry, monopolies, and the general absence of market competition reduce both the incentive and capacity of potential new market entrants to undermine and eliminate previous, less efficient companies with lower quality production methods or technology. Chinese state-owned companies (SEOs), which are financially and otherwise privileged, are notoriously inefficient, but they are here to stay.[84]

Acemoglu and Robinson illustrate these issues with a simple example:

> Dai Guofang recognized the coming urban boom in China early on. New highways, business centers, residences, and skyscrapers were sprawling everywhere

around China in the 1990s, and Dai thought this growth would only pick up speed in the next decade. He reasoned that his company, Jingsu Tieben Iron and Steel, could capture a large market as a low-cost producer, especially compared with the inefficient state-owned steel factories. Dai planned to build a true steel giant, and with support from the local party bosses in Changzhou, he started building in 2003. By March 2004, however, the project had been stopped by order of the Chinese Communist Party in Beijing, and Dai was arrested for reasons never clearly articulated. The authorities may have presumed that they would find some incriminating evidence in Dai's accounts. In the event, he spent the next five years in jail and home detention, and was found guilty on a minor charge in 2009. His real crime was to start a large project that would compete with state-sponsored companies and do so without the approval of the higher-ups in the Communist Party. This was certainly the lesson that others drew from the case.[85]

Other examples abound. From the government closing down one of the biggest Chinese open markets, *de facto* owned by small stallholders, and transferring its ownership to a politically well-connected businessman, to the near wholesale political eradication of small, innovative Township Village Enterprises (TVEs) so that the state-protected, lumbering SOEs could relax as they no longer faced stiff competition from below.[86]

This is the first horn of the dilemma which Xi Jinping and his elite might soon face. In fact, its early signs are already visible. The Chinese economy is slowing down. Since 2007 when its growth rate was almost 14% or since 2010 when the economy expanded by 10%, the rate has been steadily declining for the past nine years such that it has hovered around 6% since 2014.[87] In the past few years China has no longer been growing faster than India which, between 1991 and 2015, it had been outpacing by at least a few but usually five or more percentage points. Moreover, economists estimate that Beijing is overstating Chinese growth in its official reports. Some estimates suggest that the actual growth rate is only half of what is reported.[88] The rate of productivity growth has also slowed down in the past five years. Between 1995 and 2013 the average rate stood at 15.5%. Since 2014, the average fell to only 5.7%[89]

The second scenario Beijing can undertake is the obverse of the first. *If it wants to forestall popular protests, it will have to allow long-term economic development by reforming the economic system and opening up its censorious regime.* But here the danger is that democracy ensues and the regime falls merely by a different route than in the first scenario.

This is so for three reasons. First, profound economic reform simply cannot happen unless China at least partially democratizes first or does so concurrently with the introduction of economic reforms. Simply declaring that from now on, in China, property rights will be respected and secure will not work as there is nothing preventing the ruling elite from going back on its word. In other words, citizens will not be incentivized to change their economic behaviour due to a simple declaration, as such an announcement within a dictatorial system is not credible. It would become credible only if the ruling elite actually renounced some of its political power by democratizing, which of course it does not want to do.

Second, the censorious nature of the regime, which is stifling its long-term economic prospects more and more, cannot be significantly toned down unless China also at least partially democratizes. This is so because democracies can structurally withstand free speech and free information flows, but dictatorships cannot. It is not only that here, too, issues of credible commitments inconveniently rear their heads but also that if censorship were to actually be suspended, and so long-term economic prospects improved, the regime would be in great danger of being swept over by democratic pressure from below. A dictator without censorship powers is a dictator that does not last.

Third, if China nevertheless somehow magically managed to engender long-term economic development even as a dictatorship (which is highly unlikely), a democratic transition would then still become more likely down the road precisely due to that long-term economic modernization and the standard mechanisms proffered by modernization theory.

In sum, the ruling Chinese elite seems to be confronted with two unattractive possibilities which, were one or the other to actually occur, might lead to the sort of political change unwanted by the political elite. State-led capitalism turns out, after all, not to be the great solution to dictatorial woes that it has been touted to be.

Conclusion

Modern economic development raises the chances of transition to democracy and contributes to the consolidation of a newly formed democratic regime. This empirical fact, or statistical correlation, is quite theoretically sensible. It should not surprise us that, historically, mass democracies primarily emerged in the 19th and 20th centuries with the arrival of the modern economic system, and particularly where it was and is most developed. This is because deep social structural change that happened with the transition from pre-capitalist to capitalist economies fundamentally transformed both the incentives and capacities that different social groups have in fighting for or against democracy. Furthermore, and precisely because of this, it should not surprise us if democracies that are either externally imposed in less developed and poor countries, or suddenly emerge there due to exogenous shocks, are much less likely to succeed. Successful democracies are usually the product of deep and relatively slow changes in the social structure. Such democracies come to be as a result of a compromise between a stable set of power relations among the elite and ordinary citizens. This, of course, is not the only way for a democracy to spring up. Top-down, elite-led transitions are possible and have happened. However, where democracy was not fought for in a popular struggle and on the basis of profound social structural change in favour of ordinary citizens, the resulting equilibrium is not stable and is thus prone to collapse.[90]

Notes

1. Boix 2011.
2. On the controversy see Przeworski et al. 2000; Faria et al. 2014.
3. Lipset 1959.
4. Acemoglu and Robinson 2006, 82.
5. Usmani 2018, 667.
6. Finding evidence for: Boix and Stokes 2003; Boix 2011; Che et al. 2013; Benhabib et al. 2013; Heid et al. 2012; Faria et al. 2014; Treisman 2020a. Finding evidence against: Przeworski et al. 2000; Acemoglu et al. 2009.
7. Broderstad 2018.
8. van Noort 2019.
9. Treisman 2020a.
10. Clark et al. 2013, 183. Original figures are expressed in constant 1985 dollars, PPP (purchasing power parity), and amount to $1,000, $4,000, $6,000, and $8,000.
11. Therborn 1979; Rueschemeyer et al. 1992; Acemoglu and Robinson 2006; Boix 2003.
12. Chenoweth and Stephan 2011.
13. Acemoglu and Robinson 2012; North et al. 2009; Brenner 2007.
14. Moore 1966.
15. Dahlum et al. 2019.
16. Acemoglu and Robinson 2006.
17. Ibid., 35–37. For a critique see Haggard and Kaufman 2015.
18. For empirical evidence see Usmani 2018; Albertus 2017.
19. For empirical evidence of the importance of collective action in democratic transitions, and industrial worker campaigns in particular, see Haggard and Kaufman 2015, chapter 2; Usmani 2018; Dahlum et al. 2019; Li Donni and Marino 2020.
20. Phillips and Wetherell 1995.
21. See https://www.britannica.com/event/Reform-Bill/.
22. Acemoglu and Robinson 2006, 4.
23. For empirical evidence, especially regarding the role of economic crises, see Haggard and Kaufman 1995; Haggard and Kaufman 2015; Geddes 1999; Acemoglu and Robinson 2006, 66; Li Donni and Marino 2020.
24. Clark et al. 2013, 199.
25. Bueno de Mesquita and Smith 2011.
26. Ezrow and Frantz 2011, 224.
27. Dickson 2016, 9.
28. Geddes 1999.
29. Abercrombie et al. 1980; Scott 1985; Chibber 2013, chapters 7 and 8.
30. Mercier 2020, 260.
31. Geddes et al. 2018, 104.
32. Ibid., 72–73.
33. Ibid., 104. See also Gandhi 2008.
34. Svolik 2012, 9.
35. Geddes 1999, 139.
36. Ibid.
37. Li Donni and Marino 2020.
38. Brancati 2016.
39. Barro 1996; Ross 2001; Ross 2013; Ross 2015.
40. Ross 2011, 4. Quoted in Clark et al. 2013, 199.
41. Ross 2011, 3–4. Quoted in Clark et al. 2013, 199.
42. Kendall-Taylor and Frantz 2014, 35–47.
43. Karatnycky and Ackerman 2005.
44. Haggard and Kaufman 2015, chapter 1.
45. Li Donni and Marino 2020.
46. Bidner et al. 2014.

47 Geddes et al. 2018, 179.
48 Kendall-Taylor and Frantz 2014.
49 Kuran 1997.
50 Geddes 2018.
51 See Kim and Kroeger 2017.
52 Bratton 2009, 347.
53 https://www.belfercenter.org/publication/selective-wilsonianism-material-interests-and-wests-support-democracy; Grigoryan 2020.
54 Levitsky and Way 2010, 46.
55 Clark et al. 2013, 290–302.
56 Ibid., 302.
57 Ibid., 304–305.
58 Treisman 2020b.
59 Przeworski and Limongi 1997; Przeworski 2005.
60 Brownlee 2017.
61 Boudreaux and Holcombe 2017, 27.
62 Brenner 2007; Lafrance and Post 2019.
63 Rueschemeyer et al. 1992, 278.
64 Ibid., 282.
65 Williamson 2009.
66 Roser and Ortiz-Ospina 2020.
67 Acemoglu and Robinson 2006, 40.
68 Ibid., 39.
69 Ibid., 312.
70 Ibid., 5–8.
71 Ibid., 7.
72 Bolt et al. 2018.
73 Hung 2016, 55.
74 Huang et al. 2008, 480.
75 Xiaojun 2012.
76 Xin 2018.
77 Felipe et al. 2016.
78 McLaughlin 2005.
79 Chan 2018.
80 Kostka 2019.
81 See also Acemoglu and Robinson 2012, chapter 15.
82 Kroenig 2020a, chapters 1 and 12.
83 Hou 2019, 4.
84 Hsieh and Klenow 2009; Zaho 2019.
85 Acemoglu and Robinson 2012, 437–438.
86 Acemoglu and Robinson 2019, chapter 7.
87 World Bank 2020.
88 Leng 2019.
89 Black and Morrison 2019.
90 Kadivar et al. 2019.

3
VOTERS ARE NOT DUMB, BUT WE DO NOT KNOW MUCH

Introduction: democracy is not magic

It is often said that a decision is correct in some way, or fair, if it was arrived at in a democratic fashion. That democratic decision-making is fair might turn out to be unobjectionable. Perhaps deciding on the *values* we want to realize in a society might really be fair, simply because one cannot be mistaken about values. They cannot be tested and researched with the purpose of finding out which ones are true and which ones are false. In contrast to facts, values do not purport what the world is like, which could be investigated if we wanted to separate ostensible facts from those that are actually true. Instead, values assert what the world *should* be like. This we cannot test. If someone claims that the Middle Ages in Europe were, for the most part, feudal and not capitalist, we can verify the claim. If someone asserts that the Middle Ages *should* have been feudal (or capitalist) or that we *should* resurrect feudalism today, this cannot be verified.

Taking advantage of psychological experiments, one might be able to test whether the person really believes this odd value they claim to support. Moreover, relying on surveys one could empirically examine whether other people agree or disagree with the person. But by doing this, one would merely be researching certain facts (about people's states of mind), not testing the veracity of the value itself. The test is not about whether the espoused value is correct, which is impossible, but about whether people assent to it.

When, then, different people hold to different values and disagree among each other which is best, there is no scientific experiment or observational study one can perform to decide who is actually correct. One obvious way they can still live together and dissolve the disagreement somewhat is to democratically decide which values a society will pursue.

Now, I was careful not to say this *is* fair, but that it *might* be fair. I did so because I am acutely aware of two key problems with the preceding way of reasoning that

DOI: 10.4324/9781003172574-3

are probably on the reader's mind right now. First, how do we know what is fair? If someone says that democratic decision-making is unfair, can we show them they are incorrect? No, value-judgements cannot be false or true in the way purported facts can be false or true. Second, even if we brush aside this meta-ethical issue, there is a yet different problem. Most people have a strong intuition that slavery is not fair. Does this intuition about the moral revulsion of slavery suddenly change if we know that slavery was instituted in a democratic way? Of course not. So, it is far from obvious that the democratic nature of a decision is what makes it fair.

However, when people vote they do not choose solely, or perhaps sometimes even primarily, what values a society will pursue. They also choose which candidate will enact their preferred values – hopefully with the *proper means*. Values can be amorphous and vague, such as 'the good of the nation', or they can be more concrete, like striving for higher economic growth, lower unemployment, easier access to healthcare, higher average education. Whatever the values of voters are, we expect them to choose, roughly, the candidate who will truly realize them. And in contrast to values, there is a matter of fact to how properly or efficiently a given value is pursued. It can be ascertained, empirically, which of the chosen means A, B, and C is the more correct way of putting value A into practice. The means with which a politician tries to, for example, lower the rate of unemployment or create more accessible healthcare can be empirically right or wrong, more proper or less proper. One cannot lower unemployment by halting all investment activity in a country. Healthcare will not be made more accessible if half of all doctors are fired. Privatization is one potential means of making healthcare cheaper, but it is an empirical question whether (and in which circumstances) privatization will actually make healthcare cheaper (and to what extent).

All this is to say that if we take, as we usually do, democratic elections to be a contest for the 'best' candidate who has the most correct way of addressing the values voters prefer, the voters themselves will probably have to possess some knowledge about basic (and even advanced) economic and political facts. If elections are to work well, voters will have to at least roughly know the following:

1. How do the competing candidates intend to take care of the problems worrying voters?
2. Are the candidates' plans the proper means of addressing a given problem or goal?
3. What is the current state of society under question, i.e. are the problems that worry voters real and do they actually have the negative consequences voters think they have?

If it turned out that many voters, perhaps even a majority, are mostly ignorant of the enumerated points, the democratic process will probably not work as well as we expect it to. It will not produce only sensible solutions to real problems but, instead, a more random result. Apart from sensible solutions to real problems, it will sometimes generate wrong solutions to real problems, sometimes wrong solutions to imagined problems, and yet other times actual sensible solutions to what are, sadly, only imagined problems.

Even in the case of voter ignorance, democracy might still produce what 'the people' wanted – but what they wanted will not reflect what they would have wanted had they known more. If voters are mistaken about the likely consequences a politician's proposed policy will have on domestic unemployment, which voters want lowered but the policy will raise, they will have *democratically* decided for *the wrong thing*. They would not have done so, had they read the relevant social scientific literature on the topic.

Democratic decision-making is not magic. It is just a process in which inputs get converted into outputs, and just like in statistics, 'garbage in, garbage out' also holds for democracy. When many people vote on the basis of bad information, bad decisions are more likely to occur – *democratic*, no doubt, but bad (even using the voters' own values as a criterion of 'bad').

Voters are, mostly, politically illiterate

How informed is the modern voter? How much does she know about politics and about the different political means for pursuing the values she thinks most important? The reader will probably not be surprised that things are not rosy, especially given Donald Trump's victory in 2016, the British decision to leave the European Union, and the recent rise of radical populist parties across Europe and Latin America. We have been witnessing quite a mess in recent times.

After decades and decades of surveys and research studies in the US, we now know in detail that the average American voter does not concern him- or herself too much with politics, be it the civic basics, who the political candidates on offer are, their proposed programs and plans, or the social scientific literature which examines the likely consequences of different policy ideas.[1] A recent poll found out that only a quarter of Americans (26%) can enumerate all three branches of the government (the legislative, executive, and judicial).[2] More than a third of them (37%) cannot think of even just one of the several rights the first amendment protects (the right to free expression, religion, assembly, etc.). Other polls reveal that about half of the electorate does not know what their state decides to dedicate the largest share of the budget to. One in three voters do not know who their governor is.[3] More than half wrongly think illegal immigrants in the US do not have the rights protected by the first amendment, which is perhaps unsurprising given how many Americans do not even know what the first amendment is.

Law professor Ilya Somin summarizes the findings of the broader literature. 'The reality that most voters are often ignorant of even very basic political information is one of the better-established findings of social science. Decades of accumulated evidence reinforces this conclusion.'[4] Among the various examples he gives, a standout is that in 2007 – in the time of the ongoing Iraqi conflict and the American war on terror – only a third (32%) of Americans were able to name Sunni Islam as one of the two major denominations of Islam, the adherents of which fought amongst each other over Iraqi rule (even though the question itself revealed the other, Shia denomination). He adds that in 1964, at the height of the Cold War, less than half of all Americans (38%) knew that the Soviet Union, America's arch nemesis, was not part of the famous Anti-Soviet alliance NATO. Political scientists concur with Somin and provide similarly bizarre examples for purposes of general illustration.[5]

But perhaps ignorance is solely the provenance of American voters. Europeans are probably likely to grab hold of such a qualification as we are no strangers to holding stereotypes about the alleged general, not just political, ignorance of the average American. Alas, evidence from Europe is quite similar to that sampled above.[6] Let us first consider Brexit, the British referendum decision to leave the EU. Research done by Ipsos MORI tells us that voter ignorance was quite heavily on display in this momentous event. As the authors pithily say in the first sentence of a report, 'The public have a number of significant misperceptions about the EU and how it affects life in the UK.'[7] Let me be more concrete.

- Citizens 'massively overestimate how many EU-born people now live in the UK. On average we think EU citizens make up 15% of the total UK population ..., when in reality it's 5%.'[8] Those that had expressed intent of voting for 'Leave' were even more wrong. They thought the proportion was 20%.
- Most (67%) correctly claim that the UK contributes more to the EU budget than it gets back from it. However, almost a quarter wrongly think that among all EU members the UK is the largest contributor. In reality, Germany is the largest, contributing twice the amount of the UK in 2014, followed by France and Italy, with the UK in fourth place.
- Almost 4 in every 10 citizens overestimate by a factor of 40 to 100 the number of children in EU countries that are receiving child benefits from the UK.
- Only 6 in 10 citizens correctly think that each EU member state elects its own candidates for the European parliament (EP). Almost a fifth wrongly think that the EP is an undemocratic institution, and a further quarter are unsure whether it is democratic or not.
- The average citizen is sure that the proportion of all investment in the UK coming from other EU member states is only 30%, while in reality it accounts for half of it (48%). They also wrongly think that China is responsible for 20% of all foreign investment in the UK, while it actually accounts for only 1%.

Two years after the 2016 referendum, the state of voter knowledgeability has not improved much.[9]

- Less than a third of the public (29%) knows that immigrants from European states contribute more to the UK state budget when paying taxes than they take out of it by using services provided by the welfare state. Most wrongly think the opposite is true.

- More than half of all citizens (56%) wrongly think European migration to their country has increased crime.
- Some 4 in 10 wrongly think that European immigrants have caused a reduction in the quality of UK healthcare.
- Roughly half of the British public (47%) wrongly claim that British unemployment among low-skilled workers has increased due to incoming migrants. The silver lining is that most correctly opine that migrants have not had a negative effect on the employment opportunities of high-skilled workers.

With all this in mind, it is not hard to understand why so many British voters decided to support the 'Leave' referendum option, which is otherwise quite incomprehensible to those voting 'Stay'. If a British citizen has the (false) impression that UK is being flooded with foreigners who, besides stealing jobs from low-skilled natives, are also criminals and are destroying the national healthcare system, he will be quite attracted to the idea that the country has to finally internationally insulate itself by putting up a (symbolic) border wall to keep all of this nasty business out. If millions upon millions of British voters think that the EP is an unaccountable, undemocratic institution sucking the British budget dry with no imaginable recompense, a winning 'Leave' decision is much more understandable.

Yet, political ignorance is a state of mind not only afflicting the Americans and the British. In fact, according to the Ipsos MORI 'Misperceptions Index', the latter are among the *least ignorant*.[10] In France, where political knowledge is somewhat worse, the typical voter in 2016 felt that a whole third (31%) of the population is Muslim, while in reality their share sat at 7.5%.[11] In Canada, people thought Muslims account for five-times as much of the population (17%) as they did in fact (3.2%). The French also claimed that the proportion of Muslim population will have increased to 40% in 2020, while the official forecast in 2016 when the study was performed had it at 8.3%. Among all the countries included in the survey, voters on average wrongly held that the state allots more than a fifth of its budget to healthcare, while the actual figure is 8%.

Now, before we dismiss all of this by blaming it on the recent rise of social media and the Millennials, or perhaps Gen Z who have, we are tempted to say, understandably disengaged from politics due to the precarities and vicissitudes of contemporary life, we might first want to look in the past. The famed political scientist Philip Converse, noted especially for his studies of public opinion, long ago diagnosed the frailty of voter knowledge. As he summarized his work and that of others 30 years ago, 'The two simple truths I know about the distribution of political information in modern electorates are that the mean is low and the variance is high.'[12] In 2000 he issued a slight modification of his statement, saying, 'The pithiest truth I have achieved about electorates is that where political information is concerned, the mean level is *very* low but the variance is *very* high.'[13] What he is saying is that the typical voter is quite uninformed, but that there is also a group of voters at the top who are strongly informed and a group of voters at the bottom who know less than nothing. Putting this more precisely, and drawing on a different work, 'the top 25 percent of voters are well informed, the next 25 percent are badly informed, the next 25 percent are know-nothings, and the bottom 25 percent are systematically misinformed.'[14]

Two good and two bad explanations

Now that we know the extent of voter ignorance, we need to explain it somehow. Why is it widespread and why does it exist at all? Two common-sense explanations that spring to mind immediately are simply (1) *stupidity* and (2) *the lack of opportunities to gather reliable information*.

Can most citizens who do not know much about politics really be called stupid? This does not seem likely, even putting aside any rhetorical misgivings about the term's impropriety. First, the same people who are voters are also workers, students, and consumers. If we are to accept the proposition that voters are simply cognitively incompetent, then that should also hold for them in their other everyday roles. But it does not hold. As consumers, people think, decide, and behave differently than they do as voters, even though the role of a consumer seems trivial while that of the voter singularly important. When buying an expensive family car or a new house, consumers usually take some effort to inform themselves about the choices at their disposal. They fret about the ratio between price and quality of a car, they want to examine, in person and for themselves, what the state of the house they are buying actually is, or they hire a professional to do it for them. They consult their mechanic for advice, ask friends and family who know a thing or two about cars to help, they flip through a catalogue which rates different cars on different dimensions. If a person is buying a house in a rainy and damp geographical region and sees black mold forming while walking through the basement, they are not likely to spend hundreds of thousands of dollars on it.

Second, in the 20th century many parts of the world experienced what is called the 'Flynn effect'. This is a phenomenon of quite large long-term increase in human intelligence as measured by IQ tests. For example, between 1942 and 2008 British children have seen their IQ scores rise by 14 points on average.[15] There are many proposed explanations for the phenomenon, such as improvements in health, nutrition, education, and living standards.[16] For our purposes, the precise causes and mechanisms of the Flynn effect are not particularly relevant. Rather, the important fact is that it happened. And even though IQ tests are certainly not the only, nor the best way of measuring human intelligence, it would have been really surprising had the cognitive ability of the average person stayed the same or even declined in the meantime.

Voter ignorance, therefore, is not best explained with simple stupidity. But what if voters do not lack cognitive ability, but rather are not equipped with the proper means to use it? That this is similarly unlikely as a candidate explanation for ignorance should become obvious once we remember how drastically the chances of properly informing and educating oneself on a particular topic have increased in the past century, especially in the last few decades. With the rise of mass media and the internet, information has become ubiquitous, cheap, fast, and easy to access. Before voting on Brexit, a voter can quickly find out in a reliable way – making use of official websites – whether EP representatives are elected or not. She can be instantly informed on how many Muslims there are in the UK, and whether perhaps Europe (instead of China) is the country's most important investor. The voter would have to expend more energy and time on finding out whether recent immigrants cause more crime than domestic-born citizens, or if they are 'stealing' jobs from domestic workers, because information such as this is not necessarily accessible through simple figures on official governmental sites. However, the internet now provides, as has never before been the case, instant access for the lay public to decades and decades of social scientific literature on the topic. Yes, a voter may have to pay for access, but given how academics increasingly put their pre-print (or even official, post-print) papers up on their personal or institutional websites for free this cannot be a real issue. Moreover, an enormous amount of important, policy-relevant social science research is nowadays released with a brief summary of the main results that is publicly available and even written with the public in mind.

Cognitive inability and a dearth of information can, at most, explain a small part of the general puzzle that is voter ignorance. Let us, therefore, turn to two better explanations. Both flow from a single empirical fact but from then on start diverging. The fact is this: an individual voter in a typical democracy has an astronomically small, or at least an exceedingly small, chance of actually changing something with the vote they cast.[17] If a particular voter informs herself and, come election day, votes for the candidate who truly has the most appropriate plan for improving economic growth and lowering unemployment, while also protecting a part of the environment, the final result of the election will have been the same as if she had abstained from casting her informed vote. The candidate would have won, or not, regardless of what one particular voter did. If in 2016, on the day of the Brexit referendum, a certain John Smith voted against Brexit, the outcome would have been the same as if he voted for it. The same goes for Trump's, or Bolsonaro's, or Orbán's, victory in the US, Brazil, and Hungarian case, respectively. Brexit did not turn, as no national election ever has, on a single vote.

Rational ignorance

Voters do not know much, on average, because we tend to be *rationally ignorant*.[18] This is so for two reasons. First, many voters correctly feel that it is almost impossible to affect who, or which party, wins when casting their individual vote (and each voter can only cast their own vote). Second, they also correctly intuit that robustly informing oneself on all of the important topics that are in play when election season rolls around takes time and energy. I claimed before that gathering the relevant information is not as hard today as it once was. Information is readily available. However, given the sheer amount of issues one has to wade through, it definitely still takes time and energy. Informing oneself on the extant candidates, their programs, how reliable their plans are, the likely consequences they will have if implemented as they have been written, etc., takes more than a minute. Moreover, time spent gathering political information is time that cannot be spent relaxing, spending quality time with one's children, finding an effective altruism charity organization and donating to it, or anything else for that matter. In short, becoming politically informed has costs and it has opportunity costs.

Now, if a voter connects the first feeling of individual insignificance with that of information-gathering being costly, he or she will likely become rationally ignorant. Note that we are not talking about sheer, ordinary ignorance here. A voter can choose to be ignorant because *he feels* becoming knowledgeable is pointless. If he has set out to become informed and so engages in a process of gathering all the relevant data and social science theories in order to form an evidence-based political opinion, he has gone through a lot of trouble for … what benefit? Neither he, at least if he is not personally passionate about being objectively, impartially informed on politics (and most of us are not), nor society at large, will have been made better-off due to him casting an informed vote. After all, a single voter in a typical national democratic election cannot change a thing.

On the other hand, if a voter does not make the effort of becoming informed, nothing will change for the worse come election day, but at least he will have not wasted his time. No benefits (like in the first case), but also no costs (unlike in the first case). Almost whatever the circumstances, when it comes to national elections, it is irrational for each individual voter to engage in political education. Note, importantly, that this even holds for altruistic voters who are not disincentivized by suffering personal costs. It holds because even they know that casting an informed vote is highly unlikely to benefit society.

Up until now I have put us in the shoes of *individual* voters, where we as individual persons usually are. However, *a collective* of individually rationally ignorant voters can, as we all know, wreak tremendous havoc. When many people are politically uninformed, because for each of them taken individually this is sensible, we sometimes get Brexit and Trump. Sadly, because an individual voter can only decide for *herself* (not for everyone else) whether to become informed or not in what is in the end a collective endeavour, what is individually rational for her can lead in such circumstances to collectively irrational outcomes. Can this tragedy be prevented, now that we know of it? No, it cannot, because whatever I do on election day, I still have no control of what other people do. And elections are decided not by me, or any individual, but by a collective over which no one voter has control.

Think of why consumers are usually *not* rationally ignorant. It is because a consumer feels that when buying a service or a product, making an informed decision results in greater benefits for the consumer, while being uninformed usually costs them. Consumers, as opposed to voters, have a quite strong incentive not to be ignorant about what they are buying. As I have already pointed out, when a parent is buying an expensive family car, pouring into it all their hard-earned savings, they know that being informed about different cars will pay off, while being ignorant can result in a bad decision which they will regret for years on end. It is, of course, still possible for a buyer not to know what he is buying and to make a bad decision. But in this case the buyer was *irrationally*, not rationally, *ignorant*. The incentives all pointed in the direction of gathering information, but he refused to follow them. This is irrational. In elections, the incentives are not pointing in the direction of becoming politically knowledgeable, so it is more likely, more rational, and more easily explained, that voters remain ignorant.

The theory of rational ignorance is a much more plausible account of voter ignorance than the preceding two candidate explanations. However, on its own it is insufficient. It does not explain why some voters are not just ignorant but are, quite the opposite, deeply convinced of being knowledgeable when they are, in fact, not. Rational ignorance is not able to explain misinformation and dogmatism. There is a profound difference between a voter simply not knowing the state of the country's economy, or the literature on the lack of criminogenic characteristics of immigration, and positively holding strong beliefs on these matters one way or the other without regard to actual evidence.

Rational irrationality

Here, a paradoxically sounding concept of *rational irrationality* can be of help.[19] Let us distinguish between two general types of rationality.

If a person is *instrumentally rational*, they are pursuing their goals, whatever they are, with the appropriate means. If the goal is to save money, a person who does not buy lots of luxury goods is instrumentally rational. If the goal is to feel relaxed and at peace, a person who takes a short, stress-free trip with their close friends is instrumentally rational. If a person is *epistemically rational*, they form their beliefs on the basis of best available evidence and without succumbing to distorting biases. If a voter thinks that the minimum wage does not increase unemployment, because they read a variety of contemporary meta-analyses on the topic which summarize hundreds and hundreds of empirical studies, they are epistemically rational. If, on the other hand, they believe the minimum wage has no negative employment effects because they feel like it, or because a random friend told them that, they are not epistemically rational.

You can be instrumentally rational and epistemically irrational at the same time. If the goal you are after is not the truth but simply feeling good or being accepted by your friends, and if the means of achieving that goal in a given situation is to affirm claims without evidence, or even in contrast to evidence, proclaiming baseless beliefs is completely instrumentally rational. Put differently, incentives can be such that it is instrumentally rational for a person to act in an epistemically irrational way. When this is the case, we say that someone is being *rationally irrational*.

If the only, or the most important, goal that human beings pursued was finding out the truth, rational irrationality would be in short supply. But 'the truth' is far from the only thing people want. As already intimated, we usually want to be recognized by others, we like to publicly display our identity, want to be accepted by friends, especially by close friends, be a part of a community of people who share ties of solidarity, etc. We achieve these goals by forming beliefs and by expressing them. If a John Smith belongs to a group of informal political enthusiasts, he will collect numerous opinions on politics that are congruent with, or simply copied from, those of his enthusiast friends. By forming and showing off his in-group beliefs, he will reap the benefits in terms of feeling comradery and solidarity with other members, of anchoring his identity, and perhaps even of experiencing grandiosity – especially when politics is concerned, with its grand ideas of what the good life is, what is 'truly' righteous, and who occupies 'the right side of history'.

In many such cases, being instrumentally rational will demand an immodest degree of epistemic irrationality. Solidifying one's political identity, having the feeling of being on the right side of history, and generating communal solidarity, usually pushes one not to primarily care about facts and evidence but rather to just accept what others around oneself believe.

I said previously that the two conditions generating rational irrationality are the twin facts of an individual having almost no chance of affecting electoral results and of information-gathering costs always being significantly higher than zero. Rational irrationality is caused by something similar. First, the ineffectiveness of a single vote, and second, the various psychological benefits of forming and expressing what often turn out to be incorrect beliefs.

Both rational ignorance and rational irrationality can be found in copious amounts where they do not cause a lot of material harm to people. People are, after all, responsive to incentives. Most are not epistemically irrational about what happens in the event of jumping out of a 51st floor onto the street below. Here, instrumental and epistemic rationality are aligned. If an individual wants to survive (which is one of the most important goals of the vast majority of people), they will usually not believe that jumping out of a window is followed by magically flying and landing on the ground without a scratch. Believing so would be a case of *irrational irrationality*.

Where politics is concerned, however, instrumental rationality is oftentimes opposed to epistemic rationality. That is especially so if we are talking about politics as enacted through informal social media debates, pub talks, political rallies, and voting. In contrast to jumping out the window, there are no negative material consequences for the voter personally, or even anyone else for that matter, if he decides to follow his fantastic notions about Trump and votes for him. After all, *one single vote* (as opposed to one single jump out of a sky-scraper) changes virtually nothing, either for better or worse. There are also usually no bad material consequences for the guys in the pub discussing, evidence-free, the alleged virtues of resurrecting Soviet-style communism, or Southern-style racial segregation, for the 21st century. But there is a whole lot to be gained, psychologically, by doing so.

In sum, rational ignorance helps explain why the average voter tends not to know much of the important political information out there, even though the average voter is neither stupid nor carelessly oblivious. Rational irrationality helps explain why some voters, and political enthusiasts on Twitter, nevertheless go on dogmatically forming various political beliefs without regard to well-established social science theories and evidence.

Is political irrationality really an issue?

Voter ignorance and irrationality are widespread, and by understanding the perverse incentives at play we now understand why they are widespread. However, what if there are certain mechanisms, either social or psychological, that might nevertheless prevent ignorance and irrationality driving electoral results? If this is true, the fact that voters do not know much is still a fact – but an irrelevant one. Two potentially relevant mechanisms come to mind.

The miracle of aggregation

Let us imagine that the majority of voters, say 80%, are politically ignorant. Let us further suppose that the remaining 20% are properly informed, hold representative values, i.e. they strive toward the same goals a typical citizen does, and are not biased in processing their information.

In this case, the 80% majority would be led by their ignorance to random mistakes when evaluating the various candidates, their policies, and their likely consequences. The remaining 20% would evaluate the political terrain properly. When all voters cast their votes, the decisions made by the 80% would, due to randomness and the law of big numbers, roughly cancel each other out. Some in the 80% voted for candidate A, some for B, others for C, etc. That could make the remaining 20%, the informed and unbiased voters, decisive. The candidate X they chose would electorally stand out among all the other candidates, as she received the most votes – the same proportion of the 80% of random votes as all other candidates did, and the extra 20% of informed votes. This, in a nutshell, is the miracle of aggregation.

It is a 'miracle' because, despite the majority being uninformed, the election produced a responsible outcome mirroring both the desires of the majority *and* the socio-political facts on the ground. If this really worked, political ignorance would no longer be a serious issue as at least its dangerous electoral consequences would be prevented.

The obvious problem with this reasoning is that even though the above scenario can be made to work, mathematically, there are multiple reasons why it is unlikely to happen in the real world. First, one of the assumptions of the described scenario is that mistakes are randomly distributed among the electorate, instead of being asymmetric and concentrated. I assumed that the 80% of voters will proportionally spread out among each of the candidates (for example, 10 percentage points of 80% for each of the 8 possible candidates). This is unlikely, because ignorant voters are not choosing blindly, wholly randomly, but rely on various feelings and intuition when deciding. They might choose the politician who seemed the most charismatic, well-dressed, or nice, during media and public appearances. Whatever the particular characteristic that voters choose to focus on, the fact is that not all candidates will appear equally charismatic or 'presidential', which means that the votes of ignorant voters will not be distributed proportionally.

Second, I assumed that the politically informed minority process their information unbiasedly. But as we have already seen when examining rational irrationality, and as we shall see in the next part of this chapter, this is rare. Voters who have some, or even a lot of, information are not guaranteed to use it responsibly, impartially, and judiciously. There is no necessity, or even high likelihood, that the informed minority will decide with respect to the truth instead of ideology.

Third, there is the assumption of the informed minority having representative values. This might be so, but again there are no guarantees or even high likelihoods. As Ilya Somin summarizes: 'The small minority of well-informed voters differ systematically from the rest in gender, income, race, age, religion, ideology, and a host of other politically relevant attributes It would be remarkable if the interests of this small, unrepresentative subset of the population coincided more than very roughly with those of the population at large.'[20]

Smart heuristics

The second saving grace of otherwise ignorant voters might be their reliance on unconscious mental shortcuts, also called heuristics, on the basis of which people sometimes act.[21] As I show in the next section, innate and acquired heuristics help individuals make a non-random decision to act even when information is for some reason lacking. If it turns out that reliance on these mental shortcuts systematically leads to good decisions – decisions that would have been made had the actor been sufficiently informed – political ignorance might not be an issue.

In principle, this could theoretically be true. But in the end it comes down to an empirical case-by-case investigation. There has been a debate raging in social psychology and behavioural economics, and still is, on this very question. In the 1990s, Gerd Gigerenzer and his colleagues critiqued Daniel Kahneman and Amos Tversky's work on how many heuristics lead to irrational or at least suboptimal decisions. Gigerenzer tried to either dispel the most egregious examples of human bias Kahneman and Tversky uncovered, or to show how they are actually quite 'ecologically' rational. By this he meant that many human mental shortcuts evolved in, and for, environments where the beliefs and behaviour they led to made sense.

Without going into detail, it is true that some heuristics are, in certain situations and according to certain definitions, rational. However, there are many heuristics that are not, such as the availability heuristic about which I will have more to say later on.[22] The unreliability of heuristics is even more striking when it comes to politics and the complex, highly unintuitive, or even counter-intuitive macrosocial processes involved in modern life that voters should probably have a handle on when casting a vote. Gigerenzer's ecologically rational heuristics that were naturally selected in humans because they helped them survive and reproduce are not likely to be of much help in deciding on which candidate has the more appropriate and feasible healthcare reform plan. If voters evaluate the sincerity of a candidate on the basis of her charisma or his looks (which is certainly a heuristic), this is not a very reliable decision-making algorithm. The same goes for reasoning in anecdotes, which we often tend to do. Generalizing about social trends on the basis of unrepresentative individual experiences is simply not reliable. If it were, specialized social scientists would be superfluous and thus out of a job. I agree with Somin that, 'While it would be foolish to deny that some helpful information can be derived from ordinary life, its usefulness to otherwise ill-informed voters is often greatly overestimated.'[23]

As with the miracle of aggregation, heuristics are not likely to take the edge out of political ignorance. This is not to say that mental shortcuts are completely useless, just that even with them various demagogic populisms and similar misinformed political movements are – quite apparently – not electorally short-circuited.

The psychology of political fallacies and dogmatism

When participating in an election, or just engaging in a political discussion, people rarely actively think that they are going to argue in favour of a position that is in reality indefensible *just so that* they can feel good. This would, after all, make them insincere, or inauthentic, which feels uncomfortable. It is much more likely for a person to deceive themselves and to think that they are actually pursuing the truth by supporting a lie a politician made, arguing for a conspiracy theory, or simply spouting political talking points with no real evidentiary justification. Nobody wants to think themselves misinformed, a liar, or a party hack.

But how come we can fool ourselves so easily? How is it possible that despite the lack of information, or by using it in such an emotionally charged, biased way, we vehemently defend our beliefs as the absolute truth? How come we are unaware of our own bluffing? Why do we not stop and think, for a second at least, that perhaps we are way off, especially given how little we have read on the topic, or how unscientific our sources?

The answer, in most general terms, comes from social psychology. In contrast to a pervasive Enlightenment myth – or, ironically, *a mythologized depiction of* Enlightenment ideas – about how the human minds work, people are not wholly rational, transparent, self-aware, disembodied minds. Human cognition is quite a limited and powerless thing, at least when it comes to reliably mirroring the world around it, *itself* included. Behavioural economics, social psychology, and evolutionary psychology have all been systematically revealing for a while now that the human brain is naturally created in a way that we tend to fool ourselves, are not aware of our real motives, selectively interpret data, underestimate danger, overestimate the frequency of rare events, unwittingly generalize on the basis of anecdotes instead of statistics, etc.

Human behaviour and beliefs are formed by what can be roughly classified as two different, even if overlapping, processes or systems.[24] System 2 encompasses conscious, slow, deliberate reasoning, which takes up a lot of energy and is more likely to be activated when the consequences of a wrong decision are dire. From afar, this system roughly approximates the idea that people are rational reasoners who are able to somewhat reliably examine the world around them. Even so, System 2 is rarely activated in banal, everyday situations. Then there is System 1 which entails unconscious, swift, intuitive information processing, involving sheer gut feeling and similar mechanisms. As already intimated, it is more likely to be triggered in routine, uninteresting circumstances people find themselves in during everyday life, where energy can be usefully conserved by not deliberating too much. System 1 tends to work automatically, without the need for long deliberation, instead serving us ideas, courses of action, and information through various mental shortcuts that we have already met – heuristics – and biases – about which I will have more to say later.

The 'availability heuristic' is a standard example. When System 1 is fired up and a person is forming their beliefs mostly by relying on unconscious mental shortcuts, they tend to evaluate the frequency of an event based on how easy an example of it comes to mind. The easier the recall, the greater the perceived importance or frequency of an event is. If one is lackadaisically engaged in a conversation on airplane travel safety, and a famous airplane crash quickly springs to mind, one tends to characterize flying as more dangerous or crashes as more likely. Statistics are put to the side, and there is no question of calmly, deliberately thinking through (System 2) what the various methods of transportation are and how comparatively dangerous they each are. A recent tragic airplane crash which was sensationally and vividly reported on in the media is all that it takes to generate a misleading feeling about how dangerous planes probably are, perhaps even in comparison to the objectively much less safe travel by car, for which no similar recent striking example is at hand.

Now swap out 'terrorism' for 'flying', and 'climate change' for 'travelling by car', and it should become clear why people engaging in political discussions often unwittingly and unconsciously overestimate events that are statistically unlikely but experientially vivid, and why they underestimate statistically likely events which are not as vivid.

So much for the general answer to the question about why we are so easily led astray in our thinking. Now let me give a more concrete explanation, involving several different steps, with an eye specifically to politically charged, polarized, and dogmatic beliefs and thinking.

I have mentioned again and again that, when it comes to politics, people have a strong need to belong to a community, to express loyalty to it, to reap the approval provided to them by its members, and even to demonize members of other groups, all the while arguing against facts or at least in obliviousness to them. This is sometimes called 'tribalism' or 'tribal psychology'. This psychological tendency and its behavioural outcomes, so readily on display in contemporary political life – not least in the US and Europe –, are probably not solely the result of current socialization patterns or the arbitrary decision of a few individuals, but are rather a resilient part of human nature.[25] It seems that people might be attracted to tribalism due to standard evolutionary reasons having to do with, at first, random variation and, later on, selective survival and reproduction. Recently, a team of social and evolutionary psychologists has concisely proposed the thesis, synthesizing a vast body of extant research:

The human mind was forged by the crucible of coalitional conflict. For many thousands of years, human tribes have competed against each other. Coalitions that were more cooperative and cohesive not only survived but also appropriated land and resources from other coalitions and therefore reproduced more prolifically, thus passing their genes (and their loyalty traits) to later generations. Because coalitional coordination and commitment were crucial to group success, tribes punished and ostracized defectors and rewarded loyal members with status and resources (as they continue to do today). Thus, displays of loyalty and commitment to other members of the tribe also enhanced individual-level fitness (by increasing status and resources and minimizing risks of ostracism). Over time, this practice would select for traits that signal and enhance coalitional commitment, such as in-group favouritism.[26]

An important implication follows if this is correct. Because if people are naturally tribal creatures, our tendency to form groups, display loyalty to them, and demonize others will not easily be rooted out and will, to an extent, hold for most people. Furthermore, politics seems like the most obvious terrain for tribalistic human behaviour to play out. Political enthusiasts in group A (and every other group) will at least *tend to* process political information in a way that strengthens their ideology and signals in-group loyalty. At the same time, they will tend to utilize facts and theories in a way that mars the image of members of group B. Such demonization will, in turn, strengthen in-group loyalty on the part of members of group A. Tribalistic psychology explains, at least in part, why in politics both at the lay and the professional level we usually do not care about evidence and do not consider whether we are right or wrong. For most people engaged in politics, a much more important goal, which is both psychologically beneficial and motivationally strong, is to display loyalty and toe the line. Now, none of this means that tribalism is inevitable and that we cannot do anything about it. It just means that we naturally gravitate towards it and that it will, therefore, take a lot of willpower and effort to circumvent.[27]

Tribalism is far from the whole story. Apart from it, and in conjunction with it – further fanning its flames – are the myriad cognitive biases that human also possess, in part, due to natural selection. One such bias is the 'confirmation bias'. It nudges us to, unwittingly, search for, interpret, and remember information 'in such a way that it systematically impedes the possibility that the hypothesis could be rejected – that is, it fosters the immunity of the hypothesis.'[28] Confirmation bias 'helps us' to hold on to beliefs we already have and cherish, without the guilty feeling of knowing that what we believe is actually false.

Confirmation bias helps explain why being tribalistic is so easy and guilt-free. It allows individuals to accept otherwise dubious in-group beliefs without, at the same time, feeling like a cheat. It allows individuals to intellectually fortify and protect their beliefs from any potential onslaught from outside. It allows them to display group loyalty, all the while thinking that doing so is completely congruent with truth and facts. Over time, this obviously leads to dogmatism, especially when it comes to moral beliefs, grand political ideas, and encountering disbelievers. A person's loyalty to the tribe is now secure, as is their hatred of the other tribe. Tribalism has been unleashed and is in full effect.

Then there is the extremely well-replicated and undisputed 'Dunning-Kruger effect'. This is another example of a cognitive bias human beings suffer from. More specifically, it is the psychological tendency of people not to realize the extent of their own ignorance or incompetence. 'In short, those who are incompetent, for lack of a better term, should have little insight into their incompetence.'[29] People are not just ignorant on certain topics, for example how the economy works or what the laws of physical motion are, but are ignorant of their own ignorance. In other words, there is plain old ignorance, and then there is also meta-ignorance.

This cognitive bug can cause problems. Those who are not competent in a certain activity, or who do not know much on a given topic, tend to wrongly overestimate their competence or knowledge. Instead of a person facing their own ignorance, recognizing it, and being epistemically humbled as a result, they might think they are *much less* ignorant than they really are. For example, a voter who does not know much about economics but nevertheless engages in economic reasoning will commit glaring errors that are to him – due to not knowing a whole lot about economics – simply invisible and therefore not obvious at all. Moreover, such a voter will not be able to successfully assess the correctness of a professional economist's claim, because due to his own economics illiteracy he lacks the necessary skills to do so. David Dunning sums up the intractableness of the issue:

> Want to know if one has constructed a logically sound argument? That act of evaluation depends on the exact same know-how needed to construct a sound argument. Thus, if poor performers suffer deficits in knowledge that failed them when it came time to form correct responses, those exact same deficits would similarly fail them when it came time to judge the worth of those responses. They would not know when their responses were incorrect; they would not know when others formed better ones.[30]

An interesting question that arises after all this is whether different political groups are similarly likely to suffer from tribalism and cognitive biases. Both are widespread, but it is completely possible that they are more concentrated in parts of the political landscape than in others. Currently available meta-studies in political psychology do not point to as clear cut a picture as we might want them to. Some researchers consistently find that conservatives are more dogmatic and loyal to the in-group than liberals. Not surprisingly, this is the 'ideological asymmetry' thesis. Other researchers demur. They point to evidence that shows systematic differences between both groups to be small or non-existent. One important recent meta-study, which examined 51 psychological experiments designed to uncover degrees of political bias, found evidence suggestive of 'ideological symmetry'.[31] As they conclude, 'both liberals and conservatives show a consistent tendency to be less sceptical consumers of information that supports rather than challenges their political beliefs. The fact that neither side is immune to partisan bias may be the more important point than whether one side falls prey to it slightly more than the other.'[32] However, just a few years ago, a different and even bigger meta-analysis found evidence on the side of the ideological asymmetry thesis.[33] Conservatives were found to be markedly more dogmatic than liberals. Simply, but sadly, not enough evidence has been gathered and not enough time has passed for the field to start generating a consensus view on the matter.

Cognitive capacity is no safeguard against dogmatism, but curiosity is

If people did not systematically succumb to tribal and other biases, the problem of political irrationality might be solved by education and exhortation designed to shift people's thinking more in the direction of System 2 reasoning. We would then expect those that are more able to engage in conscious reflection to be less dogmatic and less prone to making errors. But, tribalism and cognitive biases are real and strong. Therefore, education and higher cognitive capacity on the part of political partisans will probably not work. In fact, it might make things worse by enabling the better informed and more able reasoners to achieve even higher degrees of success in their partisan political endeavours and their tribal quest of selective truth-seeking.

Multiple recent and well-regarded psychological experiments attest to this. In one such study, participants' cognitive ability (System 2 thinking) was first examined via a standard test of cognitive reflection. Then, participants were scored on their willingness to accept evidence showing their political 'enemies' to be undogmatic and reflective. The main conclusion of the study was that the individuals who received the highest scores on the cognitive reflection test were the most likely to be biased, or to process information in a way 'that promotes individuals' interests in forming and maintaining beliefs that signify their loyalty to important affinity groups.'[34] The most able reasoners were the most successful in being rationally irrational. This finding holds for both liberals and conservatives.[35]

Other studies come to similar conclusions. In a recent experiment, participants were given a counter-intuitive quantitative problem to solve which required them to engage in careful inferential reasoning from the provided evidence.[36] The same maths problem was presented in two different tests to two separate (but equally representative) groups, and the cognitive ability of all participants was measured beforehand. Their political affiliations (Democrat or Republican) were also established in advance. The first test was designed in a politically neutral way. The second test, quantitatively the same, was dressed up in political terms so that it was 'about' open-carry gun laws and their likely consequences. Three key conclusions were reached.

First, as we would expect, the successful solution of the first test was dependent on how capable an individual is in inferential reasoning. Those who scored lower on the measure of cognitive ability were also more likely to answer the quantitative puzzle wrongly. Participants' political beliefs had no effect and did not cloud the correct judgement of the more able individuals. Democrats and Republicans answered correctly or incorrectly in congruence with their abilities, not their political affiliation.

Second, political beliefs started having strong effects in the second test that was administered, even though it was quantitatively the same as the first one. Due to their political affiliation, Democrats wanted the correct answer to be the one that suggests that banning open-carry laws reduces gun deaths. Republicans wanted the truth to be the reverse. All this even though it was made clear to them that the quantitative puzzle they were solving was fictional, merely a hypothetical numerical example of maths logic, having no relation to the real world.

Third and most importantly, while solving the second, politically charged test, those with greater cognitive ability turned out to be *more politically biased* than the less able participants. Politics had a stronger effect in leading them to the mathematically wrong, but politically 'sound', conclusion. This is not, in fact, surprising. The more proficient Democrats and Republicans had, due to their higher ability, an easier time of finding the correct answer in cases where this was also ideologically appropriate. Their less capable comrades on both sides had a harder time figuring out the maths when it served them to figure it out.

When we are evaluating the truth but are also in the thrall of tribalism and cognitive biases, we are not acting as dispassionate truth-seekers who just want to find out what is the case. Instead, we act like a lawyer trying to get his client off the hook, while smearing the prosecution, witnesses, and other evidence. Lawyers are not neutral arbiters of the truth, trying to collect all the relevant evidence for and against. They are not guided solely, or even primarily, by the evidence wherever it may lead. So, it comes as no surprise when psychological experiments tell us that things do not get better when injecting extra education and cognitive ability into such a (political) lawyer. A capable lawyer is just as motivated to win (not find the truth) as is his incapable counterpart. The difference is that the capable one is much more likely to get his metaphorical mob boss client off the hook than the incapable one is.

If cognitive ability does not help with political dogmatism and bias, what does? Well, going by the experimental evidence above one would think that something having to do not with the ability, but the motivation, goals, and interests of a person should help. More precisely, the research is telling us that, even though scientific literacy is not necessarily helpful, *science curiosity* is.[37] The people who are, for whatever reasons, more *interested* in the truth than in displaying tribal loyalty tend also to be less biased and even less polarized across party lines as a result:

> our data showed that right-leaning subjects were substantially less likely to believe that human activity is causing global temperatures to rise than were left-leaning ones *and* that this differential grew substantially as respondents' science-comprehension scores increased. Higher levels of science curiosity, in contrast, were associated with greater acceptance of human-caused climate change among *both* right-leaning and left-leaning study subjects.[38]

The gap in beliefs about climate change is substantially higher among scientifically literate left-leaning and right-leaning subjects as compared to the gap that exists among less scientifically literate people on both sides of the political divide. The gap widens with scientific comprehension and narrows with science curiosity. In principle, this is good news for democracy. The only problem is that in the real world many people are under the sway of tribalism, and there are strong psychological and material incentives for this to persist. Curiosity is, both in lay and elite politics, an exceedingly rare commodity. We are, most of us, political partisans less interested in the truth and more interested in playing make-believe lawyers.

Voters are misguided even about each other

Rational ignorance and rational irrationality unleash political ignorance and political fallacies. Tribalism and cognitive biases explain why we feel so nice when, by being politically partisan and misinformed, we show off our unwavering loyalty to the tribe, and why we tend to not recognize how misguided and dogmatic we are being in doing so. With all this in mind, it should not shock us to find out that voters are not only wrong on the general political facts but that they also misperceive the basic beliefs for which the members of the other side stand.

According to an influential 2019 study, Democrats wrongly think that only about half of all Republicans approve of 'properly controlled legal immigration' to the US. In fact, the real share is around 85%.[39] Democrats are also wrong about how many Republicans believe that American racism is still a thing. They say that only about 50% of Republicans think so, while in reality around 80% do. The perceptions of Democrats on how xenophobic and racist Republicans are do not approximate the truth.

On the other hand, Republicans are just as wrong in thinking that less than half of Democrats take police officers to be generally good people.[40] In reality, 85% of Democrats think so. Republicans are similarly misguided in estimating how many Democrats would call themselves proud patriots while recognizing the mistakes the US has made. Republicans are of the opinion than only 1 in 2 Democrats are like this, when in fact 8 in 10 are. The perceptions of Republicans on how anti-police and anti-American the ostensibly rootless cosmopolitan Democrats are, are way off.

In a similar study that was published in 2018, two researchers found out that the typical American is badly mistaken in thinking that a whopping 38% of Republicans are very rich, i.e. making more than $250,000 a year, as the real share of such Republicans is only at 2%.[41] They uncovered that the average American significantly overestimates how many Democrats belong to the LGBT community. The real share is 6%, while the on-the-ground overestimate has it at 32%. They conclude that these mistakes are not generated so much by a general inability to think straight. Rather, they are caused by belonging to, and identifying with, one or the other side and by being interested in politics. The more a person is interested in politics, the more mistaken their perceptions about both parties.

One explanation for these mistakes which flows directly from the preceding discussion involves what can be termed 'echo chambers'. Tribalism and cognitive biases nudge people to create social situations in which members of a political group A talk mostly with one another and not with their political opponents who belong to group B. In these metaphorical chambers, which started spreading especially after the emergence of television and radio programs devoted wholly to a particular political side, and were further exacerbated by the internet and social media, members of group A generate *their own distorted views* on what the views of group B are. Instead of coming into contact with the real members of group B and their actual views, those belonging to group A increasingly form their opinions on B in a vacuum and by confirming each other's opinions and stereotypes. The link between reality and perception starts to fragment.

This explanation of the political perception gap by reference to echo chambers is congruent with the extant evidence on the matter. Researchers found a strong correlation between exposure to partisan media and misperception. The more intensely people follow the media, the bigger the gap between their perception of the opposite political side and the actual views of the opposite side. The nature of the medium is, of course, highly important. A more radical medium – both on the right and the left – is tied to a bigger perception gap. It is important to note that this is only a simple correlation that does not allow us to draw any robust causal inference. We do not know whether more exposure to news media *causes* a bigger gap between perception and reality, but something like that does seem theoretically plausible and both variables are strongly statistically correlated.

Nevertheless, there is something that we do get right

In chapter 2, I noted that the correlation between economic development and the democratic nature of a social system is strong and robust. Now, there exists yet another famous correlation uncovered by political science – *retrospective voting*. This is again a strong and robust correlation, but this time it occurs between the state of the economy and the support for the incumbent party. The worse shape the economy is in, the higher the likelihood of voters not supporting the incumbent in the coming elections. The lower the unemployment, or the larger the growth of the economy, the more likely it is for the incumbent to be re-elected. Here is the conclusion of a classic meta-analysis done on various studies of retrospective voting in the US and in multiple Western-European countries:

> For all democratic nations that have received a reasonable amount of study, plausible economic indicators, objective and subjective, can be shown to account for much of the variance in government support. In multivariate competition, controlling for other aggregate issue measures, the economic indicators hold their own. Indeed, the savvy modeller, given the choice of only one predictor, would do well to select an economic measure.[42]

It seems, therefore, that despite their general ignorance and even misinformation, voters somehow succeed at least in reliably catching on to how the economy is doing and whether it is high time to throw the old rascals out. This is interesting and gives one hope in light of all that has been said previously.

However, too much optimism might be unfounded. Before happily concluding that voter ignorance is dispelled by the fact of retrospective voting, we have to confront an uncomfortable question. Is it really appropriate that voters punish governments under whose rule the economy soured, while rewarding those that presided over a booming economy? Might it not be misguided for voters to infer causality (government A has *caused* economic growth) from what could be a mere coincidence (the economy was growing *while* government A ruled)? The answer the literature provides on this question is mixed.

Some political scientists, like Achen and Bartels, quite convincingly show that retrospective voting is not such a democratic panacea as it might at first seem.[43] They charge retrospective voters with myopia and with misguidedly showering praise or casting blame on the wrong actors, the ruling politicians. It is myopic, they say, because retrospective voters focus solely on the past few months or, at most, a year of movement in the economy. They are not considering the whole period four of five-year period a particular party was in power. This means that even if voters are correctly inferring causality from correlation, their perceptions are likely to be highly skewed and unrepresentative of the whole term. If a ruling party significantly improved the economy in the first three years but then a sudden downturn occurs in the months leading to election, it will be punished by the voters even though it really should not have been judged so harshly. And, of course, the reverse scenario can also happen and is just as unfair. Moreover, putting myopia aside, retrospective voting assigns responsibility for economic events to politicians even though, barring extraordinary circumstances and radical policies, politicians rarely significantly affect economic outlook in developed countries.

Other researchers are less worried, as a recent meta-analysis showed.[44] To take just one example, Duch and Stevenson looked at more than 150 surveys from 18 different countries and found that voters tend to vote retrospectively more 'when it is easier to assign responsibility for economic outcomes to a given party.'[45] In their opinion voters do not look to politicians for all good and bad economic outcomes that happen, but are more nuanced and therefore more precise in their judgement.

Fair or unfair, it is a fact that voters vote retrospectively. Let me transition to the next section by briefly considering where voters get all the information that is enabling them to vote retrospectively. There are two sources of information – and they are again not as reliable as we might want them to be.[46] First, voters rely on their perceptions of what is going on in the broader region in which the live. They look around and wonder what is happening to other people in their neighbourhood or the town they live in. If regional unemployment is high and increasing, they estimate – despite, for example, personally still having a job – that the economy has turned for the worse and that something has to be done. Second, they rely on news reports about the state of the regional or even the national economy. At least a part of their economic perceptions are formed on the basis of what newscasters tell them.

Selfish egocentrics or altruistic sociotropes?

In the first part of this chapter, where I discussed a potential mechanism for reducing voter ignorance called the miracle of aggregation, I presented three reasons why the mechanism short-circuits in practice. The last reason was that even an unbiased and informed minority might not have representative values, which is why their voting decision would not be of help to the majority of uninformed voters – their goals simply differ too much. It seems self-evident that different groups of voters with differing demographic or economic characteristics pursue different goals when voting.

For example, it seems obvious that poor people probably overwhelmingly support candidates fighting for higher taxes and much more wealth redistribution, while the rich vote strongly against both. We would expect that unemployed people want new jobs to be created, and that blue-collar workers working in those sectors of the economy that are forced to compete with foreign firms are firmly against free international trade that economically endangers them. In contrast, government and public employees, or private-sector workers not facing international competition, are not expected to necessarily support high tariffs and erecting other trade barriers, simply because international trade does not hurt them but rather helps them. Youth voters, we think, are likely strongly in favour of policies beneficial to young people, while older voters are much more concerned with the pension system, a robust healthcare plan, and affordable elderly care.

In short, it is intuitive to think that the decisions of voters will reflect their own personal situation in society. However, surprisingly, this is often not really the case. So-called 'pocketbook' voting is much less likely to happen than what is usually termed 'sociotropic' voting. When deciding, voters think more broadly and ask themselves what would ostensibly benefit the whole nation, or a region where they live, and not what would make the most sense given their individual, personal position in society.

To make this more concrete, let us look at voting patterns of voters who have been, and those who have not been, personally influenced by, say, the negative effects of international trade competition with China. Surprisingly, there is no important difference between groups. Here are the findings of two studies from 2018 examining the case of Western Europe and Brexit:

> our evidence suggests that the effect of import competition is not confined to specific groups—such as the unemployed or manufacturing workers—which might be more directly affected by Chinese imports. To the contrary, there is evidence of a significant effect even for service workers and public-sector employees, who are in principle more sheltered from foreign competition in manufacturing activities. As globalization threatens the success and survival of entire industrial districts, the affected communities seem to respond with their voting behavior sociotropically.[47]

[T]he impact of import competition is not restricted to a specific category of voters, for example, the unemployed, who might be most directly affected by the shock. ... By and large, this evidence is consistent with a sociotropic reaction of voters to the globalization shock, rather than a purely pocketbook one. In other words, individuals seem to respond broadly to the general economic situation of their region, regardless of their specific condition.[48]

These findings are pretty robust. A 2012 meta-analysis found similar results. '[E]mpirical analyses find that industry affiliation is an inconsistent or weak predictor of individual attitudes on trade.'[49] A voter's personal, individual position is not important. At least when it comes to the issue of international trade, voters are not egocentrics.[50]

The same sociotropic conclusions appear elsewhere in the literature. Take a look at an important 2014 meta-analysis in which the researchers combed through the extant studies on citizens' immigration views:

Consistently, immigration attitudes show little evidence of being strongly correlated with personal economic circumstances. Instead, research finds that immigration attitudes are shaped by sociotropic concerns about its cultural impacts—and to a lesser extent its economic impacts—on the nation as a whole. This pattern of results has held up as scholars have increasingly turned to experimental tests, and it holds for the United States, Canada, and Western Europe.[51]

Again, I find it very intuitively plausible that workers employed in sectors where employers have an interest in replacing them with cheaper foreign workers would form anti-immigration electoral views. This would be standard pocketbook voting. It seems, however, not to pan out. As the authors of the aforementioned 2014 meta-analysis bluntly put it, 'Although the labor market competition mechanism might operate under special circumstances of pronounced economic threat, the significant majority of prior work finds that labor market competition does not shape attitudes of the mass public.' In a recent study of voter support for Donald Trump in the 2016 election, Diana Mutz reviewed the existing literature on the topic and came to the same conclusions. We have heard a lot from news media about how Trump being successfully elected president occurred due to poor working-class revenge fostered by US international trade with China. Mutz denies this and reviews the literature thus:

over many decades of scholarship, evidence of voters politicizing personal economic hardship has been exceedingly rare. Although aggregate-level evidence has been suggestive of a public that blames incumbents for general economic downturns and rewards incumbents for economic gains, these relationships seldom hold up at the level of individual economic hardship. Across a wide range of issues, scholars have found that citizens seldom form policy or candidate preferences on the basis of their family's personal economic self-interest.[52]

Even studies finding some support for the pocketbook thesis are quite reserved about their results. According to one such study carried out between July 2007 and April 2009, only 59% of workers who lost their jobs during the crisis wanted funds for governmental programs designed to help the poor and the unemployed to increase.[53] At the same time, almost half (47%) of the workers who *did not lose* their jobs also supported increasing funding. Even though this is a statistically significant difference and it points in the right direction, one would expect a much larger difference if the pocketbook thesis is true. In fact, the author of the study himself notes that 'it would be misguided to interpret the findings of this study as indicating that voters' welfare policy preferences are simply a function of self-interested considerations; such an interpretation ignores a set of the findings that, taken together, suggest otherwise.'[54] Among these other findings is that 'despite the dramatic changes in people's economic fortunes during the years of the crisis, a large majority still maintained their prior views on welfare policy.'[55]

A different study focused on the period between 2006 and 2010, and similarly examined the economic views of workers who just lost their jobs (and those who did not) and their opinion on wealth redistribution policies.[56] They wanted to find out whether there is an important difference in subjective support for such policies among people with significantly different objective economic positions. They concluded that there is a difference and that it is important. Nevertheless, the difference is not consistently strong. For example, comparing both groups in the 2008–2010 period we can see that the difference is no more than 10 percentage points: 33% of newly unemployed supported redistribution, while 23% of the still employed did so. Comparing workers who suffered significant income reductions, but kept their jobs, with those who did not lose any income, the differences were smaller still: redistribution was supported by 27% of the former and 23% of the latter.

Voters are mostly sociotropic, not egocentric. But why, exactly? There are two plausible explanations. First, voters might use elections (and other opportunities of expressing their political preferences) to signal how altruistic, unselfish, and concerned with the welfare of their fellow citizens they are. Even though I claimed in chapter 1 that most people should descriptively be thought of as tilting towards self-interestedness, there are social situations in which altruism is more likely. Elections and merely talking about politics are examples of precisely such situations. This is so because talk is cheap and because a voter is not personally hurt if deciding in an altruistic manner when casting a vote. After all, a single voter's decision does not change the outcome of the election. Some researchers are convinced this is the case, i.e. that sociotropic voters are altruistic voters. In fact, they run together sociotropy with altruism. For example, this is how Yotam Margalit interprets the literature on sociotropic voting: 'substantial public opinion research indicates that preference formation is often *not* based on one's material self-interest.'[57] Jason Brennan comes to the same conclusion: 'Political scientists have conducted numerous empirical studies of voter behavior, using a wide variety of methods. They overwhelmingly conclude that voters do *not* vote selfishly.'[58]

It is, of course, possible that lurking behind sociotropic voting are authentic altruistic preferences. However, it is also at least *logically* possible that sociotropy is just self-interest in different garb. This would be the second explanation mentioned above. Perhaps voters *are* self-interested, but make their decisions on who to vote for on the seemingly altruistic basis of national or regional indicators of 'wellbeing' simply because they reason that improving broader regional welfare translates to better economic and social opportunities, and more safety, for *themselves* as well. As two pioneers of the sociotropic voting thesis emphasize, we must take care not to conflate 'sociotropic voters with altruistic ones. Voters might be voting in favor of politicians or parties that they think will further the public interest as an indirect route to furthering their own interests, as members of the public.'[59]

We need more fine-grained, precise empirical studies of voter behaviour to know for sure whether sociotropy is altruistic or self-interested.[60] For now, all we really know is that voters usually decide on their perception not of their own social position (being employed or unemployed, exposed to foreign competition or not) but that of the wider region or even the nation of which they are a part.

Conclusion

We, the voters, are not dumb. Despite that, however, we are on average not very, or properly, informed about political matters. That this is so is not inexplicable in the slightest. An individual voter's vote has an infinitesimally small chance of deciding who assumes presidency or which party gets the majority in parliament. This means that however informed an individual voter decides to become, her effort, time, and energy are spent doing something that will not matter, electorally, in the end. Most ordinary people are, then, quite instrumentally rational when they never take the time to become highly educated on politics.

There are those who are, for some reason, personally passionate about politics and derive great delight in becoming more informed on various political topics. Sadly, as we have seen, many of them tend to acquire and process political information akin to how a hardcore football fan would go about it. They use the wealth of information at their disposal in a highly skewed, partisan way so that they are able to root for their favourite team even more, all the while mocking their opponents, not taking them seriously, and demonizing them. Various human psychological traits, such as tribalism and various cognitive biases, are fanning the flames of political hooliganism and making things even worse. Such epistemic irrationality is in high demand in endless bar-room discussions and even when it comes time to cast a vote, simply because people deep down know, or at least feel, that they individually cannot really change anything for the worse but they can gain much, psychologically, by doing so.

Of course, the major social problem with this is that such 'social dilemmas' definitely do have (bad) consequences when a whole lot of people are participating in them. Even though for each individual uninformed or highly biased voter it is rational to behave like that, because they *themselves* cannot change anything either for the better or worse, this behaviour is highly irrational when looking at it from a broader social perspective, i.e. when there is a large collective body of uninformed or biased voters. Elections can turn out to be a sort of political tragedy of the commons. They can be tragic not because they might produce 'bad outcomes' but because – as in classic Greek tragedies – they might produce bad outcomes without any single individual being able to stop that.

None of this should be taken, necessarily, as a strong indictment of democracy. At least for now democracy is, to paraphrase the well-known quote somewhat, the best political system ever invented in human history, as far as realistic and mass-scale political regimes go, and if our criterion of 'good' is the welfare of the typical person. In general, democracies are, in comparison to non-democracies, more responsive to the needs of ordinary citizens (even though these needs sometimes produce Brexit or a Trump presidency), more transparent, more egalitarian, richer, and more strongly correlated with various indexes of human welfare. I will have more to say on this in the next chapter. However, it is important to also acknowledge that democracies have their own share of structural issues, and that these can be used to explain certain phenomena which might otherwise, had we been romanticising democracy, either be overlooked or explained away as surprising anomalies.

Notes

1 Somin 2013, chapter 1.
2 Annenberg Public Policy Center 2017.
3 Rosen 2018.
4 Somin 2013, 17.
5 See Achen and Bartels 2017; Althaus 2003.
6 See surveys by the agency Ipsos MORI.
7 Ipsos MORI 2016a.
8 Ibid.
9 Ipsos MORI 2018a.
10 Ipsos MORI 2016b. See also Ipsos MORI 2018b.
11 Ipsos MORI 2016b. Other figures in this paragraph are also sourced from here.
12 Converse 1990, 369.
13 Converse 2000, 331. Emphases added.
14 Brennan 2016, 32.
15 Flynn 2009.
16 Rindermann et al. 2017.
17 Brennan 2016, 31.
18 Downs 1957.
19 Caplan 2001; Caplan 2007.
20 Somin 2013, 113.
21 Kahneman 2011.
22 Somin 2013, chapter 4.
23 Ibid., 91.
24 Evans 2008; Kahneman 2011.
25 Clark et al. 2019.
26 Ibid.
27 Let me also add that it does not follow from the above discussion that it is *morally good* that people are tribalistic, or that by referencing evolution I am insinuating that people

should engage in tribalism. As is always the case with evolutionary claims, they only pertain to what people are probably *like* and what they tend to do. Keep in mind the distinction between descriptive and normative.
28 Oswald and Grosjean 2004, 79.
29 Dunning 2011, 260.
30 Ibid., 261.
31 Ditto et al. 2019.
32 Ibid., 386.
33 Jost 2017.
34 Kahan 2013.
35 Ibid., 417
36 Kahan et al. 2017.
37 Kahan et al. 2017.
38 Ibid., 187–188.
39 Yudkin et al. 2019, 15.
40 Ibid., 16.
41 Ahler and Sood 2018.
42 Lewis-Beck 2000, 211.
43 Achen and Bartels 2017.
44 Healy and Malhotra 2013.
45 Ibid., 291.
46 Mansfield and Mutz 2009, 432.
47 Colantone and Stanig 2018a.
48 Colantone and Stanig 2018b, 214–215.
49 Margalit 2012, 486.
50 Rho and Tomz 2017.
51 Hainmueller and Hopkins 2014, 225.
52 Mutz 2018, E4331.
53 Margalit 2013.
54 Ibid., 98.
55 Ibid.
56 Owens and Pedulla 2014.
57 Margalit 2019, 289. Emphasis in original.
58 Brennan 2016, 49
59 Kiewiet and Lewis-Beck 2011, 303.
60 But see Chong et al. 2001.

4
POLITICIANS ARE PEOPLE, NOT ANGELS

Introduction: 'if it is too good to be true ...'

In discussions on the appropriateness of the two most infamous modern economic systems one regularly encounters an interesting mistake known as the 'nirvana fallacy'.

The fallacy occurs because people tend to compare the functioning of an imperfect, realistic system A with how a perfect, non-realistic system B works. For example, capitalism is usually presented as a system in which real people, such as selfish entrepreneurs, want to take advantage and sometimes succeed in taking advantage of imperfect market mechanisms so that they themselves end up benefiting instead of, or more than, the consumers. This is a realistic portrait of capitalists and capitalism. However, we are then subsequently tempted to compare this capitalist system with a socialist one which, we presume, is populated by imaginary people, such as angelic politicians and wholly responsible, unselfish workers who will use the socialist economic mechanisms of the future with fairness and will make decisions with the public interest in mind. In capitalism, capitalists are selfish, so when an opportunity arises to not act responsibly and to benefit themselves at the expense of others, they will do so – for example, they will dump toxic waste in a nearby river, polluting it. In socialism, socialists are altruistic and so even when they are structurally incentivized to benefit themselves at the public's costs, they will remain firm and will unwaveringly maintain the public interest – for example, they simply do not exploit workers or invest in polluting sources of energy.

Such a comparison is faulty. If we want to reliably, consistently, and fairly evaluate how two different systems A and B work, and what their likely consequences are, we have to compare them – well, consistently. That means that, at least for the initial purposes of getting the analysis off the ground, one should compare two different sets of institutions (capitalist and socialist institutions in our example) *without changing the psychology* of actors populating both institutional systems. If we want to find out how socialism would probably work had it been implemented in the here and now, we need to assume that people living in it are motivationally, or psychologically, similar to people living right now. They are responsive to incentives, and the average person is primarily concerned with their own welfare and that of their close family and friends, not millions of anonymous strangers.

Now, it might turn out that socialist institutions are sufficiently different from capitalist ones so that the former manage to always, or at least more frequently than the latter, translate private selfish acts into the public common good. Or, it might turn out that this is not the case and that socialist institutions are no better or worse than capitalism is in producing collective welfare from individuals pursuing their own welfare. It might even turn out that the logic of socialist institutions has a tougher time aligning individual interests with the public interest. Whatever the concrete conclusion, if we were led to it by carrying out a consistent comparative analysis of different institutional frameworks, this would have been more appropriate than simply committing the nirvana fallacy.[1]

Governments, not merely markets, fail

One might succumb to a similar error when, taking the existing democratic capitalist framework as given, one is discussing how the market and the government perform *within it*. One might start off by appropriately noting, as I have already pointed out, that market mechanisms are imperfect, meaning that they do not produce as much of common welfare as they ideally could. Markets fail in their otherwise beneficial functioning.

If a whole bunch of conditions are satisfied, markets are highly competitive and tend to produce two important outcomes – even if, or precisely because, entrepreneurs are generally self-interested. If there are a lot of sellers on the market among which buyers can freely choose; if the buyers are properly informed; if new sellers can freely enter the market; if property rights are clearly defined; and if the price of goods is determined in a decentralized fashion, markets tend toward what might for our purposes be called 'cost efficiency' and 'price efficiency'.[2] Both of these outcomes are in the public interest.

How can these two cold, technical, economistic outcomes aid the public interest? What do I even mean by them? What I have called *cost efficiency* means that economic actors produce goods or services in a way that uses the least amount possible of natural resources, time, labour, etc., while still meeting the existing demand for the products. Such efficiency is in the public interest because it enables us – the society – to either conserve the extra resources we now have due to higher efficiency and which would otherwise be gone, or to put the extra resources to other uses, producing other goods and services the people also want. Put succinctly, at least one important element of the public interest seems to be for a given society to use up as little of physical and human resources as possible, holding production constant. Now, what I have termed *price efficiency* is simply the fact that goods and services sold on a competitive market tend to sell at a price that is near the actual production costs. Price efficiency means that prices consumers have to pay to get what they want are not rip-off prices serving no other function but lining the capitalists' pockets. Why this is in the public interests is self-evident.

Why do we think markets can work like that? Imagine a simple scenario. If producer A is producing in a cost inefficient way on a competitive market, or if he is selling his products at twice the price than is necessary to cover costs, he will soon be punished for both inefficiencies. Competitors B, C, D, and E will see A's inefficiency and bloated prices, and recognize a profit opportunity. If they manage to produce the same product in a more efficient way than A, or if they can sell it at a lower price, their income will rise either because their costs fell or because they attracted more buyers to their outlets, seeing as how buyers usually prefer less expensive goods, holding quality constant.

Producer A can react to this in one of the following ways. First, he can accept the terms of the competitive game that is being played. That is, he can redirect his production so that it becomes more efficient, and he can lower his artificially bloated price, bringing it down to actual production costs. Both strategies will help him survive on the market. Of course, he can, secondly, resist the competitive pull and stick to his old ways. But, over time, this means mounting costs and loss of customers, leading to lower profit and bankruptcy, i.e., being eliminated from the market. Whichever of the two scenarios happen, under the stipulated conditions the market will tend to produce benefits for all, even though economic actors are, on the whole, selfishly oriented. A competitive market tends to align the private interest of the seller with the interests of all the other market participants.

It is commonly said that the neoclassical economic theory suggesting what I have just laid out is apologetic of capitalism, papering over its flaws and exaggerating its benefits. I do not think this is quite right. After all, the same economic theory points to precisely those social conditions that, if present, lead markets to *fail*. The standard example is the presence of a monopoly. When a firm has a certain level of market power, it does not produce as much as the consumers demand, and the prices it charges are higher than suggested by efficiency. Moreover, the beneficial functioning of the market I have described above tends to, according to economics, at least partially break down even when there are no monopolies. This happens if, for example, there are externalities on the market, if the nature of a good is public (not private), or when the costumers are uninformed about what they are buying. Markets can definitely fail in producing cost and price efficiencies. They can cause various socially suboptimal or harmful consequences that they, ideally, should not.

The standard case of market failure due to *externalities* is air pollution. The costs of pollution are not spontaneously registered on the market because no one owns air. What happens to the air, therefore, is not something that will directly affect the economic decisions of entrepreneurs (or consumers for that matter). More air pollution will be created than if its producers (again, both capitalists with their factories as well as consumers with their car-buying and driving) *individually suffered* the costs of their own pollution. If that happened, they would be incentivized to act more prudently. But it does not happen, and because economic actors are generally self-interested, they do not care about the negative externality they produce, the costs of which are only infinitesimally borne by themselves. Economic actors would act much more 'responsibly' had the externality been internalized, i.e. had it been included in the costs the producer or consumer faces.

A standard example of market failure resulting from the *public nature of the good* under consideration is a lighthouse. A lighthouse is not a typical private good but is rather a public good. By this I do not mean the standard 'healthcare/schooling is a public good' claim. I mean something more technical and economistic. A lighthouse is a public good because it is *non-excludable* and *non-rival*. That it is *non-excludable* simply means that when it exists everyone can use it; access to it cannot be restricted. Even if they wanted to, providers of lighthouses cannot make every single ship pay for their service that is emitting light and signalling useful information to seamen, because the ships are far away and the light is there for all to see. Sellers of cinema tickets, for example, face a very different situation. They have no problem charging every single moviegoer for tickets before they enter the theatre.

That a lighthouse is a *non-rival good* means that when a ship uses its light to navigate it does not, by doing so, reduce the available quantity of light for other ships. This is again a very different situation compared to selling cinema tickets for a 200-person theatre room. Because a lighthouse is such a doubly atypical good, the market cannot properly deal with it. More precisely, because market actors are self-interested they will, from the public interest point of view, tend to invest too little in building lighthouses. This is so because they, unlike a cinema-ticket seller, know they cannot capture all the potential benefits of providing a lighthouse service. Their incentive is not strong enough, so supply will not meet the social demand.

Asymmetric information also distorts the efficient operation of the market.[3] A seller of used cars knows her goods quite well. She knows what the particular issues with the different cars are and how long they can be expected to still work. The everyday buyer of a used car has much less information and must sometimes simply rely on the seller to tell the truth. The problem with this is that the selfish used-car salesperson, given asymmetric information, does not necessarily have the incentive to tell the truth. Quite the opposite, she has the incentive to somewhat overprice the car. Moreover, the seller will not necessarily be afraid to overemphasize the car's ostensible quality, especially if she knows that issues will arise only months after the purchase and could plausibly be attributable to chance or the driver's mistake. If this is the case, consumers will be ripped-off. They will be buying lesser quality, or overpriced, cars than they wanted and that they could, in fact, have gotten had they possessed the same information as the seller.

In short, markets definitely fail in their task of fully serving the public interest through generating various efficiencies. The 'First Fundamental Theorem of Welfare Economics', which states that perfectly competitive markets exhaust every possible positive-sum transaction, producing a social situation under which no further exchange could make any person better off without making another worse off, is correct – but only, and it is a big 'only', under perfect conditions. Criticizing real-world capitalist markets for not being optimal, therefore, is a completely reasonable first step in the comparative evaluation of how governments and markets work. However, the next step that tends to happen in our evaluative endeavour is mistaken.

Too often, the next step is a leap in logic straight to the conclusion that governments will definitely, or at least very likely, succeed where markets have failed. The market failed because economic actors are selfish, and in certain conditions (say, where pollution is free for the capitalist) their selfishness does not lead to social benefits but rather causes damage (for example, polluted air for all). This, we are wont to say, can easily be fixed if only government were allowed to handle the situation. After all, in contrast to economic actors, political actors are not self-interested and will act, even in structurally suboptimal conditions, to further the public interest. The natural answer to market failure is government success. The government can, and will, create a public good that is undersupplied by the market. The government can, and will, use regulation to make firms internalize what are otherwise negative externalities, thus fixing their oversupply. The government can, and will, break up monopolies and fix information asymmetries by educating and informing the public, so that consumers will not be eluded by potential price and quality benefits on the market.

Something akin to this argument is what a member of the Slovenian parliament advocated during a session of the committee on health in the time of my writing this very chapter. He said: 'A private entrepreneur is pursuing their own private interest. Where money rules, in the sphere of economic activity, this private interest is profit. But if we are talking about an activity run under public auspices, what is in principle pursued is the public interest.'[4]

Here, the same fallacy I pointed to at beginning of the chapter tends to be committed. For the politician or the bureaucrat are, in fact, no less sensitive to their own personal welfare than the entrepreneur is. When a propitious opportunity arises, political actors can very much be expected to act in their own interest even if that means endangering and reducing the public interest. Just as we have market failure, there also exists government failure.[5] And without performing a thoroughgoing theoretical and empirical analysis, one should not simply declare that government failure is merely a marginal occurrence, whereas markets fail all the time and to a very significant extent. As Richard Posner warns, 'Mainstream economists were preoccupied with market failures and saw efficient regulation as an essentially costless method of rectifying such failures; they did not consider the obstacles to efficient regulation. They saw market failures everywhere, but tended to be blind to government failures.'[6] The political scientist Bruce Bueno de Mesquita and his colleagues note something similar: 'For many economists, leaders are *assumed* to be interested in enhancing the welfare of their citizenry. Failure to do so is thought to be a product of ignorance or the result of constraints beyond their control that prevent them from implementing the necessary reforms.'[7]

None of this should be taken to mean that the government cannot fix market failures or that it is wrong for the government to try. Governments do fix market failures and it is good that they try and sometimes succeed. Internalizing externalities through taxation is the obvious example, as is correcting information asymmetries through mandating nutritional labels on food. It is crucial, however, that there is nothing necessary or automatic, and in certain circumstances even likely, about this process. Moreover, even apart from the question of how well governments can be expected to fix market failures, there is the issue of them – just like markets – usually not operating with full efficiency and optimally serving the public interest. Just as ideal markets do not exist in the real world, so too are ideal governments imaginary creatures.

Three areas of government failure and their various causes

Politicians, officials, and bureaucrats can happen to produce cost, price, and other inefficiencies that undermine the public interest. Roughly speaking, government failure can happen in three key areas under the domain of the government:

1. When *offering non-market alternatives* to a market service.
2. When *issuing subsidies* (or, conversely, when *taxing*).
3. When *regulating* market activities.

In the next few pages, I briefly focus on the first two areas, while I consider the third in more detail in a separate section following this one. My thinking on the first two areas has been strongly shaped by Julian Le Grand's general theory of government failure.[8]

There are, roughly, four specific reasons for government failure as it manifests in (1) and (2):

i The absence of competitive pressure.
ii The artificial changing of supply and demand.
iii The absence of the price mechanism.
iv The 'short-sightedness effect'.

Apart from these more specific causes, there is also the already mentioned general contributing cause, i.e. the fact that politicians are not altruistic saints working solely, or even primarily, with the intention of serving the public interest. I will mostly leave this fact aside for now, but will come back to it in the next section when discussing regulatory capture.

When the government offers (1) non-market alternatives (like the postal service), it tends do so in a monopolistic manner. This means that (i) the usual competitive market pressure is strongly reduced or wholly absent. The government is not facing either current or potential future competitors, as it has forbidden market entry for private firms. That this might be a problem should not be hard to understand. If the usual competitive pressures are curtailed, state actors, such as politicians and bureaucrats, are not facing the usual market incentives that would otherwise induce them to be cost and price efficient simply due to their own self-interest in surviving on the market and attracting more customers. Instead, it seems we will have to rely on them – the state actors – to be *personally committed* to efficiency, which is a much less reliable, i.e. a weaker and scarcer, motive than the marriage of competition and self-interest.

There are, of course, other structural incentives apart from the (now absent) threat of economic competition that might prod politicians and bureaucrats to act in the public interest when providing a monopoly service. For example, they are worried about their reputation and the likelihood of being re-elected. This is perhaps why even when it comes to monopolistic non-market alternatives provided by the government, mounting cost and price inefficiencies are usually somewhat kept in check. However, they do occur and voter ignorance might be one important explanation why state actors can indulge in inefficiencies without being worried about the wrath of the voters.

When the government (2) issues subsidies to certain firms, or taxes others, it (ii) changes the amount of supply and demand that would otherwise obtain, had the prices been determined under competitive conditions.[9] For example, if providers of healthcare receive large subsidies, the price of their goods and services falls under the standard competitive price, which leads to increased demand for these goods and services. Now, demand can outstrip the amount of supply currently existing, or the amount the government deems appropriate. This, in turn, necessitates a response so that the excess demand is handled somehow. The government is likely to create waiting lists to spread out the excess demand. The potential problem with this is well known. Think of one of the key pitfalls of the otherwise important public healthcare system. In many cases, coincidences and personal connections – not the actual healthcare need or at least some imperfect proxy for it – determine who goes first and who comes last. This is neither fair nor efficient. Here, I am not trying to suggest that a public healthcare system (with long waiting lists) is necessarily worse than a private system (without waiting lists but with a host of other problems, like inaccessibility). I am just pointing out that in the real world both solutions have their own pitfalls and trade-offs, of which we must be mindful. Let us not suppose, *a priori*, that the public option is always, or even usually, better – nor the reverse.

If the government (iii) abstains, or is prevented, from relying on the price mechanism, it gives up an otherwise important source of incentives and information. First, prices act as a strong motive to buy more (if the price is low or falling) or less (if the price is high or rising), which further leads people to – usually unwittingly – act as if they care about the relative scarcity of a given good. High prices, mirroring high relative scarcity, motivate low consumption, thus protecting the scarce good from being excessively consumed. This goes for both consumers and producers. Prices motivate producers to buy resources for production and to shift their production in accordance with their relative scarcity. They are motivated to conserve the use of those resources that cost a lot, and to seek out those resources that are abundant and therefore cheap. Moreover, the price mechanism incentivizes producers to produce more of what consumers want, and less of what they are not keen of buying. This is because it pays producers to produce the good for which the demand is rising (increasing demand means higher prices and higher profits), while it is not as economically attractive to produce goods for which the demand is falling (falling demand means falling prices and lower profits).

In all these various ways, prices can incentivize socially responsible behaviour even if (or precisely because) individuals are not altruistic and personally committed to being socially responsible. This is the first and most well-known role of the price mechanism. However, secondly and just as importantly, prices are also information about what consumers want more or less of, and which resources are scarce or abundant. Producers rely on competitively determined prices to find out what consumers want and in roughly what quantity they want it. The thing that is currently very pricey is either in high demand or very rare and hard to produce. The classic example are diamonds. The thing that is cheap is in lesser demand or is already available in abundance. The classic example is wheat or water, at least in locations where deserts and droughts are not common. In sum, prices contain important information for the economy and, therefore, for pursuing at least one crucial dimension of the public interest.

This crucial and complex network of information can be improperly distorted for achieving efficiency if there are (2) too many subsidies or too high taxes, barring certain market failures that require subsidies and taxes in order to be fixed. Subsidies artificially lower the price of goods, while taxes raise them. This means that, as Le Grand notes, 'the government will find it very difficult to assess the overall efficient level of production of a commodity; for, in the absence of a price mechanism, it has few, and not very reliable, ways of assessing the social benefit from that production and relating it to its social cost.'[10] Why? Because providing subsidies means giving money to producers if they are willing to produce what the government wants, for example, corn. Because corn producers receive additional funds from the state, they can now afford to sell corn cheaper on the market than they otherwise would; it benefits them to lower the price so that they attract more buyers. This, in turn, means that the price of the corn no longer reflects the actual, material production costs of the crop. Rather, the lower corn price signals to consumers that its production costs are lower than they really are. Taxes work the other way round. In either case, prices are no longer reliable signals of information about the relative scarcity of resources and commodities.

The last reason for government failure is (iv) the 'short-sightedness effect'. I already said that when offering (i) non-market alternatives, political actors might still face some important incentives – not least of which is due to democratic oversight – not to produce mounting social costs with their state enterprise, even though the standard competitive discipline is absent. However, I also intimated that this might not work as well as hoped for because voters are by and large rationally ignorant, making the discipline of democratic oversight weak, at least when it comes to the more opaque inefficiencies of various government services. But how about retrospective voting? Is this not an important incentive for politicians to get things right?

Not necessarily. Precisely due to retrospective voting, politicians have in some cases strong reasons to enact, in the last year of their term when voters are most sensitive to economic conditions, irresponsible economic policies that are unsustainable in the long-term with the intention of boosting their short-term chances of re-election. This is the short-sightedness effect. Many political actors have quite short time horizons. Staying in power for another term is at the top of their priorities, because without this they have no power and so cannot enact either their self-interested or altruistic preferences.

The discussion up until now has been of a theoretical nature. As with most things, however, the question of government (and market) failure is, in the end, an empirical question. I have pointed out the various ways in which things can go badly wrong both within markets and in governments. Neither are *guaranteed* to be safe havens for the public interest. At the same time, both social spheres can protect and promote it, given certain conditions. Their failure to do so has to be examined in each individual instance when it happens.

One exhaustive empirical review of government failure in the US, where these are especially acute, paints the following image:

> First, government policy has created economic inefficiencies where significant market failures do not appear to exist, such as with antitrust laws and economic regulations that have raised firms' costs and generated economic rents for various interest groups at the expense of consumer welfare. To be sure, antitrust enforcement may be deterring anticompetitive behavior, especially collusion, but this potentially important benefit has not been verified empirically. ... Second, in situations where market failures do exist, government policy has either achieved expensive successes by correcting these failures in a way that sacrifices substantial net benefits or in some cases has actually reduced social welfare.[11]

The review also notes that, although in the *US case* market failure springing from imperfect information does not seem to create large efficiency losses, in general 'market failures arising from externalities such as air and water pollution, hazardous wastes, and traffic congestion do impose significant social costs that government policy could reduce efficiently.'[12] This tells us, first, that in the US both market and government failures exist and are not to be taken lightly. Second, that at least some instances of government failure, although far from optimal, create less efficiency losses when fixing market failure than would result if the government had not tried to fix it. In other words, even though government failure always creates costs to society, these costs are sometimes outweighed by the benefits gained when that market failure has been addressed. The obverse is, of course, also true. I will return to this point below.

Regulatory capture

We have just examined a couple of important conditions where government failure might happen. However, I have yet to touch on perhaps the most tantalizing areas of government failure: that of interest groups and the nefarious marriage between political and economic actors. It is not just that political actors – on their own – sometimes have a hard time of figuring out how to fix market failures, nor only that they can lack the proper incentives to do so. Rather, governments sometimes fail because it might be in their interest – and the interest of some entrepreneurs – to actively *cause* market failure. This is not specifically limited to the phenomenon of regulatory capture, which we will now examine in detail, but it is most obviously revealed by it.

Regulatory capture happens when a state agency that has been created with the intent of protecting and promoting the public interest in fact helps special interest groups leading certain economic sectors, which the agency was supposed to regulate in accordance with the public interest.[13] The classic example is the regulation of taxis in New York, legally limiting their number to around 13,000, which is half of what it had been during the Great Depression.[14] As Butler notes, 'Because new competition is outlawed, taxi drivers make more money and New Yorkers pay more and wait longer for taxis than they otherwise would.' The price of milk in the US had been another staple example. Due to what Joseph Stiglitz called a 'legally sanctioned cartel-like arrangement' by the government, the price of milk had been 'well above its competitive market price.'[15] As he notes, the resulting annual welfare cost to society is high and mostly affects poor children, as it 'seriously erodes a substantial fraction of the value of the government subsidy for Women, Infants, and Children (WIC) and for school lunches.'[16]

Of course, not every regulatory capture is the same. We have to distinguish between a weak and a strong version.[17] *Strong regulatory capture* occurs when interest groups and politicians distort a given regulation to such an extent that it would have been better for the public not to have regulation at all. *Weak regulatory capture* occurs when interest groups and politicians reduce the ability of a given regulation to promote the public interest but do not subvert it completely. In this case, it is still better for the public to have the regulation even though it is not optimal and therefore generates costs as well as benefits. On net, the regulation has more benefits than costs.

The authors of a contemporary handbook that advocates for this distinction and empirically investigates cases of regulatory capture suspect that strong regulatory capture definitely exists but is not widespread. According to them, weak regulatory capture dominates in most cases. This view is in contrast to the famous claim made by George Stigler who founded the theoretical basis for understanding regulatory capture. He claimed that *strong regulatory* capture is, in fact, omnipresent.[18] Systematic reviews of empirical evidence that could settle this disagreement are, for now, scarce.

How does regulatory capture work? There are two main mechanisms underlying the phenomenon, which both create it and help it persist. They are also the causes of various other forms of government failure and can be added to the enumerated list from the previous section.

The first mechanism is known under the general heading of 'rent-seeking'. This is a process in which a group of entrepreneurs A (or any other interest group, say a trade union) offers a politician, or a group of politicians, B certain benefits in exchange for a rent that surpasses the ordinary profit that might be generated by the entrepreneurs on the open market. To make this more workable, we must understand what a rent is, how politicians can generate it, and what interest groups can offer politicians in exchange for a newly minted rent.

In this context, rent is the 'unnecessary' extra income that entrepreneurs can collect in certain circumstances, for example, with the helping hand of the government, without producing an extra amount of a given good, improving the quality of their product, offering something new that consumers want but nobody else was yet able to create, etc. Rent is the income generated not by direct or indirect productive activity, and not by contributing any social benefits, but by a mere transfer of wealth from one pocket to another.

This unproductive type of income can be captured outside the competitive market with the help of state actors in three main ways. First, politicians can award a group of entrepreneurs new monopoly privileges. They can do this, for example, by legally barring new potential competitors from entering the market. Because competition is stifled, the existing entrepreneurs are not forced to bid down the prices of their products so that they align with production costs. The goods are now more expensive than they would have been in competitive conditions. Second, rents can be created by the government taxing competitors of a certain entrepreneurial group. That puts the former in a worse economic position than the latter, thus reducing their competition and helping them. Tariffs and other protectionist measures against foreign competition can have such an effect, enabling domestic companies to produce at lower efficiency and higher prices. Third, rents can be generated by a simple monetary transfer, a subsidy, to a given group of capitalists or other interest groups.

What can those clamouring for rents offer to politicians in exchange for such favours? The means of exchange can be both legal and illegal: money, electoral support, campaign contributions, information, promises of a comfortable job after the end of a politician's career, etc.

As we are all painfully aware when watching the news and snickering at the immorality of politicians and their economic hangers-on, rent-seeking behaviour is not quite as exceedingly rare as one would hope. As the authors of the aforementioned handbook on regulatory capture note, 'The historical and statistical annals of legislative studies are filled with evidence for how business interests and other special interests (including labor unions) use their resources … to induce politicians to bend.'[19] This, of course, does not mean that there is as much regulatory capture as there are rent-seeking efforts. Not all who try are successful, so there should always be less capture than there are efforts to generate capture.

Rent-seeking behaviour answers part of the question about why regulatory capture (and other active forms of government failure) happen when they do. Both political and economic actors tend to be self-interested, which means that when they feel an appropriate opportunity for mutual gain has arisen – an opportunity in which such a deal will likely go unpunished by the public, even though it comes at the public's expense – they will grab hold of it. However, this answers only the *motivational* part of the puzzle. We also want to know how come politicians and entrepreneurs are *able* to get away with it. Why does democratic oversight fail? Why do the voters, or the taxpayers, who are the harmed party not resist and prevent such government failure?

Here, the second mechanism of regulatory capture kicks in: the principle of concentrated benefits and diffused costs. The rents economic actors receive are usually quite substantial for the small group that fought for them. Usually, a nimble rent-seeking group does not involve tens of thousands or even millions of entrepreneurs, which means that even a relatively humble rent of tens or hundreds of millions of dollars represents a hugely substantial amount per person. The benefits generated are highly concentrated within a small group of people. This further means that each individual has a strong incentive to act, i.e. to contribute his share of the effort in rent-seeking. However, the social costs caused by rent generation are typically extremely dispersed. They fall on the shoulders of tens or even hundreds of millions of citizens. Even huge social costs amount to no more than a few tens of dollars per citizen. The costs are, taken individually, so inconsequential that most of the time the citizens do not even take notice. And even if they do notice the costs, they correctly judge them to be lower than what it would take (in terms of time, effort, and money) to try and defeat them through informing oneself, writing to one's congressperson, or either taking part in, or organizing, a protest. Simply swallowing the small costs seems the most rational course for an individual citizen, which leads them to be rationally ignorant and rationally passive.

Consider the following illustrative example. If domestic producers of sugar lobby the government and succeed in getting an import quota passed, stifling foreign competition, they are able to charge their domestic consumers a higher price per kilogram of sugar. Instead of the price being 10 cents, it is now 19 cents. In the US, sugar actually costs about twice the world average.[20] If we tally up all the domestic consumers of sugar, the annual amount of sugar they buy, and its artificially bloated price, we get a whole lot of rent-seeking benefits. Depending on the size of the country, this might reach into the hundreds of millions, if not a billion, dollars. That is a lot of money, annually, if it is divided solely among a few companies. But it is mere change per the individual sugar consumer, not merely enough to lose sleep over and be motivated to fight against.

Estimates of social costs of rent-seeking behaviour are hard to come by, but a few researchers have tried to estimate them roughly. In the US case, the highest annual estimate found in one study was 22.6% of GDP, amounting to trillions of dollars lost or, better yet, misallocated.[21]

The limits of public choice

We have seen that governments, like markets, fail. We have come to understand the reasons for both. Much of what I have argued about government failure is associated with public choice theory, both as the general application of the principles of rational choice theory to politics (instead of solely restricting its scope to markets) and as a scholarly tradition specifically associated with economists such as James Buchanan, Gordon Tullock, and others. The romanticizing, naïve democrat must come to grips with these insights, just as the romanticizing, naïve libertarian must recognize the possibility, and indeed actuality, of market failure.

I stand by the analysis from preceding sections. There are, however, also certain nuances that have to be added. First, as will be discussed below, we must delve deeper into the empirical evidence corroborating the applicability of rational choice theory to politics. Second, an important modification of rational choice has to be made so that it can deal with the fact that many people actually go out and vote, even though it seems they have no material reason to do so. Third, even though governments fail, not all failures happen to the same extent. On average, rich democratic states significantly outperform poor democracies and both poor and rich autocracies on a variety of measures of social welfare. This must be, and can be, explained through the same rational choice apparatus that I have used throughout the book; the last section of this chapter is devoted to precisely this issue.

As an explicit theoretical research program, public choice is not well known in sociology. Nevertheless, some sociologists, such as Lars Udehn, who are intimately acquainted with the endeavour, tend also to be its harshest critics. They reject the methodological individualism of public choice and its reliance on foundational assumptions of self-interest, responsiveness to incentives, and strategic decision-making.[22] Pointing out that voters are sociotropic, Udehn insists that the evidence on political behaviour flatly contradicts the assumption of self-interest. I have already dealt with the potential merits and demerits of methodological individualism in chapter 1, and I have nothing more to add. Similarly, I already pointed out in chapter 3 that sociotropic voters are neither necessarily altruistic nor is altruistic voting, if it happens, an inexplicable phenomenon for public choice. That is why in this section I will only take a closer look at what the empirical evidence on political behaviour shows regarding the assumption of self-interest and responsiveness to incentives.

Consider, first, experimental game theory and behavioural economics evidence on people's preferences. When researchers ask subjects to play various games that can either mirror social dilemmas described in chapter 1, or not, such as the Ultimatum Game or the Public Goods Game, the standard result is that, on average, subjects do not optimally maximize their own welfare. That is so because they tend to share some of the money with their partner or the group, depending on the game. Typically, slightly more than half of all participants share around half of the money they were endowed with by the experimenters. At first glance, this seems to be an obvious refutation of the self-interest assumption. There are, however, many confounding variables in such experiments that make it hard to infer what precisely is going on with people's preferences. Do they share the money in the Public Goods Game because they are afraid of being punished by the group otherwise? Do they share the money because they fear their partner is going to reject the (stingy) offer in the Ultimatum Game, thus dooming them both to receiving no money from the researchers? Do they hide their self-interest because they know they are being studied and watched by other people who might think badly of them if they do not express other-regarding preferences?

There are experiments that try to better control for these issues. Many of them reveal a somewhat different picture of human behaviour, one closer to what rational choice would predict.[23] First, if a subject has to earn his money instead of being given it by the experimenter, offers to the partner in the Ultimatum Game are lower.[24] Second, if the experiment is moved out of the laboratory setting and if the subjects are unaware that they are being watched, self-interested behaviour rises.[25] For example, comparing charitable behaviour outside the lab with the one that is observed in a lab reveals a striking negative difference. People are less charitable in the real world. Third, when the trade-off between being fair and being materially better off changes so that one has to forego much more money (say, $100 instead of $10) to maintain the appearance of being kind, the average offer to a partner in an Ultimatum Game drops sharply.[26] Fourth, when punishment in the Public Goods Game is forbidden and subjects are anonymous, contributions start dwindling over repeated rounds, indicating that previously fair and sharing behaviour might have been more a result of prudent, strategic, self-interested reciprocity ('Given the rules of the game, I can get what I want by playing fair with others') than sheer altruism.

One sceptical response to all this is to point out what happens in certain one-off, i.e. non-repeated, anonymous games. There, subjects are *still* willing to share, even though no strategic and self-interested reciprocal behaviour is possible, even in principle, in such a strict game. Is this not evidence of robust altruism?

Not necessarily. The are two things to note here. First, it seems highly plausible that such a contrived experiment is so artificial in comparison to the actual ordinary human environment of non-anonymity and repeated interactions that, unless subjects are really thinking through the situation and adapting to it in real time, people's intuitions on what to do will 'misfire' in these strange conditions. That is, in the usual, everyday social circumstances people know (or feel) that it pays to be pro-social and reciprocal. Otherwise, punishments of various kinds follow, i.e. missing out on positive-sum transactions, losing friends, ostracism, etc. The heuristic one typically develops through life in the modern world is that, when in doubt, you are better off behaving nicely to others. This is the prudent default setting given the circumstances. People might be nice not because they are altruistic but because, being primarily self-interested, reciprocity in ordinary circumstances tends roughly to pay off for them. It is true that it does not pay off in the artificially one-off and anonymous experimental game, but subjects, having little time to think and adapt to such a weird environment, are probably just relying on their otherwise prudent heuristic.

Second, we know that this is precisely what is happening in these experiments because if experimenters give their subjects the opportunity to think the situation through, and if they prime them to reflect on it and strategize, subjects no longer tend to act as cooperatively and fairly as before.[27]

In short, humans are indeed a highly cooperative and reciprocal species, as evolutionary psychology, social psychology, and behavioural economics continuously reveal, but this does not necessarily, or even likely, suggest selfless altruism instead of self-interest as our motivational bedrock. Especially when having the opportunity and the motivation to engage in deliberative reasoning.

How about *politicians'* behaviour, specifically? Do we have evidence of it being fundamentally altruistic or self-interested? Consider, first, empirical studies on how politicians tend to change the rules of the electoral system.[28] One would theoretically predict that winning politicians are not likely to change the very rules that enabled them to win. They are expected to change them primarily in cases where such a change would benefit them. Moreover, one would expect the losers to want to change the system in such a manner that they are more likely to win the next time around. These predictions, based on the assumption of self-interest, turn out to quite correct. Of course, certain complexities also emerge. Self-interest is not the *only* motivational force behind politicians' actions. Ideology and values count as well.[29] Importantly, however, their effect is not as systematic or strong as the effect of self-interest.[30]

Consider, next, the literature on corruption in less developed states. In their political campaigns and public life, most politicians (and ordinary citizens) are, rhetorically, strongly critical of corrupt behaviour. They know corruption to be a selfish, immoral strategy which is almost universally condemned from a neutral and impersonal standpoint. That is why they also know that it would benefit them to present themselves as fighters against corruption, or at least as not being in favour of corrupt behaviour. For example, a majority of Africans says it is wrong for a politician to place a development project in the region where his friends and supporters live; a majority disapproves of politicians doling out jobs to their kin, if they are unqualified for the job; a majority condemns a politician's request for additional funds for performing a service that is already considered a part of his regular job.[31] Are these noble words later translated into actual good practice on the ground? No. A majority of ruling politicians (and ordinary citizens) in less developed countries partakes either directly or indirectly in corrupt activities.[32] That this is not true in the most developed countries is, in part, a consequence of their better institutions that manage to better align private interests with the public interest. This, in turn, leads even self-interested actors, who would like to behave corruptly given the chance, to promote the public interest instead of destroying it.

The second major sociological critique of public choice is the charge that political behaviour cannot be studied as rational behaviour that is responsive to incentives. In other words, quite apart from the question of whether politicians are self-interested, we can ask if they really consciously form goals and pursue them with the most appropriate means. Some of the studies already considered above implicitly reveal that this second critique is not all that strong. For example, Carles Boix shows, in detail, how strategically politicians behave. As he summarizes his conclusions:

> The electoral system (structured around plurality or majority rules) remained unchanged during the era of limited suffrage. As soon as universal suffrage was adopted, which led to the massive entry of mostly left-wing voters and, hence, to a radically new electoral arena, the ruling elites followed different solutions. The plurality/majority system survived under two circumstances. First, it remained in place in those countries in which the new entrant (a socialist

party) was weak and, itself the victim of strategic voting, could not challenge any of the established parties. Second, it was maintained in those countries in which, although the new entrant became strong, one of the established or nonsocialist parties retained a dominant position in the nonsocialist camp. Since it could easily attract the strategic vote of all nonsocialist voters (mostly worried about blocking the victory of social democracy), the dominant party acted rationally in maintaining a highly constraining electoral rule. By contrast, proportional representation was adopted in those countries in which the socialist party was strong and nonsocialist parties controlled roughly similar shares of the electorate. Failure to reduce the electoral threshold would have led to an overwhelming victory of the socialist party. As soon as the electoral arena became stable and the party system froze along certain cleavages, policymakers lost interest in modifying the electoral regime.[33]

A swathe of other studies examining how term limits affect political behaviour likewise suggest strong responsiveness to incentives on the part of politicians.[34] For example, Claudio Ferraz and Frederico Finan looked at how corrupt the elected politicians who can get another term are compared to those who cannot.[35] Public choice analysis suggests the latter will engage in more corruption than the former as the incentives obviously point in this direction. Politicians who are in their last possible term have nothing, electorally, to lose by being corrupt. Politicians who can, and want to, run for another term have to be more careful not to hurt their chances of re-election. Empirical evidence suggests this is the case. Last-term politicians illegitimately appropriate a whole third more of state funds than those faced with the possibility of re-election. The conclusion remains even if we statistically control for potential confounding variables besides term limits. Further strengthening the case for politicians being responsive to incentives, Ferraz and Finan also found that the difference between the two groups of elected officials is substantially smaller if we look only at subtle forms of corruption that are more opaque to the public. This is precisely the result one would expect, because the personal risks of engaging in subtle corruption are equally low both for politicians at the end of their career and those still trying to get re-elected.

So, then, what are the real limitations of public choice? One of them relates to the assumption just under discussion. Standard public choice is, or was in the past, somewhat blind to the fact that when people are deciding on an action in a situation where, *whatever their particular action ends up being*, there are no significant material costs or benefits associated with it, we simply cannot deduce their behaviour from the principles of rational choice theory. We might say that being responsive to incentives it itself responsive to incentives. Where there are no compelling reasons to be calculating, people tend not to be calculating with their behaviour. In such 'indeterminate' social situations, it is much more likely that individuals act in accordance with their internalized duties, norms, or simply habits.[36] Elections are a good example of precisely such a situation. That is why we should expect many people to go out and vote even though there is no materially rational reason for doing so. Voters will cast their ballots because they think it is right to do so, or because it is what they were taught by their parents to do since they were children.

There are three things to note here. First, practitioners of rational and public choice theory knew from the start that they have to somehow resolve the 'paradox of voting', i.e. the theoretical prediction of nobody voting and the reality of many people voting. They did so in various ways, but the underlying logic was usually the same. That is, people were thought to not only be concerned with material payoffs but also with psychological ones. It was supposed that voting makes one feel a 'warm glow' and to be doing the right thing, which is a psychological incentive unto itself. As critics were quick to point out, the obvious problem with this 'solution' is that, even though the supposition is descriptively true, by moving rational choice theory in this direction we are in danger of losing theoretical tractability. We must not start blindly adding too many assumptions and variables to the theory if we are to use it to generate precise predictions, avoiding ad-hoc reasoning. A theory that can explain everything cannot, in fact, explain any single thing. The real, or better, solution then is to *specify in advance*, and with reliance on empirical insights from social psychology (see endnote 36), the social conditions in which people are more likely to act in accordance with the postulates of rational choice theory, and those where such action is less likely. Thus, rational choice analysis can be sustained even in light of the paradox of voting, while ad-hoc and tautologous reasoning that would weaken the explanatory power of rational choice is at the same time prevented.

Second, note that what I suggested above with regards to the paradox of voting is consistent with my arguments from the previous chapter detailing why most voters are rationally ignorant or rationally irrational. This is so because even though *the act of voting* carries very low costs with it, the same does not hold for *politically informing oneself* before voting. In the latter case, costs are high and benefits are virtually non-existent, which is why we should expect most voters, when it comes to gathering information, to act according to rational choice principles – that is, they will not seek out information because expected material benefits of doing so are vanishingly small. On the other hand, we should also expect most of them – in contrast to what standard rational choice analysis suggests – to go cast their votes on election day, seeing as how there are no significant material costs or benefits of doing so, meaning norms, duties, and habits take over as the main behavioural principle.

Third, incorporating this insight into our theory of politics is key for not overlooking an important incentive which at least politicians in liberal democracies face when governing. Because people do vote in large numbers, this fact being both empirically obvious to everyone as well as theoretically explicable under the proposed framework, politicians know that they will tend to lose their power if they systematically engage in the kind of politics that visibly harms voters or simply symbolically enrages them. Blatant corruption, obvious governmental mishandling of a natural disaster, economic scandals, etc., can spur voters to punish ruling officials and vote them out, especially when prominently exposed by the media. This is why we can expect that, at least in robust democratic systems with independent and trustworthy media, politicians will act more carefully and tend not to endanger the public interest too obviously and excessively, simply due to their own self-interest. We might even talk about a sort of 'invisible hand' of liberal democratic governments which, although as discussed above does not prevent government failure, still roughly aligns the private interests of politicians with the public interest of the electorate. I turn to a more detailed consideration of the performance of democratic and non-democratic political systems next.

The general structural logic of political behaviour

We have seen that just as economic actors are (rightly) assumed by academics and lay people to be primarily self-interested and, thus, likely to exploit an unpunished opportunity for self-enrichment at the expense of the public, so too are political actors. Let us not romanticize politics. As de Mesquita and colleagues note, it might be 'pleasant to think that the brutish behavior of a King John or a Genghis Khan, his approximate contemporary, is a thing of the past, a relic of a less civilized age.'[37] Furthermore, it might be 'pleasant to think that most contemporary political leaders are motivated by high ideals in their pursuit of office; that the opportunity to do good works – not the quest for power – is more prominent a motive today than it was centuries ago.'[38] It might be pleasant to think so, and it might even turn out to be somewhat true, but we would be wise not to pin our analysis of politics to such a rosy assumption. After all, 'Few, even among those who profess and demonstrate a strong commitment to the public welfare, leave office alive less well-off personally than they had been when they came to power.'[39]

We must, however, consider two additional issues. First, how significantly does the political behaviour of an exceptional, truly altruistically motivated politician change when the harsh structural logic of the political game asserts itself? Second, if we continue assuming, as it seems warranted to do, that politicians are – on average and primarily – self-interested, how come democracies are such thriving places?

Simplifying the work of de Mesquita and colleagues, I argue there are two major rules of politics operative today just as they were in the past, and all who seek office must heed them, even the exceptional altruist. The first rule of politics is: *get power and hold on to it for as long as possible*. Even politicians who are primarily moved by the self-sacrificing motive to do good for others cannot – must not – go against this first rule. One has to possess power before one can pursue the goal of promoting the public interest. Now, this by itself is not necessarily problematic. But it does start to bring up issues when we consider the second rule of politics, which flows directly from the first: *get key supporters on your side*. Even an exceptionally civic-natured politician cannot achieve power or, if she has already got it, hold on to it for very long without strong support from other people.

Here, two issues immediately open up. First, even if a candidate for the leader is herself exceptional, the majority of her key supporters are probably ordinary, self-interested people. And what can a potential leader do to secure the loyalty of such people? What can she offer them in exchange for their support? Regulatory capture, unreasonable subsidies, packing state institutions with one's own (but not necessarily meritorious) supporters, enacting policies that do not make sense in the medium- to long-term, etc. Everything comes in handy. Second, the brutish rules of the political game tend to eliminate, or filter out, the exceptional, civic-minded, altruistic political candidates, and instead structurally attract those who are willing to do what it takes to come to the top and secure power for themselves. Two specific mechanisms are operative here. Either most of the exceptional people are turned away from politics from the start or, barring that, they tend to get replaced in time with other, less exceptional people by their own disgruntled supporters. Structurally, at least mild government failure should be pervasive.

Nevertheless, government failure (like market failure) does not mean the public interest is *completely* undermined and destroyed; only that it is not being optimally served. Warts and all, right now rich capitalist liberal democracies are quite comfortable to live in. Liberal democracy correlates strongly with economic freedom, which is itself further statistically tied to a wide variety of welfare measures, such as high GDP per capita, high average income, exceedingly low absolute and very low moderate poverty rates, long life expectancy, gender equality, etc.[40] Decades ago, the Nobel laureate and economist Amartya Sen famously claimed that democracies prevent famines, a claim contemporary studies confirm.[41] Even more to the point, rent-seeking behaviour and regulatory capture are statistically less prevalent in democracies than in dictatorships.[42] There is even evidence that this correlation is robust to a variety of measures and confounding variables, which suggests that there is something about *democracy* that makes democratic societies less prone to intense government failure compared to dictatorships.[43]

How is this possible, when I keep insisting we should take democratic politicians' basic motivational makeup to be similar to what it has been in the past and what it still is today in dictatorships? The reason is that, although across societies politicians have the same basic *goals* (get power, keep it, attract supporters), these goals cannot be pursued effectively in the same manner under different *institutional settings*. Democratic institutions are more likely to incentivize civic-minded policies, at least in effect if not in intention, than dictatorial ones. In other words, it should not be surprising why *even the same political actor*, such as Leopold II, acted so very differently under two incredibly different sets of social structures. As Bueno de Mesquita and colleagues describe him:

> Leopold II, as king of the Belgians, was at the forefront of promoting economic growth, educational reform, and other successful policies at home in the emerging Belgian democracy while, as the personal owner of the Congo, he simultaneously promoted unspeakable oppression and exploitation in his dictatorship. ... [H]e had no change of heart, no change in culture, no change in civic-mindedness; he did have a change in fundamental political realities, and those changes altered his behavior.[44]

The typical democratic leader is not, 'by nature', more mindful of the public interest than the typical autocrat. The former just has many more, and much stronger, incentives to behave roughly in accordance with the public interest. This disparity in incentives can usefully be captured with the twin concepts of 'real selectorate' and 'winning coalition', developed by de Mesquita and colleagues.[45] The smaller these two groups are, the more removed the behaviour of political actors will be from the public interest. The larger they are, the less intensive government failure will be.

The nominal selectorate is made up of all those people who have the legal right to participate in choosing political leaders. In democracies, this group encompasses all adult citizens, the voters. In dictatorships, something similar might be the case as many such regimes now pretend to have democratic elections and to give the right to vote to all adult citizens.

The real selectorate is the group of people who actually have the power to choose political leaders. In liberal democracies, the nominal and real selectorate are roughly the same, with the only difference being the number of people who turn out to vote on election day. Even in the US, where the president is in the end chosen by special electors, not directly the voters themselves, nowadays the electors are more or less guaranteed to vote in accordance with the wish of the electoral majority in a given state. Dictatorships, in contrast, have a very different, much smaller real selectorate in comparison to their nominal one. The legal right to vote, if it exists, does not mean much when it comes to national elections. In the Soviet Union, even though everybody had 'the right' to vote, the real selectorate was made up of a section of members of the Communist party.

The winning coalition is made up by that part of the real selectorate which a politician needs, in each particular case, to secure victory and defeat her opponents. In democracies, the winning coalition is not simply the majority of the nominal selectorate, i.e. the majority of all citizens eligible to vote. It is not even simply the majority of the real selectorate, i.e. the majority of all citizens who actually cast their vote on election day. Instead, it is the smallest possible number of voters who cast their vote, just sufficient to secure the win. It is the narrowest possible slice of the real selectorate that one needs to defeat the opponent. This means that in dictatorships, where the real selectorate is itself already very small, the winning coalition, which is simply a subset of the real selectorate, is an exceedingly small group of people. Perhaps, in some circumstances, only a few thousand or even a few hundred high state officials, generals, and selected businessmen.

Now, to explain why liberal democracies are, in comparison to dictatorships, very nice places to live for the ordinary person, one simply needs to note the different institutional path to victory and maintenance of power a politician is faced with in both regime types. Where the real selectorate and especially the winning coalition are broad social groups made up of millions or even tens of millions of ordinary citizens, the aspiring politician, or an incumbent seeking re-election, cannot simply buy each of them off with various targeted private goods. Instead, what he or she has to do is offer would be supporters various public or quasi-public goods such as roads, parks, schools, hospitals, economic development, etc.[46] In a liberal democracy, offering primarily targeted private goods to (millions and millions of) individuals is a highly inefficient, wasteful strategy from the politician's point of view. Doling out non-excludable public goods is a cheaper way of securing the support of so many people because general economic growth, or a few parks, schools, and hospitals cover a whole lot of people, while individual bribes are precisely that – *specific to an individual*. Moreover, even though the running politician only cares to reward his winning coalition, not the whole real or even nominal selectorate that were not instrumental to his victory, other citizens still unintendedly profit from his offerings. Because the offered goods are public and usually cannot be restricted to just a particular group of voters, even the winner's electoral opponents, i.e. the voters who did not vote for him, or those that did not take the time to vote for anybody, can use them and benefit from them. Everybody is better-off, even if unintendedly.

In short, the democratic politician has, due to the vastness of the winning coalition, an incentive to try and make life better for roughly everyone if he wants to be in power. Of course, this is not his *only* incentive, seeing as how rent-seeking by powerful interest group also provides a strong and a very different incentive. But if we compare the situation to that in dictatorships, it is no longer surprising why rent-seeking and government failure are usually more rampant and intense over there. If an aspiring, or sitting, political leader in a dictatorship needs only the support of a few thousand powerful people, the leader can buy their continuing loyalty with promises of personalized, private benefits, privileges, jobs in high positions, power-sharing arrangements, and bribes. The vast majority of the population that is much less important for who the leading politicians are is to a significant extent left outside of this reciprocal dynamic, and is also less likely to receive abundant public goods. As we have seen in chapter 2, this is not to say that dictators can completely overlook all of the needs of the population they rule over. After all, the danger of popular uprising is always potentially lurking in the background. However, as long as the repressive arm of the state, i.e. the military and police, is under control and kept loyal, and as long as the economy is not too modern, which would structurally empower the citizenry to fight, a dictator need not worry too much about the common person. He has to keep his sights on the narrow winning coalition that is instrumental to maintaining his position. Consider Putin's Russia:

> Political leaders close to Putin have become multimillionaires, and the oligarchs around them, according to *Forbes* Russia, have become billionaires. They are able to maintain that power and wealth as long as they don't challenge Putin politically. Under this system, the state absorbs the risk, provides state funds for investment, and gives those close to the Kremlin massive monetary rewards. With the return under Putin to state capitalism, the state nationalizes the risk but continues to privatize the rewards to those closest to the president in return for their loyalty.[47]

The preceding comparative analysis explains why, in general, corruption and rent-seeking are much more rampant in dictatorships than in democracies, thus explaining why the public interest is less endangered in democracies. It does not, however, explain why some important differences remain *between democracies*. Wealthy democracies tend less toward political improprieties, and provide more public goods, than do poor democracies.[48]

One possible simple explanation for this is the following.[49] It is true that in democracies one is institutionally encouraged to provide public goods in order to keep power. Still, doing so is not inexpensive. Investing in public goods reduces the share of the state budget a politician could use, at the end of the day, to enrich herself, her family, and her cronies. In poor democracies, where owing to their poorly developed economies the state budget is likewise much humbler, politicians are more incentivized to limit the expenditure on public goods in comparison to their colleagues in rich democracies. They are more incentivized to be selective, 'careful' with how they spend state resources on the citizenry. In a rich democracy, a large share can be spent on the citizens without endangering the possibility for political actors to also take a hefty reward from the budget for themselves. Even if the *share* of the budget that remains to be plundered is *similarly small* in both rich and poor democracies, this same share represents a much bigger *absolute amount* of money in a rich country, even controlling for purchasing power differences.

Conclusion

When politicians make bad decisions that hurt the public interest, or act inefficiently in the sense that the public interest is served sub-optimally, this does not necessarily or even likely happen because they are evil or incompetent. Systemically bad political decisions are the result of bad incentives with which politicians are confronted. In a democracy, this has three general dimensions. First, government failure sometimes happens because certain beneficial informational market mechanisms are skewed or absent in the state sector. Second, politicians can intendedly and self-interestedly indulge in certain forms of opaque government failure because voters tend to be rationally ignorant and because the principle of concentrated benefits and dispersed costs further exacerbates this unfortunate tendency. Third, even if exceptional and altruistic politicians are normatively and ideologically committed to abstain from self-interested action, they face the problem of self-interested action one level below themselves. In contrast to a few exceptional politicians, their ordinary supporters and powerful interest groups do tend to be self-interested, and their loyalty, if the leader wishes to remain in power and act out her altruistic motives, must sometimes be secured by engaging in forms of government failure.

Politics is not an idyllic fairy tale. As Randall Holcombe pithily puts it:

> In the abstract, everyone would want for policies to further the public interest, but as the political process actually works, individuals and interest groups have an incentive to work toward furthering their own interests rather than looking

out for the more general public interest. Firms that benefit from participating in a market economy do not lobby for more economic freedom, but rather for special interest benefits targeted at their own firms. The policies those interests lobby for promote their own interests, but at the expense of the general public interest. They engage in rent-seeking activities and capture the regulatory agencies that are charged with promoting the public interest, offering political support for those who are empowered to design public policy.[50]

Nevertheless, all is not lost. As I have discussed, in comparison to non-democracies the typical democratic regime usually prevents blatant exploitation of the public interest and intense forms of government failure. Among the usual bad incentives there are also a few strong positive incentives in democracies – incentives having to do with the extent of the winning coalition, free press and media, and the ever-present electoral democratic mechanism of voting out the really bad political actors. These mechanisms can all discipline rulers and politicians in advance to not be as bad as they would otherwise want to be, and these same mechanisms can also act to replace them if it comes to that. Liberal democracy is far from perfect but, somewhat akin to what I have argued with regards to the capitalist market, it is the best realistic social mechanism of accountability we currently possess.

One final note. In this chapter, I have been evaluating how markets and governments work with respect to (Pareto) efficiency, not *fairness*. The former is important because, as I have argued, it represents an important dimension of the public interest. However, it is certainly true that efficiency is not synonymous with fairness. Therefore, it is possible to argue that even though certain regulations or government action in general create inefficient outcomes, thus hurting the public interest in one sense, they do contribute to some fairness criterion (for example, wealth redistribution), thus improving the public interest in a different sense. One might further argue that government failure is tolerable precisely due to this fact, or that the overall net effect, taking both dimensions into account, is positive in the end. My response to this is that, first, this can be a completely coherent and plausible argument. But, second, that it will tend not to hold in those cases where government failure occurred unintendedly, simply due to the lack of proper information, or where it was caused by self-interested actors trying to benefit themselves at the expense of the public. My purpose in the chapter was primarily to bring these latter social phenomena to the front and to put them side by side with the well-known facts of market failure.

Notes

1. On this see Brennan 2014.
2. See, e.g., Gwartney et al. 2011, chapter 3; Cowen and Tabarrok 2015, chapter 12.
3. Akerlof 1970.
4. Recording 2019. As I have said, in everyday talk we tend to support this argument by simply assuming entrepreneurs are self-interested, while politicians are not. The member of the parliament under consideration correctly avoided this assumption and said that the

mechanism which nevertheless guarantees an important asymmetry between entrepreneurial and governmental action is the 'democratic supervision'. The government is, indirectly, in the hands of the people while the economy is not. This seems to be a more reasonable argument but as we have seen in the preceding chapter and as will be show in this chapter, it does not necessarily and sometimes even likely hold.

5 Le Grand 1991.
6 Posner 2013, 50.
7 Bueno de Mesquita et al. 2003, 19.
8 Le Grand 1991, 431.
9 Ibid., 434–435.
10 Ibid., 436.
11 Winston 2006, 73, 75.
12 Ibid., 73.
13 Carpenter and Moss 2013, 13.
14 Butler 2012, 75.
15 Stiglitz 1998, 10.
16 Ibid.
17 Carpenter and Moss 2013, 11–12.
18 Stigler 1971.
19 Carpenter and Moss 2013, 19.
20 Cowen and Tabarrok 2015, 373.
21 Laband and Sophocleus 1988.
22 Udehn 1995; Zafirovski 1999.
23 Levitt and List 2007.
24 Hoffman et al. 1994.
25 List 2006, 1–37.
26 Carpenter et al. 2005.
27 Rand and Nowak 2013; Bear and Rand 2016; Mifune et al. 2010.
28 Bowler et al. 2006; Boix 1999.
29 Bowler et al. 2006.
30 Ibid.
31 Persson et al. 2012.
32 Ibid.
33 Boix 1999, 609.
34 Alt et al. 2011; Ferraz and Finan 2008; Aruoba et al. 2019.
35 Ferraz and Finan 2011.
36 Chaiken and Trope 1999; Chong et al. 2001.
37 Bueno de Mesquita et al. 2003, 18.
38 Ibid.
39 Ibid., 22.
40 Gwartney et al. 2018, 18–22.
41 Burchi 2011.
42 Bueno de Mesquita et al. 2003, 20; Wintrobe 1998.
43 Lake and Baum 2001.
44 Bueno de Mesquita et al. 2003, 33.
45 Ibid.
46 Ibid., 91.
47 Dawisha 2014, 2.
48 Roessler 2019.
49 Ibid.
50 Holcombe 2016, 83.

5
FOR AND AGAINST DEMOCRATIC PEACE

Introduction: an iron law of international relations?

Since at least the Neolithic Revolution onward, warfare has been a recurrent phenomenon in many, if not most, small-scale hunter-gatherer communities and horticultural tribes.[1] Likewise, warring definitely does not escape the more well-known larger-scale state societies that have first emerged some 5,000 years ago and in which we still live today. Some researchers, particularly in the past, attributed this humanity's less fortunate inclination to human nature, seeing humans as inherently prone to interpersonal and intergroup violence. Others caution that, depending on the particular circumstances, people can be attracted to both war and peace, with war itself resulting from either benign or malign intentions. Still others ascribe the propensity to wage war to sheer irrationality and ideological blinkeredness.

However this debate will be settled – and the second position of humans being inclined both toward war and peace, depending on the particulars of the environment, seems to be winning out – one thing is clear.[2] Although humanity has certainly not gotten rid of either murders, terrorism, civil wars, militarized interstate disputes, or most other forms of violence in social life, the singularly blood-soaked large-scale war between great powers has now been absent for around ¾ of a century. Since 1945, we have been witnessing a 'Long Peace' between the otherwise scary looking contemporary behemoth states.[3] Moreover, specifically with the rise of the *democratic* state, even the tendency to smaller-scale, ordinary interstate war seems to be almost completely vanishing – at least between democracies. Dan Reiter recently summarized the vast empirical literature on the topic: 'One of the most indisputable, nontrivial, observed patterns in international relations is that democracies almost never fight each other.'[4]

This statistical correlation should fill one with hope – hope of increasing likelihood of world peace as our planet becomes more democratic. Nevertheless, it has also tragically and ironically helped inspire American and European neo-conservatives to try and spread democracy across the world through the barrel of the gun. They reasoned that if democracies do not fight each other and if we turned the whole globe into a blooming field of democracies, war would be either banished out of existence or at least become incredibly unlikely. What they did not concern themselves too much with is whether this noble goal of world peace justifies the not-so-noble means of foreign occupation, or what grim unintended consequences might ensue in pursuing such a grand goal as spreading freedom. They were also not very consistent with their project, seeing as how they applied it only to certain specific regions of the world.

Apart from the terrible mistakes and even crimes of the neocons, the democratic peace correlation itself is strong. It is robust to various definitions of democracy and it holds under the standard definition of interstate war – 'a series of sustained battles, between or among the military forces of two or more states, resulting in a total of 1,000 or more battle-related deaths'.[5] Democratic peace is an extremely important phenomenon for any student of democracy. However, as I have warned repeatedly in chapter 2, correlation is not causation. It is not surprising, therefore, that the field of international relations has seen in the last few decades a quite vigorous debate about the precise causal nature of democratic peace.

There are at least two general topics of contention. First, some researchers try to show that introducing various omitted variables into statistical models of democratic peace overturns the correlation's pretension to causal status. As we shall see at the end of the chapter, this type of a critique is becoming less and less convincing with study after study confirming the relationship. However, second and more interestingly, democratic peace is also the battle-scarred terrain on which serious, even grand theoretical clashes are occurring continuously. On the one hand, various researchers are disputing amongst themselves the precise causal mechanisms underlying the correlation. On the other, major international relations paradigms are weighing in, either supporting or undermining the ostensibly causal nature of democratic peace as either its presence or absence ties in with how legitimate the different paradigms themselves are. Here, the winner is less obvious, and it is this topic that we will be concerned with for a significant portion of this chapter.

Liberalism: between democracy and capitalism

Liberalism and realism are, and have been for quite some time, the two major theoretical frameworks for understanding international relations (IR); constructivism is usually also rightly mentioned in IR textbooks, but it is less a tractable social science theory than a meta-philosophical meditation. Both paradigms share important similarities but are also divided by significant differences. Both contain a variety of smaller, more fine-grained or middle-range theories which flow from the general assumptions of each paradigm but then also specify a host of more concrete hypotheses about international relations in the here and now. For example, and most relevant for our purposes, liberalism encompasses both the democratic as well as the capitalist peace theory.

Democratic peace theory considers the empirical correlation between democracy and international peace as a causal connection. That is, it claims that democracy is a significant cause of peace, and then details a set of plausible causal mechanisms which could theoretically ground the ostensibly causal status of the correlation. *Capitalist peace theory* at least partly, but sometimes wholly, rejects the notion that the above correlation is causal. Instead, it suggests that there are other variables – especially economic, capitalist factors – to which democracy's ostensible impact on peace reduces to with a properly performed statistical analysis. Supporters of the theory accept the seeming connection between democracy and peace, but claim that this appearance is generated by a third common cause, capitalism, that somehow produces both democracy and peace.

Both theories are instances of the general liberal paradigm, which is why both accept as their methodological bedrock rational choice theory and the idea that state actors, not non-state ones, are the proximate causes of international phenomena.[6] State actors are seen as following their self-interest and acting strategically, which means that they try to anticipate the actions and reactions of their opponents, and act accordingly. These assumptions are made by the realist paradigm and its off-shoots as well. Moreover, both the liberal and the realist paradigm accept that the particular structure of the international system, i.e. how power is divided between states and whether the system is either anarchic or hierarchic, helps shape how states act. However, the most significant difference between both paradigms is that in the liberal case the domestic structure of a given state is just as, if not more, important than what the valence of the whole international system is.[7] Whether two *democratic* states come into contact on the world stage, or whether a *democracy* and an *autocracy* collide, is a very important distinction for liberal IR theorists, which realist scholars tend not to care about. Liberal scholars insist that different countries have differing institutional frameworks which generate very different incentives for their statespersons when making decisions, which can further lead to very different international relations behaviour.

This seems completely unobjectionable. Why would anyone tolerate ignoring a whole dimension of social interaction when investigating international relations phenomena? Well, realists offer two interrelated justifications. First, as we have already discussed in chapter 1, every theory must make tough decisions on what to abstract away so as not to drown in the incomprehensible complexity of the real world. It is not that realism is sweeping in its abstraction, while liberalism controls its temper and holds back. Both abstract away a lot from reality. So then the question is reduced down simply to who performs the more appropriate abstraction. Here, secondly, realists claim that their own abstraction is the proper one, because the causal influence of the domestic sphere, even though it is real, is overwhelmed by the international sphere in most cases. We shall see in the second section of the chapter why they think so. Note, for now, that the fact that realists are 'forgetting' about the domestic institutional pressure is not necessarily an issue.

This fundamental difference between the two paradigms generates another key distinction. As we will explore later in detail, realists think that states (especially great powers) compete among each other for power, which is why cooperation between them is always limited and transitory, never more than a temporary function of the overarching power-competition.[8] In the final analysis, states have fundamentally different interests and do not trust each other. War is therefore a constantly recurring phenomenon in international relations, always potentially lurking in the background even in times of peace. It is not, according to realism, that conflict and warfare are anomalous, the brief exceptional periods between the normality of peace. It is more the reverse, with peace being the happy temporary period between the natural condition of mistrust and war-prone competition. Liberals, in contrast, reason that in certain conditions, which are potentially quite general, power competition simply ceases to be the main interest and behaviour of states, significantly increasing the likelihood of peace in a region or the whole world. We are inching closer and closer to such circumstances with the spread of democracy and capitalism. Cooperation between states, although never *guaranteed*, can be a lasting phenomenon and not only the temporary outgrowth of states securing more power for themselves, inevitably giving way to future conflict.[9]

Democratic peace theory

Democracies might be peace-loving toward each other for two sets of reasons. First, because they have vastly different formal domestic institutions than non-democratic states. Second, because democratic politicians have been socialized to respect very different norms compared to their autocratic counterparts.

There are many proposed institutional reasons for the democratic peace, which is why I will focus here only on two of the most plausible and discussed ones. The first mechanism can be called (1) *popular power constraints*, while the second one has to do with (2) *credible signalling* in which democracies can engage but autocracies cannot.

The first mechanism works in the following manner. Due to their democratic nature, democratic societies can easily get rid of a ruling politician or political party if their popularity falls sharply. In democracies, politicians rule as long as they enjoy sufficient popular support, and they are keenly aware of this fact. When going over the different policies they might enact, they know that usually one should not experiment with policies which are highly unpopular if one wants to keep power. Now, because at least *prima facie* war is typically not attractive to the general public, politicians in democracies can usually be expected not to cause wars.

That the ordinary citizen will not welcome warfare with open arms is theoretically plausible for two reasons. First, because wars are expensive and reduce state budget which the ordinary citizen would rather was expended on him, and because wars are destructive of capital and the private property of the whole of population. Second, the ordinary citizen must surely know the simple fact that both battle deaths and civil casualties of war flow from one single source – the ordinary citizenry. These are all the multifarious costs of war for the typical person. How about the potential benefits? These are rather small, dispersed as they are throughout the population. Moreover, they are dependent on whether 'our' side wins the war. So, the liberal theorist expects that warmongering will not be cheered on by the electorate, thus the first institutional mechanisms kicks into action and reduces the likelihood of democratic wars at least *between* two democracies.

The second institutional mechanism has to do with information.[10] To understand how it works, we need to first take a step back and recognize that wars are most immediately brought about by two factors. First, there has to occur a conflict of interests between two states. Second, the conflict must be irresolvable with peaceful diplomatic methods. Why does diplomacy sometimes not work? Either because the issue at contention is indivisible or because both sides have, at the start of the dispute, good reasons to bluff regarding their power and willingness to go to war. More concretely put, even if a state is not very powerful and even if it is not completely resolved to wage war, bluffing that it is, in fact, very strong and determined can pay off by scaring the opponent into peacefully submitting to the offered terms. This is especially true in situations where information is scarce and uncertain. If the bluff succeeds, a state gets what it wants (i.e. territory, access to strategically important docks, etc.) while also avoiding the great costs of war. A double whammy.

However, because *both sides* know that the other side has a strong incentive to bluff, one or both actors might unintentionally underestimate the real threat of war they are faced with. It is completely possible that state A is *in reality* militarily stronger and more committed to warfare than state B thinks is the case, being mindful of how self-serving it is of state A to boldly declare its might and resolve. Because state B (rationally) underestimates A's threat, B does not offer enough to A in negotiations and other diplomatic attempts to ameliorate the crisis, thinking that A is not that strong or determined. Had B correctly assessed the threat posed by A, it would have given away more at negotiations. This would have been better for both parties in the dispute. B would have lost less territory and wealth due to happily avoiding war in which it is destined to lose anyway. A would have also been better off because even though it could win the war, there are significant financial, human, and opportunity costs associated with this process – costs that can be avoided by successfully warning the opponent of what will happen if it does not offer enough in negotiations. In this case, A's goal would have been successfully pursued without the unnecessary costs of war.

Now back to the second institutional mechanism. I have just illustrated how the lack of proper information, generated in part by bad incentives for bluffing, makes peaceful diplomatic solutions which are better for both sides of a dispute harder to achieve. But if two *democracies* find themselves in a tiff, this might yet be avoided. When a state observes a democracy letting its opponent in a dispute (and everyone else) know that it is ready and willing to go to war, the first state in the dispute can be quite sure that its democratic opponent is not bluffing. Why? Because if the democracy was not really either strong or truly committed to war, and thus its loud proclamation of war was a mere bluff, that would be a highly irrational and therefore unlikely course of action for the political leadership. Such behaviour would be exceedingly costly for democrats (but not autocrats) to pull off. If a militarily weak democratic leader insincerely escalates to the brink of war, hoping that his bluff works, he is likely to find himself in an actual war which he will then tend to lose because his proclaimed strength and commitment was a mere ruse. And if he loses, the people are likely to throw him out of office and bury his future political career – this is a democracy, after all.

Something similar is unlikely to happen to leaders of autocracies. The autocratic leader can bluff all he wants and then, if he stumbles into war without sufficient strength and commitment, this blunder and the resulting loss is not all that costly for him. The people will suffer and be enraged, but they cannot as easily replace and punish the leader as their counterparts in democracies can. In comparison to dictators, democratic leaders will tend to choose wars much more carefully because they are incentivized to do so. And if their opponents know this, they know that when a democrat calls for war he is most likely not bluffing. A weak and uncommitted democrat's bluff is too costly for him to make in comparison to a strong and resolved democrat's escalation to war, which is not the case for a weak dictator compared to a strong dictator.

In sum, the second institutional mechanism for democratic peace is the ability for democratic states to send credible signals to their opponents regarding the former's true intentions, thus circumventing at least some of the otherwise omnipresent trouble with non-credible information in international relations. Think of it this way. It is much more likely, in reality, that only students who are actually competent and committed to studying receive a diploma or a graduate degree. That is why the degree is a credible, trustworthy signal of competence to their potential employers, revealing that a candidate's claims of competence are not a bluff. It is credible because it is too costly to fake, i.e. too hard to also be sent by incompetent students. Because in this case there exists a *separating equilibrium*, i.e. graduate degrees separating the population of would-be employees into the more and the less competent students, credible signalling is made possible.

It is the same way in international relations. Only those democratic leaders who are truly resolved, and strong enough in reality, to go to war and win are likely to proclaim so and escalate a crisis. That is why the democratic threat is credible, and will not be mistaken for a bluff, in the eyes of the opponent. It is credible because it is too costly to fake, i.e. too hard to be sent by democratic leaders who are in fact weak and uncommitted. Because here again the equilibrium is separating (committed versus uncommitted leaders), signalling is possible. In the dictatorial case, the equilibrium is *pooling*, which means the 'signal' can equally likely be sent both by uncommitted and committed leaders, so uncertainty in the eyes of the opponent remains, and stumbling into war is likely. In the dictator's case, but not the democrat's, words are cheap and therefore unreliable as an indicator of what the dictator really intends.

The last remaining mechanism of democratic peace to consider is the normative one. Especially in liberal democracies, contractual and impersonal norms are an almost unquestioning part of everyday life. Moreover and relatedly, people are used to norms of non-violent resolution of conflicts when, for example, they get into a car accident, their property is stolen, etc. Further still, most people in democracies have throughout their lives internalized, at least somewhat, the norm of value and idea pluralism according to which each individual can think and write almost whatever she wants. The normative mechanism for democratic peace is thought to flow from the fact that *political leaders* in democracies have also grown up and internalized all of these norms, and will act in accordance with them on the international terrain. When it comes to blows, they will be the first to pull back and de-escalate.

What is more, because democratic leaders from various democracies all know each other to share these fundamental values, they are more likely to be trusting of one another and to respect each other. They are trusting because they can count on their democratic opponent to be normatively committed to the same value of non-violent conflict resolution and pluralism as they, themselves, are. They are respectful of each other because all of them are *democratic* (instead of autocratic) politicians presiding over the same, and to their mind the only legitimate, democratic type of political regime. Therefore, we can expect peace to prevail or at least be significantly more likely among democratic dyads.

Note that all three mechanisms explain not only why one can observe peace between democracies, but also why peace is much more precarious among mixed dyads (democracy–autocracy) and between autocratic dyads. First, non-democracies are not institutionally constrained by the will of the people, which is why a dictator has a much easier time waging war against other non-democracies or against democracies themselves. Second, non-democracies are not really in possession of mechanisms of credible signalling which means that, even though a democracy can truthfully signal its intentions to an autocracy, the reverse does not hold and so a war might still break out. Third, democracies do not normatively respect or trust non-democratic regimes, which is why the third mechanism should be expected to break down if we step outside of democratic dyads, so the fact that mixed dyads are similarly likely to go to war as non-democratic dyads are, does not contradict the logic of the normative mechanism.

Capitalist peace theory

In chapter 2, I discussed at length both the empirical and theoretical status of the ostensibly causal connection between capitalism and democracy. If the connection really exists, the correlation between democracy and peace might be spurious. Perhaps what is really at play here is that the third variable of capitalism produces both democracy and peace at the same time. Perhaps capitalism, not democracy, is the real cause of peace, while democracy is a mere causally inert by-product tagging along for the ride, statistically.

If democratic peace wholly, or at least partly, reduces to capitalism, we would also expect that not every democracy will have as strong an inclination toward international peace. The more capitalist and developed democracies should be more peace-loving than their less economically free and less rich counterparts. In fact, there is some evidence in support of this asymmetric conclusion.[11]

There are at least four plausible mechanisms by which capitalism might generate, or raise the likelihood of, international peace.

I call the first mechanism (1) *lesser benefits of war*. Developed capitalist societies have the type of economic backbone that makes it much less beneficial for political elites to engage in war than it was in the past when they presided over non-capitalist or only weakly developed capitalist economies. Before capitalism, when the level of economic freedom was low all around the world, wars were at least partly a means to an economic end. Through wars, one could accumulate land and labour, two factors of production without which economic growth was virtually impossible. Expanding the economy and growing rich through technological development we all know today was well-nigh impossible. It was so due to the particular incentive structure of the pre-capitalist, Malthusian economy, in which property rights were far from secure and market competition (both in labour, goods, and capital) non-existent, that rapid and systematic technological improvement and innovation were highly unlikely.

The world today is very different. Developed capitalist economies grow primarily through technological progress and innovation in ideas about what and, most importantly, *how* to produce. Both of these processes raise labour and land productivity, i.e. the amount of output produced *per given* amount of labour or land input, thus generating sustained, year-on-year, continuous growth. As a means of economic growth, war has lost most of its plundering appeal in these changed social circumstances, replaced as it was with other cheaper and more efficient alternatives. Particularly in a *post-industrial* capitalist economy, which is not primarily based either on agrarian or industrial production, territorial conquest is simply anachronistic. Developed capitalist societies have an easier, faster, and cheaper time reaping benefits for themselves through technological development, and both domestic and international trade competition, than they do by taking land and killing potential customers at home and abroad.

Is sum, war is less economically attractive today (i) because developed capitalist societies can grow without territorial expansion (this is the difference between past extensive and contemporary intensive growth, or between past zero-sum and contemporary positive-sum economy). Furthermore, war is not as attractive (ii) because in today's developed capitalist economies stealing land and labour from abroad does not generate great benefits anymore.

The second mechanism is (2) *credible economic signalling*. Just as political leaders in democratic states are able to send a trustworthy message about their own strength and resolve to the opponent, so too can politicians in advanced capitalist societies – regardless of the fact that almost all advanced economies are also at the same time democracies. The logic here is that, in societies with greater degrees of economic freedom, investors are free (or at least more free) to voluntarily choose whether they will start, and keep, investing in a certain country's economy both now and in the future. If politicians in a given country are ramping up a particular conflict, foreshadowing war, then markets and investors will quickly get spooked and start pulling out their investments. Falling investment leads to lesser economic growth, which in turn angers voters and makes them hostile to the incumbents due to vanishing economic opportunities, higher unemployment, and reduced wages.

Moreover, a slowdown in economic growth reduces the state's capacity to perform, to pay off debts, to enact policies, etc. simply due to a concomitant reduction in the state's budget.

In sum, under conditions of high economic freedom, i.e. in advanced capitalism, the actions of politicians in state A provide for a costly and therefore credible signal to the leaders of state B that A means business – ironically, even to the point of losing actual business – and is not bluffing. This gives the opportunity for B to back off from crisis escalation and return to diplomacy or negotiation, offering A better terms than it previously did so that a compromise acceptable to the stronger and more resolved A can be achieved, with both countries avoiding war in the process. There is some empirical evidence of this being the case, although the specific findings tend to be mixed.[12]

The third mechanism has to do with (3) climbing *opportunity costs of war* for the economically developed states. Advanced capitalist countries that have a whole lot of built and working infrastructure, accumulated physical capital, and an exceeding amount of valuable market transactions, risk losing significantly more in the process of a destructive war than an economically less developed state. This is true both in the sense of direct destruction of existing infrastructure, capital, and wealth, as well as in the more indirect sense of losing out on potential capital accumulation and positive-sum market opportunities *while undergoing war*. If the country had not been busy with war, it could have engaged in more market transactions. Therefore, businesspeople, ordinary citizens, and even politicians, dependent as their budget is on market transactions, will have a lesser incentive to support war. This mechanism also has some empirical support.[13]

The fourth mechanism is the well-known process of (4) *economic interdependence*. Economically freer, more advanced capitalist economies are usually also highly dependent for their wealth and welfare on other countries they trade with and on the success or stability of their economies. If an advanced economy geopolitically attacks other capitalist states with which it shares markets and trades, it either starts materially destroying them, hurting its own beneficial trading opportunities in the process, or it spooks their investors which again also indirectly hurts the attacker, economically. And as I have explained before, a state undermining its own economy is a huge cost which political leaders usually do not want to indulge. A swathe of statistical studies supports this last mechanism.[14]

It is, of course, true that large economically advanced states are also the ones which, owing to their development, usually have the bigger military might or at least the potential to achieve it. This is one characteristic of advanced economies that points, as far as war is concerned, in the 'wrong' direction of lesser peace. Nevertheless, the state's capacity to wage war does not cause war unless it is activated by statespersons. And the four proposed mechanisms make us think, theoretically, that advanced economies are less likely to *motivationally trigger* their otherwise large violent potentiality.

Realism and the bellicose tragedy of international relations

Due to their paradigmatic commitment to realism, realists try to reject liberal theories of peace in any way possible. The main issue of contention is that realism sees states as black boxes, the internal structural makeup of which we are unaware of and disinterested in because it is, by hypothesis, only of marginal causal import. States are presumed to be internally homogenous just like billiard balls are, varying only in size, i.e. power. It follows that how democratic or capitalistic a regime is, cannot importantly shape whether peace or war prevails in international relations, so theories referencing these variable must be shown to be wrong. Aside from this and similar theoretical concerns, there are also empirical reasons for why realists want to debunk liberal theories of peace. I turn to this at the end.

At base, all contemporary realist theories of international relations spring from four substantive and one methodological assumption, arriving at three general conclusions about the likely dynamic of the international system.[15]

1. *Anarchy.* There is no overarching authority in the international system in which states act, no supreme sovereign who would systematically and impartially pursue and punish wrong-doer states that are in violation of the rules of the system. In contrast to what social life looks like *inside* states, where hierarchy is present, meaning police and the judiciary pursue and punish citizens who violate the law, life in the international order is anarchic. In this sense, citizens are not sovereigns, states are, and there is no one above states.
2. *War-making capacity.* All states possess at least some form of military capacity. They all have soldiers, or at least potential soldiers, weapons, and other technological devices with which they could, in principle, hurt other states. Miniscule states, such as Slovenia, have an incomparably small war-making capacity considered alongside, say, France. Still, all sovereign states have some ability to attack other political units in the international system.
3. *Uncertain intentions.* Just as people within states can never be completely sure what the intentions of others around them are, because intentions are only directly observable by each individual herself, so too states can never be certain what other states intend to do either now or especially in the future. It is always possible that a neighbouring state has malign intentions or that it is peaceful today but will start plotting an attack tomorrow. Of course, one can try to gather the best possible indirect information about the intentions of others, both within and between states. However, one never arrives at a complete picture of what others are planning on doing.
4. *The primacy of survival.* The first and the most fundamental goal of every state is to secure its own survival. Realists assume this not only because they are committed to rational choice theory, which itself assumes actors primarily care about themselves and their own interests, but also because of a simple fact, i.e. if a state does not survive, it cannot pursue any other goal it might have. States, or people staffing them, definitely have other goals, such as getting

rich, achieving great status, or even altruistically helping others. But they can realize these other goals only if they first survive to live another day.

5. *Rationality*. The last assumption is the acceptance of rational choice theory. People running states are considered by realists to be rational actors, who are responsive to incentives, and strategize.

Combining all these assumptions results in three general conclusions about international relations.

First, fear is pervasive in the international order. At times, fear rises or subsides, but it is always at least somewhat present. States fear each other, realists claim, because they know the following facts: that it is always possible that other, especially neighbouring, states might become stronger in the future; that other states might have bad, militaristic intentions; that if a state stumbles into trouble, there is no impartial police or the judiciary to call for help. Fear is always more acute in *anarchic* international relations than in *hierarchic* domestic relations. Even though people in both spheres have the potential to hurt each other and can never be sure of the other's intentions, this is a much more intractable problem in the international sphere because there is no supreme sovereign to intervene and because the capacity to cause harm is orders of magnitude greater than on the street.

Second, states are destined for politics of self-help. States know that, at the end of the day, they cannot rely on anybody but themselves when it comes to security and help in times of trouble. Alliances are, it is true, commonplace but alliances just as commonly shift or break down. Alliances form and persist because, if, and until each individual state stands to benefit from them. They are not permanent.

Third, states (especially great powers and aspiring great powers) are obsessed with finding ways of increasing their own security. Here, realism breaks down into two general subgroups: (a) defensive and (b) offensive realism.

According to *defensive realism*, states as security-seekers will usually not tend to actively accumulate more power and territory but will rather try to maintain the existing balance of power in the system. They will strive to prevent other states from gaining more power, and they will increase their own power when others do so, but that is all. Typically, most states are 'status quo' powers. In other words, states that want to survive maximize security.

According to *offensive realism*, states as security-seekers will usually tend to actively accumulate more power and territory. Instead of maintaining the existing balance of power, they will try to tilt it to their advantage. Typically, the more powerful sates are 'revisionist' powers. Becoming more powerful, or the most powerful state in a region, tends to be according to offensive realism the only rational way for gaining security in the uncertain world of international politics. States that want to survive maximize power.

Why the difference? Defensive realists reason in the following way. A state knows that if it pursues aggressive politics, expansion, and regional hegemony, that will almost certainly scare other powers. Furthermore, a state knows that by scaring off others it will just bring them together in an alliance, a balancing coalition, rationally formed with the intention of stopping the expansionist zeal of the first state dead in its tracks. Therefore, the initial act of unsettling the balance of power and pursuing regional hegemony is a highly risky strategy that a rational state should not play with. After all, of all the attempts by individual states at becoming a hegemon in the past 200 years, only one – the American one – was successful, and even that owing partly to the unusual geographic position of the US. Expansionist France was defeated in the Napoleonic wars, Imperial Germany in World War I, Nazi Germany and Imperial Japan in World War II, and the Soviet Union in the Cold War. Defensive realists insist that the rational state will, in usual circumstances at least, not upset the balance of power and will rather try to credibly signal to other states that its intentions are pure and non-aggressive.

It might seem here that defensive realists reason similarly to liberals, as they are obviously not as pessimistic about the future of international relations as their offensive counterparts. It is true that they are less pessimistic, but not because of any fundamental agreement with liberals. To the contrary, defensive realists warn that, even though states are not simply destined for war as in the offensive case, their benign, defensive security-seeking can lead to serious and recurring instabilities in the system and, in the end, even unintended war. Perhaps the most famous concept that captures and explains this dynamic is the notion of the 'security dilemma'.[16]

The security dilemma is a situation in which the actions of a state, intended only to increase its own security by, say, drafting more soldiers and buying new military technology, decrease the relative security of other states which, in turn, prompts *them* to act similarly, i.e. to build up their army if only for defensive security reasons. The situation can spiral out, with the first state now feeling even more threatened, thus further boosting its security apparatus, which then only confirms, seemingly, that the suspicions the other states had in the beginning were correct, prompting *them* to increase their military capacity, and so on. The final result of this downwards spiralling dynamic can be a serious international conflict or even preventive war from one of the participating sides – even though nobody had aggressive intentions at the start and everybody *intended* to avoid war.

According to defensive realists, the security dilemma is pervasive but not intractable. One solution is communication through credible signalling. This happens when a state engaging in costly action *displays* (instead of merely *declaring* on the cheap) that it does not have aggressive intentions. Another solution is for a state to increase its security by arming itself in a clearly defence-biased way. This should make other states less edgy and more convinced that either the former state has benign intentions or, if it happens to have malign intentions, that it cannot do much to hurt them as it has armed itself in such a defence-tilted manner. The problem with this is that, at least in the past, most arms and technology could be used in either offence or defence.

Offensive realists also accept the logic of the security dilemma, but frame it in a much more pessimistic way. They claim the tragic situation is not solvable, because states simply cannot ever be wholly certain about others' intentions. In conditions of high mistrust, which according to them are pervasive in the international system, signalling cannot work because it cannot be credible. States, if rational, will have to assume that other states usually want to hurt them, and they will have to respond accordingly, i.e. with power-maximization wherever possible, striving for that ever elusive hegemonic position where they can finally rest (somewhat) at peace as no one can hurt them, regardless of their intentions.

Who is closer to the truth? My general evaluation proceeds in three steps. First, we have to note that offensive realists reason as they do because they smuggle in an extra, less explicit assumption into their analytic mix.[17] If we know what it is, we can examine how justified they are in making it. The extra supposition is that the absence of *certainty* in international politics necessarily (or at least in high likelihood) leads states not only to be uncertain, which is completely reasonable, but also to think the worst of other states. The international system is, according to offensive realists, not only pervaded by fear but also by radical fear. However, what they seemingly forget in asserting this is that certainty is precluded even in the domestic, hierarchic sphere. Things are always and everywhere only *more or less certain*. Of course, we can say that in international politics things are less certain, due to standard realist reasons, than in domestic social relations. But 'lesser certainty' does not mean 'no certainty'. The absence of total certainty does not automatically lead to the presence of total uncertainty, which would then, had it existed, generate radical fear. In other words, because we do not have to assume, as offensive realists do, that states cannot ever at least somewhat reliably know the intentions of others, we do not have to paint such a tragically bellicose picture of international relations as they do. States wanting security will not inexorably be led to maximize relative power, because even though they know that it is always *possible* that others want to hurt them, they also know that in certain circumstances this is *not very likely*. And when it is not very likely, a rational state will tend to maintain, not maximize, power so as not to trigger the security dilemma.

Second, it follows from this that defensive realists actually expect international politics to be relatively non-bellicose in quite a range of circumstances. Put less politely, defensive realism has what is sometimes called a 'status-quo bias'. This is not a normative charge. The potential issue with an IR theory being status-quo biased is not that it is ethically odious, say that it ostensibly wrongly advocates against radical change of the present social system and in favour of political quietism. Rather, status-quo bias means that defensive realism explains too little. It does not really explain why international relations often *are*, or have been in the past, soaked through and through in intentional aggression. To circumvent this awkward problem, defensive realists try to explain conflicts and major wars in the preceding centuries by invoking more concrete, middle-range theories once or twice removed from defensive realism itself, such as various foreign policy theories, psychological profiles of (pathological) political leaders, the offence–defence balance in military technology, etc. In a sense, then, the core logic of defensive realism is, unlike that of offensive realism, theoretically underdetermined. It needs supplemental aid that can only be provided by other theories, which are not always tightly connected to its core propositions. This is one of the key reasons why the offensive realist John Mearsheimer decided to develop his alternative theory of international relations that does not suffer from status-quo bias, implicitly including as it does aggressiveness and expansionism in the first premises of the theory.

Third, in spite of only a single state's aspiration for hegemonic status being achieved in the past 200 years, which suggests defensive realism is correct in pointing out that counterbalancing will tend to occur and so prevent would-be hegemons in succeeding – punishing as it does aggressive behaviour and making it less rational – we must heed the opposite side of this coin as well. That is to say that 19th and 20th century international politics also shows important congruence with the offensive realist idea that great powers do, indeed, seek hegemonic status.[18] More specifically, even though almost all attempts at achieving hegemony failed, they were nevertheless *carried out*, just as offensive realism predicts. States obviously thought that it is rational to act in accordance with the dictates of offensive realism. One can try to counter this by noting that such course of action turned out, in the end, to be self-destructive and therefore irrational, and that aspiring hegemons of the past were in fact just anomalies that can better be explained with the various defensive realist sub-theories, say, the weird psychology of Hitler or Stalin. One could further say that if the typical state today is rational, and especially if it is aware of how terribly past hegemonic projects ended, it is more likely to act in ways codified by defensive, not offensive, realism.

Now, despite all the differences and disagreements among the realisms, one thing is clear: they all reject democratic and capitalist peace theory. This is what should concern us the most. They are convinced that due to anarchy and its related phenomena of fear, self-help, security (or power) maximization, and the security dilemma, potential domestic causes of peace will simply be trumped by grander causes flowing from the structure of the international order. As perhaps the most famous defensive realist of the 20th century, Kenneth Waltz, points out:

> Democracies may live at peace with democracies, but even if all states became democratic, the structure of international politics would remain anarchic. The structure of international politics is not transformed by changes internal to states, however widespread the changes may be. In the absence of an external authority, a state cannot be sure that today's friend will not be tomorrow's enemy. ... What can we conclude? Democracies rarely fight democracies, we might say, and then add as a word of essential caution that the internal excellence of states is a brittle basis of peace.[19]

The already mentioned Mearsheimer, probably the most famous offensive realist of the late 20th and early 21st century, is just as clear:

> For any of these theories to dominate realism, its proponents have to argue that it makes war certain not to occur. It is not enough for them to argue that their theories lead to enhanced interstate cooperation or make war much less likely. One might think I am setting the bar too high. But as long as there is

some chance of war between any two states in the system, every state has little choice but to privilege survival and act in accordance with realist principles. Even if the likelihood of war is judged to be only 1 or 2 percent, states must think and act according to balance-of-power logic because the dire consequences of losing a major war require them to worry about their survival.[20]

The debate on democratic (or capitalist) peace will not be resolved with lofty, grand theoretical paradigms battling it out with each other at a high level of abstraction. Instead, one must dig deeper and consider the various ostensible shortcomings of concrete theories propounded by the liberal and realist paradigm. After all, realists themselves admit of certain recalcitrant exceptions that do not submit to the general logic of their explanation.[21] Here, perhaps, one might argue that a space opens up for liberal theories – even if we assume, for the sake of argument, the truth of the general realist paradigm.

Realist critique of democratic peace theory

Well, realists are definitely not willing to go down without a fight. Turning first to democratic peace theory, they allege that one fault with the first proposed institutional mechanism (*popular power constraints*) is its asymmetric nature.[22] They claim that if it were really the case that citizens in democracies are usually not supportive of wars and can constrain any warlike ambitions their political leaders might have, then mixed dyad wars in which a democracy and a non-democracy participate, should be just as scarce as wars among democratic dyads are. But, realists continue, they are not just as scarce. Mixed dyad wars are common, thus the logic of the first mechanism collapses.

By itself, this argument is a *non sequitur*. According to the logic of the first institutional mechanism, ambitions for war are constrained only on one side – the democratic side. So if a non-democracy, which is not similarly constrained, launches a war against a democracy, thus producing a case of mixed dyad war, this says nothing about the validity of the first mechanism. The sheer frequency of war between mixed regimes is not enough to indict democratic peace theory. However, realists are correct that if, taking a closer look at mixed dyads wars, we observe *democracies* to be just as likely to start wars against non-democracies as non-democracies are, the first institutional mechanism loses its credibility. And seeing how since the end of the Cold War the democratic US has started no less than seven wars against non-democracies, one does become somewhat suspicious.

Pressing on, realists add that it is simply naïve to believe that citizens in democracies are not fond of warfare. In other words, they dispute an ostensible fact, which needs to be true for the first institutional mechanism of democratic peace to hold. It might be true that politicians are constrained with the popular will, realists say, but the popular will itself is not necessarily unwelcoming towards war. And even if the electorate is not spontaneously clamouring for war, a dab of political demagoguery can provide the appropriate 'fix'. As Mearsheimer points out, democratic leaders are often adept at convincing reticent publics that war is necessary, even when it is not.[23] Liberals, of course, reject these claims and point out that we have both theoretical and empirical reasons to think otherwise. For instance, they claim that political leaders in democracies have usually not tended to mislead the public on matters of war in the past.[24] This should not be theoretically surprising, as the twin facts of a stark political competition and a free and transparent media terrain in democratic states ostensibly provide all the necessary incentives for politicians not to lie and mislead the public too much.

The results of a comprehensive experimental study from 2013 are interesting in this respect. It found that both the American and British public opinion is, indeed, not fond of war-like behaviour. More specifically, both publics showed significantly reduced support for a military strike against a democracy, compared to an otherwise identical autocratic society.[25] This is at least partly in tension with Mearsheimer's critique and in congruence with the democratic peace theory. I say 'partly' for two reasons. First, Mearsheimer might still be right that public opinion swings the other way in special situations in which politicians systematically and unrelentingly strive to convince the electorate to change its mind. Second, the results of the study causally support the democratic peace thesis – democracies tend not to fight each other – by providing a specific mechanism for it, i.e. the public for some reason does not want to hurt other democracies, although it does not have a problem with striking autocratic states. However, the causal logic of the first institutional mechanism *in particular* is not strengthened. That is so because the mechanism proposes that the public is wary of war *in general*, due to being concerned with its economic and human costs, not just when it comes to staring down democracies.

Of course, we can simply rework the particular logic of the mechanism in accordance with the study's findings. We might say that democratic peace still comes about because democratic politicians are constrained with the popular will, and that the public is unlikely to throw its support behind a war with another democracy. However, now we cannot ground this by pointing to the general costs of war. Rather, going by the study, it is simply a brute fact that democratic publics are unwilling to fight with other democracies. Thus, the first mechanism is saved, the price being that it is now less theoretically grounded than before.

The second institutional mechanism (*credible signalling*) is charged by realists with being empirically unjustified. There are older studies from the 1990s, which in general supported the mechanism, but newer studies reveal that democratic political leaders do not tend to make clear threats during crises that would send a trustworthy signal of strength and resolve, helping to avoid misperceptions caused by incentives to bluff, and thus averting possible unwanted wars.[26]

The normative mechanism (*the spirit of non-violent conflict resolution*) is, according to realists, both theoretically and empirically faulty. Theoretically, rational choice analysis which is accepted by both the realist and liberal camp gives us good *a priori* reasons to believe that democratic (or any other) norms work in triggering behaviour mostly when they are backed up by various sanctions and, ultimately, by the threat of force – that is, when they are anchored to incentives. Think of how democratic and liberal norms work *within* states. They work because if one breaks them, one is fined or sent to jail. But in the world of *international relations* where there is no higher authority to back up acting in accordance with democratic and liberal norms, actors do not usually have strong external incentives to follow norms they otherwise would not like to follow voluntarily. So, especially in cases where the stakes are high and where a democracy can capture important benefits for itself by acting in violation of the norms it (and other states) otherwise purports to support, one should cynically expect cold interest to prevail over romantic norms.[27]

Backing up these realist theoretical concerns about the effectiveness of incentive-less norms in international relations are various notable empirical cases. Liberal-democratic states, even leading ones such as the US, do not have too many qualms over whether to continue respecting their own norms when it suites them not to. As Mearsheimer summarizes: 'The United States, for example, has a rich history of toppling democratically elected governments, especially during the Cold War. The more prominent cases include Iran in 1953, Guatemala in 1954, Brazil in 1964, and Chile in 1973.'[28] He adds that similar anti-normative behaviour of democratic powers is on display in the 21st century. Consider the destabilization (by the democratic US and Israel) of the democratically elected Hamas in 2006, or how during the Arab Spring the US helped topple the democratically elected Muslim Brotherhood in Egypt in 2013. Now, a liberal might retort that the US is a special case, being the regional hegemon and by far the most powerful state in the world, and that it therefore does not count. However, it is precisely the powerful US that throws into sharp relief what happens when one's own lofty norms come into conflict with one's own (perceived) geopolitical interests. The latter usually win out over the former. In sum, the normative mechanism of democratic peace is probably the weakest of all three.[29]

Realist critique of the capitalist peace theory

The democratic peace theory has been dealt quite a severe blow by the realists.[30] How about the capitalist peace theory? What do realists have to say about *it*?

Their critique of the theory is, interestingly, less striking and all-encompassing. As Mearsheimer puts it, 'It would be wrong to say that economic interdependence does not matter at all. There will surely be cases where it tips the balance away from war, especially when the economic costs of fighting are great but the political stakes are not. Nevertheless, in many circumstances it will not sway policymakers, and thus it does not come close to guaranteeing peace between economically interdependent states.' Also interesting is that in his critique of liberalism, Mearsheimer does not touch upon other mechanisms of capitalist peace theory besides economic interdependence.

Let us start here. Why should one typically expect economic interdependence not to significantly reduce the likelihood of war? In congruence with his offensive-realist thinking, Mearsheimer primarily claims that this is so politics trumps economics.[31] The main goal of a state is not economic welfare but survival, and surviving in anarchic international relations requires a state to maximize its relative power and, if possible, achieve regional hegemony. Put differently, security reasons force states, if rational, to concern themselves with geopolitical competition, side-lining economic concerns when making decisions about international politics.

What is one to think of this? Well, if we accept the underlying logic of offensive realism, it seems correct. But we do not have to accept it. There are, as we have seen, good reasons to be doubtful of at least an important part of what offensive realists claim about international relations. Nevertheless, we cannot sidestep the classic empirical example realists usually marshal in support of their critique. Economic interdependence did not manage to prevent the outbreak of World War I, even though the world has never before in history been as economically interdependent as it had been on the eve of the war. The major belligerents of World War I had been trading more and more in the decades leading up to the fateful events of 1914. The rate of trade engaged in by Great Britain, Germany, France, and Italy had increased between 1870 and 1914 by 2-times (Britain), 4-times (Germany), 3-times (France), and 2-times (Italy).[32] Obviously, the seemingly pacific mechanism of economic interdependence had tragically failed at the beginning of 20th century.

Now, there exist numerous avenues of response that are available to liberals here. First, we can say that World War I is just a single example and as such cannot disprove a general statistical trend. After all, the liberals do not claim that economic interdependence *guarantees* war, only that it reduces its *likelihood*. There are no deterministic iron laws in social science, only probabilism.

Second, European nations had in fact been quite interdependent before the outbreak of war, but different regions also enjoyed quite different degrees of interdependence. The southern part of Europe was markedly less internally interdependent and, moreover, it was less integrated into the European market compared to the western and northern part. This is important because the trigger for war came from the south. War did not start among the most economically interdependent states, rather it was ignited between Austria–Hungary and Serbia. Furthermore, in the decades leading up to 1914, the economically most interdependent states found themselves, again and again, in serious international disputes which could have broken out in war – but in fact did not.[33] Perhaps the various conflicts between core European powers, such as the two Morocco crises (1905 and 1911), were peacefully resolved in part due to the states' higher economic interdependence. This seems even more likely when we consider that similar conflicts between less interdependent countries in southeast Europe resulted not in continued peace but in regional wars (both Balkan wars in 1912 and 1913).

Third, increasing trade between European great powers before the war had been accompanied by steadily accumulating protectionist measures, which negatively affected the prospects and evaluations of *future* trade cooperation. This was especially so in the case of Germany and its relationship to the increasingly protectionist France and Russia.[34] There is a further nuance at play here. It is true that if we limit our investigation only up to the 19th and the first part of 20th century, trade really was at a historical high on the eve of the war. However, extending the analysis up to today and comparing pre-1914 levels of international trade with the unprecedented booming of trade the world has witnessed in the latter half of the 20th century, especially in the last 30 years since 1990, the level of interdependence before World War I is much less historically impressive. This implies that perhaps *partial interdependence*, characterizing international relations in the early 20th century, might, as realists claim, not be able to prevent or significantly reduce war, but *significant interdependence* we know today still could – and ostensibly does. In sum, the realist critique has some bite to it, but does not go the full way.

Just as Mearsheimer does not pay too much attention to the other three mechanisms of capitalist peace theory, so too the defensive realist Waltz deals only with economic interdependence.[35] Perhaps they realize the empirical and theoretical robustness of the other mechanisms and so do not challenge them. A more charitable interpretation, however, is simply that Waltz's critique appeared in 2000, when other aspects of capitalist peace theory were not as fleshed out as they are today. What remains somewhat surprising is that Mearsheimer did not take the time to fully dissect the mechanisms in his 2018 book on liberalism.

'Realist peace theory'

Whatever the case might be, realists accept, just as liberals do, the surface statistical correlation between democracy and peace. Their theoretical account for it is, of course, very different from that of the liberals, tied as it is to the characteristics of the international and not the domestic system. Realists claim the seeming connection between democracy and peace holds for two reasons, both compatible with realism.

First, democratic peace is mostly a phenomenon which has temporally existed since the end of World War II and has been spatially tied, mostly, to the Western part of the world. Before this period, there was scarcely a democratic state in the world, and of those that existed some were arguably belligerent towards other democracies (Germany just before World War I comes to mind, though this is a weak example). After the end of World War II, most democracies have been found in the West.

Second, and closely relatedly, roughly around this time and place a bipolar international order emerged in which two opposing but similarly powerful superpowers, the US and the Soviet Union, participated. Because the system was populated by only two superpowers, the likelihood of a typical large interstate war erupting between other powers was very low. Superpowers do not, after all, tolerate chaos in their sphere of influence. And because both superpowers *themselves* were roughly balanced in strength (and armed with nuclear weapons), the likelihood of war breaking out between the two of them was likewise very low. How about the 30 years that have passed since the end of US–Soviet bipolarity? Europe started becoming more multipolar and therefore, according to realism, more likely to engage in warfare. At the same time, however, the US happened to extend its NATO alliance deep into Europe and elsewhere, maintaining its military presence in democratic regions across the world, thus reducing the dangers of multipolarity.[36] Realists speak of a US-based 'unipolar moment' since the fall of the Soviet Union.

A realist explanation for (the seemingly democratic) peace is now basically at hand. For the first 45 years it was generated by bipolar geopolitics. From then on, since 1990, 'democratic peace' continued simply due to the presence of the US 'pacifier' in Europe and elsewhere. Even though the international system is and remains anarchic, a sort of temporary quasi-hierarchy was established first through bipolarity and later by the incredible US power-projection capabilities and its interventionist tendencies, which made war unthinkable for most states (except, of course, the US). So what we have been witnessing for the past 75 years is not a democratic, or capitalist, but rather a realist peace, which will soon come to an end if the US decides to withdraw from Europe to American shores and if China continues to rise. Realists maintain that the relatively peaceful epoch might soon end even if, in the meanwhile, the whole world democratizes and increases its economic freedom.

This is an elegant explanation, but it cannot evade a simple yet very troublesome fact. Again and again, quantitative studies reveal that, even though a big power gap between democracies is known to be a factor that reduces the likelihood of war, the democratic variable nevertheless maintains its causal power and cannot be reduced to anything else one can imagine.[37] Moreover, the various standard realist factors, such as common strategic interests or alliances, are either not statistically significant or have a much weaker contribution to peace in comparison to democracy.[38]

Conclusion

Theoretically speaking, it is hard to say who wins. It seems, in fact, that the democratic peace theory is shot-through with both explanatory and empirical holes, at least as far as some of its specific mechanisms are concerned. Capitalist peace theory seems to fare comparatively better, although it does not escape the realist wrath wholly unscathed. The general realist paradigm also seems quite theoretically attractive, even though it has some empirical shortcomings when it comes to explaining peace.

Nevertheless, statistically, the democratic peace thesis turns out to be empirically sound, even more so than capitalist peace. Democracy *is* a cause of peace, at least among democracies. We do not know precisely how it works, mechanistically, but one for sure cannot statistically reduce the democratic variable to some other factor and account for why these regimes are so peaceful toward each other. In recent years, numerous scholars have tried to prove otherwise but did not succeed. In his comprehensive literature review, Reiter concludes that democratic peace remains robust despite decades of criticism. Mark Crescenzi, Kelly Kadera, Allan Dafoe, Seung-Whan Choi, James Ray, Bruce Russett, John Oneal, and Azar Gat concur. Just in the last 10 years they have either found fatal flaws in statistical models purporting to show the spuriousness of democratic peace, or they have managed to successfully replicate the positive finding.[39] Moreover, evidence for contributory effects of capitalism on peace is also solid, although capitalism is statistically a weaker cause of peace than democracy.[40]

I agree with Reiter that further progress in this area must come in at least two ways. First, defenders of democratic peace will have to plausibly rebut some of the criticism of their proposed mechanisms. If this turns out not to be possible, the existing mechanisms will either have to be reworked and patched up, or new ones will have to be invented. Here, one must be careful not to engage in unfalsifiable theorizing leading to a degenerating research program. Second, empirical testing of democratic peace will have to rely on other methods besides statistics. For example, one can empirically corroborate the various indirect patterns and events that implicitly flow from the theory. Moreover, one can utilize fine-grained historical investigation to trace the exact sequence of micro-level events in particular cases, with the sequence either conforming to the causal logic of the proposed mechanism, suggesting the mechanism might in fact be real, or deviating from it and pointing us in new directions.

Notes

1. Gat 2015; Kelly 2013; Pinker 2012.
2. Gat 2019; see also the various chapters in Fry 2013.
3. Gaddis 1986.
4. Reiter 2017.
5. Maoz et al. 2019, 818.
6. Keohane 1986, 193.
7. Ibid., 195. See also Moravcsik 1997.
8. Mearsheimer 2013.
9. Keohane 1986, 194.
10. It is tied to the famous analysis of Fearon 1995.
11. Mousseau et al. 2003.
12. Dafoe 2014.
13. Ibid.
14. Oneal and Russett 2005; Hegre 2009; Russett 2013.
15. Mearsheimer 2013.
16. Jervis 1976, 62–76; Glaser 1997.
17. Tang 2008.
18. Mearsheimer 2001.
19. Waltz 2000, 10–11.
20. Mearsheimer 2018, chapter 7.
21. Mearsheimer 2001, 10. In his lectures, Mearsheimer usually mentions that his version of realism probably accounts for roughly 75% of international relations phenomena.
22. Mearsheimer 2018, chapter 7.
23. Ibid.
24. Reiter 2012.
25. Tomz and Weeks 2013.
26. Snyder and Borghard 2011; Downes 2012.
27. Rutar 2019; Opp 2017.
28. Mearsheimer 2018, chapter 7.
29. See also Bakker 2016.
30. However, see this liberal critique of the realist critique of democratic peace theory by Kinsella 2005.
31. Mearsheimer 2018, chapter 7.
32. Gartzke and Lupu 2012, 128.
33. Ibid., 133–135.

34 Copeland 1996, 33.
35 Waltz 2000.
36 Mearsheimer 1990; Mearsheimer 2010.
37 Russett 2013, 103.
38 Maoz 1997, 176; Maoz 1998; Russett 2013, 103.
39 Crescenzi and Kadera 2016; Dafoe 2011; Choi 2011; Choi 2016; Ray and Dafoe 2017; Dafoe et al. 2013; Gat 2017, chapter 6 and 7.
40 Reiter 2017; Russett 2009; Russett 2010; Gat 2017, chapters 6 and 7.

6
CONCLUSION
Fukuyama's 'The End of History?' in social scientific retrospective

Democracy is not the *telos* of history

At the beginning of the book, I presented three general ways of thinking about democracy and politics which are personified by *romanticists, utopians,* and *activists,* and which I tried to avoid in subsequent chapters. I then claimed there exists a fourth, more *realistic* way of analysing democracy which I strived to display in the book. Now, it is doubtful whether these four types can really be thought of as completely distinct, or if one can actually subsume the whole terrain of both academic and lay thinking on the matter under these four headings. One important and infamous take on democracy that might elude my neat classification is Francis Fukuyama's teleological sounding proclamation that liberal democracy represents the end of history.

It seems that many of Fukuyama's critics, including my younger student self, who heaped scorn on his 1989 article published in *The National Interest* did not really thoroughly acquaint themselves with what he wrote in those fateful 15 pages.[1] (To be painfully honest, I myself have *carefully* read the essay for the first time only over the past two years when doing research for this book.) Fukuyama did not claim that after the end of history one can expect historical events to cease streaming in. He did not claim that the end of history implies a cessation of all human conflict. He did not even claim that history had ended in 1989 or that it will have done so in a few years.

What he did say is that, at the time of his writing, the world had been divided into two parts, one that had remained historical and one that had already become post-historical. He allowed for the possibility of conflict among states *within* the first part and *between* both parts of the world. Moreover, he added that specifically the rates of ethnic and nationalist violence will remain high and will, perhaps, even escalate. This is so, he said, because 'those are impulses incompletely played out, even in the parts of the post-historical world.'² Furthermore, although not relevant for what I presently want to do with Fukuyama's thesis, he in contrast with what his critics sometimes implied, painting him as an unflinching Pollyannish apologist of the democratic-capitalist *status quo*, lamented the coming end of history, seeing it as bringing about apathy and boredom.

What, then, did Fukuyama mean? His argument is quite simple, and to see that, I shall break it down into five main parts. First, the fundamental claim is that history shall end when capitalism and especially liberal democracy succeed in winning people over in the battle of ideas. The end will come when capitalism and liberal democracy are no longer facing practical, real-world ideological competitors such as fascism or communism. We will recognize the coming end of history when we recognize that, in contrast to other practical ways of arranging society, capitalism and democracy have no fundamental 'internal contradictions' that have time and again destroyed all previous systems. Second, presently (in 1989) this is exactly what is happening. It will not happen immediately and completely, but the trends are pointing in the right direction. Third, *in the long run* this ideational trend will cause a material shift in the world, structurally moving it more and more toward democracy and capitalism. At that time, the material battle among the systems – dictatorship against democracy, socialism against capitalism – will come to an end just as, per the second claim above, the ideational battle is currently winding down. Fourth, when history ends, large-scale interstate conflicts and warfare will slowly disappear or, at least, strongly diminish. Fifth, the claim that history has this long-run democratic tilt and end-state, and the claim that the material shifts are determined by ideational factors, holds for various Hegelian reasons.

Put like this, the main issue with Fukuyama's thesis is not, to my mind at least, that it declares the gradual ideational and, later on, material domination of capitalism and liberal democracy over other economic and political systems. If one speaks of (i) *a gradual* and not immediate change, (ii) *likelihood* and not necessity, and (iii) *a long-term* material shift, then I think this might roughly be true. (Moreover, his point about diminishing interstate war is well captured today in capitalist and democratic peace theory, as we have seen in chapter 5.) There are a couple of reasons for thinking so, not all of them available to Fukuyama 30 years ago.

First, the world today really is both ideationally and materially more capitalist and democratic than in 1989 – even despite the recent democratic recession. There are, of course, no guarantees that this trend will continue in the future. We are probably not even justified in saying that it is *very likely* to continue. But, certainly, we have been witnessing the world grow more and more capitalist over the decades without a truly feasible ideational, let alone material, economic alternative to a system of secure property rights and market competition. Moreover, in chapter 2 we have seen the various social mechanisms that make the spread and consolidation of democracy more likely with capitalist economic development. So, *on the condition that* no stable and growing ideational or material alternative to capitalism materializes (and even today's socialist politicians such as Bernie Sanders are no longer challenging it, rather setting their gaze towards the Scandinavian free-market welfare states), this economic system will likely remain triumphant – and with it democracy is not likely to lose out either.

Second, it seems that the main contemporary autocratic opponents of liberal democracy, such as Russia and China, have an important internal contradiction at the core of their system. Apart from the fact that Russia is a stagnating petrostate not likely to remake the world in its image, even the potentially challenging and seemingly miraculous Chinese amalgamation of a vibrant capitalist economy with dictatorial politics is not such a viable alternative to Fukuyama's democratic capitalism as one might think. As we have seen in chapter 2, China's growth has slowed significantly over the past decade. Its productivity growth has likewise declined sharply. A majority of Chinese entrepreneurs are afraid of expropriation and act accordingly. The necessary modernizing economic reforms are not underway. Xi Jinping has 'stalled or reversed course on eight of 10 categories of economic reforms promised by the Chinese Communist Party (CCP) itself.'[3] Is this just a fluke, waiting to be washed away in the future? Not likely. Structurally, autocratic politics almost never mixes well with long-term, sustained economic development. Once the initial industrializing spurts of growth are over, a country reaches such a level of development that, if it is to be pushed further ahead, both the capability for its citizens to freely exchange ideas as well as a government incentivized not to take care only of its closest cronies and elite supporters are required.

Third, even though there are geopolitical perks to a dictatorship that democracies lack, on net, democracies still win out over dictatorships.[4] Statistically, dictatorships start more wars than democracies, their wars last longer, and are more destructive, which hurts them both economically and geopolitically. Autocratic alliances are less stable than those formed by democracies. Moreover, in contrast to dictatorships, democracies actually win the wars they start. Over the past two centuries, democracies have won 93% of wars they initiated compared to the 60% win rate for dictatorships.[5] If the past is any guide to the future, geopolitics seems to be more on the side of democracy than dictatorship.

Fourth, another structural issue that lies at the heart of a dictatorship, but not democracy, has to do with an important artefact of human nature. Regardless of culture, people are not passive automata oblivious to their most fundamental needs and interests. The basic human need for material wellbeing can be satisfied by a dictatorship such as China. But the other fundamental need – the need for personal autonomy – can scarcely be so. The enduring, recurrent struggle against (political) oppression cannot be relegated to the 20th century, the canonical period of crumbling dictatorships. In fact, today just as before, people risk life and limb to protest against autocrats all over the world. Focusing only on 2019 and 2020, we see there were mass pro-democracy protests in Algeria, Armenia, Bolivia, Hong Kong, Iran, Belarus, and Sudan, some of them quite successful. More to the point, in 2019 a whopping 44% of all existing states experienced pro-democracy protests (compared to only 27% in 2009).[6] Democratic states can easily tolerate them and even become strengthened by such protests. Dictatorships, on the other hand, are existentially threatened by them and sometimes destabilized and even overthrown. According to one measure, there is more mass mobilization for democracy in the world today than in the time of Arab Spring or even in the tumultuous period of 1989–1991.[7]

Even though nothing is completely clear, all of the above pieces of evidence make me think Fukuyama was not that far off in his proclamation, at least as I have presented it. Now, aside from that Fukuyama also, more controversially and in line with Hegelian philosophy, emphasizes that the world of ideas dominates material reality. Even more to the point, Fukuyama intimates in a few places that history might have a set end-goal towards which it is inevitably, even if only in the long-term and gradually, driven by ideological clashes. His view of history sometimes verges on the teleological. This must be rejected. There is no good social-scientific reason to subscribe to the mystical idea that History (as apart from particular human beings) has a set end-state; let alone that it is inevitably propelled to it; or that such an end-goal is represented by liberal-democratic capitalism. Why? First, because only individuals have intentions and goals which they strive to achieve. History is nothing but a word referring to the aggregation of all past human actions. It is not a separate entity with its own intentions. Second, because there are no assurances that every single person accepts capitalism and liberal democracy, or that people will necessarily succeed in achieving their goals whatever they are.

I have argued both here and in chapter 2 that there are numerous reasons to think that the successful spread and consolidation of capitalism tends in many cases (but not all and certainly not necessarily) to be followed by democratization. However, this has less to do with the ideas generated in a capitalist society and more so with the changed structural, material circumstances brought about by development. At the same time, it has nothing to do with any kind of Hegelian (or Marxist) theory of history which assumes the existence of different and relatively fixed 'stages of consciousness' in history, 'internal contradictions' which inevitably lead to a resolution of the contradiction and thus a transition to a 'higher stage', or a sequence of 'historical epochs' moving from one to the next along a predetermined track leading from the 'primitive' to the 'progressive'.

In sum, there might be at least two different versions of Fukuyama's 'end of history' thesis, a *weak* and a *strong* one. There is a surprising amount of support for the weak version, even though it might not be very revolutionary and interesting in its vision. The strong, Hegelian version, on the other hand, is revolutionary but not reasonably warranted. Just as evolutionary biology has long ago been saved from teleological reasoning (the evolution of species is not led and has no purpose), so should historical analysis be divested of teleology, at least if what we have in mind is some kind of objective teleology divorced from the intentions and actions of particular individuals. Fukuyama's strong thesis represents its own form of unrealistic democratic romanticism. In fact, it is as if he, himself, is aware of the dilemma he is faced with which is why, despite the constant rhetorical references to Hegel and even a few explicit teleological statements, the actual content of his arguments is much more aligned with the weak version of the thesis.[8]

Key takeaways

The rise and fall of democracy

1. Mass state democracies are a huge historical exception.

The real theoretical puzzle is why they have ever emerged in the first place, not why they do not spring up more regularly or why sometimes they fall.

2. Democratic transitions in the past have frequently resulted from successful social pressure and conflict between ordinary citizens and elites.
3. The likelihood of social struggle for democracy being successful increases with modern capitalist economic development.

There are at least five causal mechanisms at work here: (i) the formal separation of politics from the economy; (ii) the emergence of the middle class; (iii) the replacement of landed elites by industrial and post-industrial capitalists; (iv) the replacement of rural peasantry by urban workers; and (v) middling levels of inequality.

4. Apart from the long-term, deep structural causes, there are also short-term, surface triggers of democratic transitions which can work by suddenly shifting the set of incentives and capacities of various social groupings towards an increased occurrence and likelihood of success of social struggle for democracy.

Usually, interstate wars, domestic and international economic crises, and a military defeat of foreign allies of an autocratic regime figure prominently among such triggers.

5. Democratic transitions can also happen in a more top-down fashion, involving elite action more than the collective action of ordinary citizens. Such transitions are less likely to be robust and will not as often lead to a consolidated liberal democracy.

Partial top-down democratization can happen in circumstances where opening up a dictatorship helps the elite with solving (i) problems of power-sharing, (ii) the dictator's dilemma, (iii) or inconveniencies stemming from its position in the international system. Top-down democratization also occurs (iv) due to mistaken elite perceptions.

6. The likelihood of a new democracy surviving and consolidating increases with, among other factors, further economic development, wealth, and opening up of economic institutions in a given society.
7. Democracies which fall tend to be economically underdeveloped and poor.

Voter behaviour

1. Most voters are politically ignorant or irrational.
2. A large part of the explanation for this phenomenon has to do with the bad incentive structure faced by voters in elections.

The costs of informing oneself before casting a vote are high, but the expected benefits are usually very low given the marginal influence of a single person's vote on the outcome. Being ignorant pays.

3. Political ignorance and irrationality are quite an intractable problem which will not likely be resolved with more political education.
4. The issue is not only the bad incentive structure but also human tribal psychology, and biased reasoning and decision-making.
5. Voters are retrospective which means they tend to electorally punish those incumbent politicians and political parties that have presided over a bad economy and reward those who have been graced by a flourishing economy.
6. Voters do not mostly vote with their pocketbooks. Rather, they vote sociotropically, meaning that they decide on what matters to them, politically, not by reflecting on their own personal situation in a society but on what they think would benefit the broader region or even the nation in which they live.

Political behaviour

1. Politicians – just like entrepreneurs – tend to primarily be motivated by their own self-interest, not the public good.
2. Nevertheless, public interest is pursued by politicians if a society's institutions manage to align the politician's private interest with the welfare of society.
3. The principle of concentrated benefits and dispersed costs, overlain with the fact of rationally ignorant voters, leads to unpunished rent-seeking behaviour and government failure even in democracies.
4. We should not characterize corruption and clientelism as esoteric, weird, and anomalous political phenomena, but as standard tools of political actors, the use of which is curtailed only in certain circumstances.
5. Democracies manage to have institutions and social incentives which reign in the most odious and excessive political behaviour, so that life in democracies for the ordinary citizen tends to be significantly better than the life of their counterparts in dictatorships. Liberal democracies are, in general, less corrupt than dictatorships, and rich democracies perform better, publicly, than poor ones.

The international effects of democracy

1. In the past two centuries since mass democratic states first emerged, they have never or almost never fought a war among each other. They do, however, regularly fight against non-democratic regimes.

2. This 'democratic peace' is in all likelihood foremost generated precisely by the democratic nature of states.
3. There are also other theoretically plausible variables that might account for the correlation between democracy and peace, such as capitalism, but they have a less strong effect.
4. Even though we are, empirically, quite sure that democracy is a strong cause of (dyadic) peace, we do not know exactly why this is. The presently proposed causal mechanisms are not completely convincing.

Notes

1 Fukuyama 1989.
2 Ibid., 18.
3 Kroenig 2020b.
4 Kroenig 2020a.
5 Bueno de Mesquita and Smith 2012; Reiter and Stam 2002.
6 Lührmann et al. 2020, 7.
7 Ibid., 21.
8 On this contradiction, see Callinicos 2007, chapter 1. See also Fukuyama's introduction to Fukuyama 1992, in which the rhetoric is unmistakably teleological, but the substance of the argument is not.

BIBLIOGRAPHY

Abercrombie, Nicholas, Hill, Stephen, and Bryan S. Turner. 1980. *The Dominant Ideology Thesis*. London: Allen & Unwin.
Acemoglu, Daron, and James A. Robinson. 2006. *Economic Origins of Dictatorship and Democracy*. New York: Cambridge University Press.
Acemoglu, Daron, and James A. Robinson. 2012. *Why Nations Fail. The Origins of Power, Prosperity, and Poverty*. London: Profile Books.
Acemoglu, Daron, and James A. Robinson. 2019. *The Narrow Corridor: States, Societies, and the Fate of Liberty*. London: Penguin.
Acemoglu, Daron, Johnson, Simon, and James A. Robinson. 2005. 'Institutions as a Fundamental Cause of Long-Run Growth,' in Philippe Aghion and Steven N. Durlauf (eds), *Handbook of Economic Growth*. New York: Elsevier, 385–472.
Acemoglu, Daron, Johnson, Simon, Robinson, James A., and Pierre Yared. 2009. 'Reevaluating the Modernization Hypothesis,' *Journal of Monetary Economics* 56, 1043–1058.
Achen, Christopher H., and Larry M. Bartels. 2017. *Democracy for Realists*. Princeton: Princeton University Press.
Ahler, Douglas J., and Gaurav Sood. 2018. 'The Parties in Our Heads: Misperceptions about Party Composition and Their Consequences,' *The Journal of Politics* 80, no. 3, 964–981.
Akerlof, George A. 1970. 'The Market for "Lemons": Quality Uncertainty and the Market Mechanisms,' *The Quarterly Journal of Economics* 84, no. 3, 488–500.
Albertus, Michael. 2017. 'Landowners and Democracy: The Social Origins of Democracy Reconsidered,' *World Politics* 69, no. 2, 233–276.
Alexander, Amy C., and Christian Welzel. 2017. 'The Myth of Deconsolidation: Rising Liberalism and the Populist Reaction,' *Journal of Democracy* Web Exchange. Accessible via: https://econpapers.repec.org/paper/zbwilewps/10.htm/.
Alt, James, Bueno de Mesquita, Ethan, and Shanna Rose. 2011. 'Disentangling Accountability and Competence in Elections: Evidence from U.S. Term Limits,' *The Journal of Politics* 73, no. 1, 171–186.
Althaus, Scott L. 2003. *Collective Preferences in Democratic Politics*. New York: Cambridge University Press.

Annenberg Public Policy Center. 2017. 'Americans Are Poorly Informed About Basic Constitutional Provisions.' Accessible via: https://www.annenbergpublicpolicycenter.org/americans-are-poorly-informed-about-basic-constitutional-provisions/.

Arrow, Kenneth J. 1963. *Social Choice and Individual Values.* London: John Wiley & Sons.

Aruoba, S. Borağan, Drazen, Allan, and Razvan Vlaicu. 2019. 'A Structural Model of Electoral Accountability,' *International Economic Review* 60, no. 2, 517–545.

Bakker, Femke E. 2016. 'Do Liberal Norms Matter? A Cross-Regime Experimental Investigation of the Normative Explanation of the Democratic Peace Thesis in China and the Netherlands,' *Acta Politica* 52, no. 4, 521–543.

Barro, Robert J. 1996. *Determinants of Economic Growth. A Cross-Country Empirical Study.* Cambridge: The MIT Press.

Bear, Adam, and David G. Rand. 2016. 'Intuition, Deliberation, and the Evolution of Cooperation,' *Proceedings of the National Academy of Sciences* 113, no. 4, 936–941.

Benhabib, Jess, Corvalan, Alejandro, and Mark M. Spiegel. 2013. 'Income and Democracy: Evidence from Nonlinear Estimations,' *Economics Letters* 118, no. 3, 489–492.

Bidner, Chris, Francois, Patrick, and Francesco Trebbi. 2014. 'A Theory of Minimalist Democracy,' National Bureau of Economic Research, Working Paper no. 20552.

Black, Duncan. 1986. *The Theory of Committees and Elections.* Boston: Kluwer, 1986.

Black, J. Stewart, and Allen J. Morrison. 2019. 'Can China Avoid a Growth Crisis,' *Harvard Business Review.* Accessible via: https://hbr.org/2019/09/can-china-avoid-a-growth-crisis/.

BLS. 2015. 'Volunteering in the United States.' Accesible via: https://www.bls.gov/news.release/pdf/volun.pdf/.

Boix, Carles. 1999. 'Setting the Rules of the Game: The Choice of Electoral Systems in Advanced Democracies,' *American Political Science Review* 93, no. 3, 609–624.

Boix, Carles. 2003. *Democracy and Redistribution.* New York: Cambridge University Press.

Boix, Carles. 2011 'Democracy, Development, and the International System,' *American Political Science Review* 105, no. 4, 809–828.

Boix, Carles, and Susan C. Stokes. 2003. 'Endogenous Democratization,' *World Politics* 55, no. 4, 517–549.

Bolt, Jutta, Inklaar, Robert, de Jong, Herman, and Jan Luiten van Zanden. 2018. 'Rebasing "Maddison": New Income Comparisons and the Shape of Long-Run Economic Development,' Maddison Project Working Paper 10.

Boudreaux, Christopher J., and Randall G. Holcombe. 2017. 'Economic Institutions and the Durability of Democracy,' *Atlantic Economic Journal* 45, 17–28.

Bowler, Shaun, Donovan, Todd, and Jeffrey A. Karp. 2006. 'Why Politicians Like Electoral Institutions: Self-Interest, Values, or Ideology?' *The Journal of Politics* 68, no. 2, 434–446.

Brancati, Dawn. 2016. *Democracy Protests: Origins, Features, and Significance.* Cambridge: Cambridge University Press.

Bratton, Michael. 2009. 'Sub-Saharan Africa', in Christian W. Haerpfer, Patrick Benhagen, Ronald F. Inglehart, and Christian Welzel (eds), *Democratization.* Oxford: Oxford University Press.

Brennan, Jason. 2014. *Why Not Capitalism?* New York: Routledge.

Brennan, Jason. 2016. *Against Democracy.* Princeton: Princeton University Press.

Brenner, Robert. 2007. 'Property and Progress: Where Adam Smith Went Wrong,' in Chris Wickham (ed.), *Marxist History-Writing for the Twenty-first Century.* Oxford: Oxford University Press, 49–111.

Broderstad, Troy Saghaug. 2018. 'A Meta-Analysis of Income and Democracy,' *Democratization* 25, no. 2, 293–311.

Brownlee, Jason. 2017. 'The Limited Reach of Authoritarian Powers,' *Democratization* 24, no. 7, 1326–1344.

Buchanan, James M., and Gordon Tullock. 1962. *The Calculus of Consent: Logical Foundations of Constitutional Democracy*. Ann Arbor: University of Michigan Press.

Bueno de Mesquita, Bruce, Smith, Alastair, Siverson, Randolph M., and James D. Morrow. 2003. *The Logic of Political Survival*. London: The MIT Press.

Bueno de Mesquita, Bruce, and Alastair Smith. 2011. *The Dictator's Handbook. Why Bad Behavior is Almost Always Good Politics*. New York: PublicAffairs.

Bueno de Mesquita, Bruce, and Alastair Smith. 2012. 'Domestic Explanations of International Relations,' *Annual Review of Political Science* 15, 161–181.

Burchi, Francesco. 2011. 'Democracy, Institutions and Famines in Developing and Emerging Countries,' *Canadian Journal of Development Studies* 32, no. 1, 17–31.

Butler, Eamonn. 2012. *Public Choice – A Primer*. London: The Institute of Economic Affairs.

Callinicos, Alex. 2007. *Theories and Narratives. Reflections on the Philosophy of History*. Cambridge: Polity.

Caplan, Bryan. 2001. 'Rational Ignorance Versus Rational Irrationality,' *Kyklos* 54, no. 1, 3–26.

Caplan, Bryan. 2007. *The Myth of the Rational Voter. Why Democracies Choose Bad Policies*. New Jersey: Princeton University Press.

Carpenter, Daniel, and David A. Moss. 2013. 'Introduction,' in Daniel Carpenter and David A. Moss (eds), *Preventing Regulatory Capture: Special Interest Influence and How to Limit It*. New York: Cambridge University Press, 1–22.

Carpenter, Jeffrey, Verhoogen, Eric, and Stephen Burks. 2005. 'The Effect of Stakes in Distribution Experiments,' *Economics Letters* 86, no. 3, 393–398.

Cartwright, Nancy. 1983. *How the Laws of Physics Lie*. Oxford: Oxford University Press.

Caughey, Devin, O'Grady, Tom, and Christopher Warshaw. 2019. 'Policy Ideology in European Mass Publics, 1981–2016,' *American Political Science Review* 113, no. 3, 674–693.

Chaiken, Shelly, and Yaacov Trope (eds). 1999. *Dual-Process Theories in Social Psychology*. New York: Guilford Press.

Chan, Tara Francis. 2018. 'China's Social Credit System Has Blocked People from Taking 11 Million Flights and 4 Million Train Trips,' *Business Insider*. Accessible via: https://www.businessinsider.com/china-social-credit-system-blocked-people-taking-flights-train-trips-2018-5?r=UK/.

Che, Yi, Lu, Yi, Tao, Zhigang, and Peng Wang. 2013. 'The Impact of Income on Democracy Revisited,' *Journal of Comparative Economics* 41, no. 1, 159–169;

Chenoweth, Erica, and Maria J. Stephan. 2011. *Why Civil Resistance Works. The Strategic Logic of Nonviolent Conflict*. New York: Columbia University Press.

Chibber, Vivek. 2013. *Postcolonial Theory and the Specter of Capital*. London: Verso.

Choi, Seung-Whan. 2011. 'Re-Evaluating Capitalist and Democratic Peace Models,' *International Studies Quarterly* 55, 759–769.

Choi, Seung-Whan. 2016. 'A Menace to the Democratic Peace? Dyadic and Systemic Difference,' *International Studies Quarterly* 60, 573–577.

Chong, Dennis. 2000. *Rational Lives. Norms and values in Politics and Society*. Chicago: Chicago University Press.

Chong, Dennis, Citrin, Jack, and Patricia Conley. 2001. 'When Self-Interest Matters,' *Political Psychology* 22, no. 3, 541–570.

Clark, Cory J., Liu, Brittany S., Winegard, Bo M., and Peter H. Ditto. 2019. 'Tribalism is Human Nature,' *Current Directions in Psychological Science* 28, no. 6, 587–592.

Clark, William Roberts, Golder, Matt, and Sona Nadenichek Golder. 2013. *Principles of Comparative Politics*. Los Angeles: Sage.

Colantone, Italo, and Piero Stanig. 2018a. 'The Trade Origins of Economic Nationalism: Import Competition and Voting Behavior in Western Europe,' *American Journal of Political Science* 62, no. 4., 936–953.

Colantone, Italo, and Piero Stanig. 2018b. 'Global Competition and Brexit,' *American Political Science Review* 112, no. 2, 201–218.
Converse, Philip. 1990. 'Popular Representation and the Distribution of Information,' in John A. Ferejohn and James H. Kuklinski (eds), *Information and Democratic Processes*. Urbana: University of Illinois Press, 369–388.
Converse, Philip. 2000. 'Assessing the Capacity of Mass Electorates,' *Annual Review of Political Science* 3, 331–353.
Copeland, Dale C. 1996. 'Economic Interdependence and War: A Theory of Trade Expectations,' *International Security* 20, no. 4, 5–41.
Coppedge, Michael, Gerring, John, Knutsen, Carl H., Lidberg, Staffan I., Teorell, Jan, Altman, David, Dernbahrd, Michael, Fish, M. Steven, Glynn, Adam, Hicken, Allen, Lührmann, Anna, Marquardt, Kyle L., McMann, Kelly, Paxton, Pamela, Pemstein, Daniel, Seim, Brigitte, Sigman, Rachel, Skaaning, Svend-Erik, Staton, Jeffrey, Wilson, Steven, Cornell, Agnes, Gastaldi, Lisa, Gjerløw, Haakon, Ilchenko, Nina, Krusell, Joshua, Maxwell, Laura, Mechkova, Valeriya, Medzihorsky, Juraj, Pernes, Josefine, von Römer, Johannes, Stepanova, Natalia, Sundström, Aksel, Tzelgov, Eitan, Wang, Yi-ting, Wig, Tore, Ziblatt, Daniel. 2019. *V-Dem [Country-Year/Country-Date] Dataset v9*. Varieties of Democracy (V-Dem) Project. Accessible via: https://www.v-dem.net/en/data/archive/previous-data/data-version-9/.
Cowen, Tyler, and Alex Tabarrok. 2015. *Modern Principles of Economics*. New York: Worth Publishers.
Crescenzi, Mark J. C., and Kelly M. Kadera. 2016. 'Built to Last: Understanding the Link between Democracy and Conflict in the International System,' *International Studies Quarterly* 60, no. 3, 565–572.
Dafoe, Allan, Oneal, John R., and Bruce Russett. 2013. 'The Democratic Peace: Weighing the Evidence and Cautious Inference,' *International Studies Quarterly* 57, no. 1, 201–214.
Dafoe, Allan. 2011. 'Statistical Critiques of the Democratic Peace: Caveat Emptor,' *American Journal of Political Science* 55, no. 2, 247–262.
Dafoe, Allan. 2014. 'Observing the Capitalist Peace: Examining Market-Mediated Signalling and Other Mechanisms,' *Journal of Peace Research* 51, no. 5, 619–633.
Dahlum, Sirianne, Knutsen, Carl Henrik, and Tore Wig. 2019. 'Who Revolts? Empirically Revisiting the Social Origins of Democracy,' *The Journal of Politics* 81, no. 4, 1494–1499.
Dawisha, Karen. 2014. *Putin's Kleptocracy. Who Owns Russia?* New York: Simon & Schuster.
Diamond, Larry. 2008. 'The Democratic Rollback – The Resurgence of the Predatory State,' *Foreign Affairs* 87.
Diamond, Larry. 2015. 'Facing Up to the Democratic Recession,' *Journal of Democracy* 26, no. 1, 141–155.
Dickson, Bruce J. 2016. *The Dictator's Dilemma. The Chinese Communist Party's Strategy for Survival*. New York: Oxford University Press.
Ditto, Petter H., Liu, Brittany S., Clark, Cory J., Wojcik, Sean P., Chen, Eric E., Grady, Rebecca H., Celniker, Jared B., and Joanne F. Zinger. 2019. 'At Least Bias Is Bipartisan: A Meta-Analytic Comparison of Partisan Bias in Liberals and Conservatives,' *Perspectives on Psychological Science* 14, no. 2, 273–291.
Downes, Alexander B. 2012. 'The Illusion of Democratic Credibility,' *International Organization* 66, no. 3, 457–489.
Downs, Anthony 1957. *An Economic Theory of Democracy*. New York: Harper & Row.
Dunning, David. 2011. 'The Dunning-Kruger Effect: On Being Ignorant of One's Own Ignorance,' *Advances in Experimental Social Psychology* 44, 247–296.
Evans, J. S. 2008. 'Dual-Process Accounts of Reasoning, Judgement, and Social Cognition,' *Annual Review of Psychology* 59, 255–278.

Ezrow, Natasha M., and Erica Frantz. 2011. *Dictators and Dictatorships. Understanding Authoritarian Regimes and Their Leaders*. London: Continuum, 2011.
Faria, Hugo J., Montesinos-Yufa, Hugo M., and Daniel R. Morales. 2014. 'Should Modernization Hypothesis Survive Acemoglu, Johnson, Robinson, and Yared? Some More Evidence,' *Econ Journal Watch* 11, no. 1, 17–36.
Farrell, Henry, and Steven M. Teles. 2017. 'When Politics Drives Scholarship,' *Boston Review*. Accessible via: https://bostonreview.net/class-inequality/henry-farrell-steven-m-teles-when-politics-drives-scholarship/.
Fearon, Jamesa D. 1995. 'Rationalist Explanations for War,' *International Organization* 49, no. 3, 379–414.
Felipe, Jesus, Bayudan-Dacuycuy, Connie, and Matteo Lanzafame. 2016. 'The Declining Share of Agricultural Employment in China: How Fast?' *Structural Change and Economic Dynamics* 37, 127–137.
Ferraz, Claudio, and Frederico Finan. 2008. 'Exposing Corrupt Politicians: The Effect of Brazil's Publicly Released Audits on Electoral Outcomes,' *Quarterly Journal of Economics* 123, no. 2, 703–745.
Ferraz, Claudio, and Frederico Finan. 2011. 'Electoral Accountability and Corruption: Evidence from the Audits of Local Governments,' *American Economic Review* 101, no. 4, 1274–1311.
Flynn, James R. 2009. 'Requiem for Nutrition as the Cause of IQ Gains: Raven's Gains in Britain 1938–2008,' *Economics and Human Biology* 7, no. 1, 18–27.
Foa, Roberto S., and Yascha Mounk. 2016. 'The Dangers of Deconsolidation: The Democratic Disconnect,' *Journal of Democracy* 27, no. 3, 5–17.
Foa, Roberto S., and Yascha Mounk. 2017. 'The Signs of Deconsolidation,' *Journal of Democracy* 28, no. 1, 5–15.
Freedom House. 2021. 'Country and Territory Ratings and Statuses, 1973–2021.' Accessible via: https://freedomhouse.org/report/freedom-world/.
Friedman, Milton. 1953. *Essays in Positive Economics*. Chicago: Chicago University Press.
Fry, Douglas (ed.). 2013. *War, Peace, and Human Nature: The Convergence of Evolutionary and Cultural Views*. Oxford: Oxford University Press.
Fukuyama, Francis. 1989. 'The End of History?' *The National Interest*, no. 16, 3–18.
Fukuyama, Francis. 1992. *The End of History and the Last Man*. New York: The Free Press.
Gaddis, John Lewis. 1986. 'The Long Peace: Elements of Stability in the Postwar International System,' *International Security* 10, no. 4, 99–142.
Gartzke, Erik, and Yonatan Lupu. 2012. 'Trading on Preconceptions. Why World War I Was Not a Failure of Economic Interdependence,' *International Security* 36, no. 4, 115–150.
Gat, Azar. 2015. 'Proving Communal Warfare Among Hunter-Gatherers: The Quasi-Rousseauan Error,' *Evolutionary Anthropology* 24, no. 3, 111–126.
Gat, Azar. 2017. *The Causes of War and The Spread of Peace: But Will War Rebound?* Oxford: Oxford University Press.
Gat, Azar. 2019. 'Is War in Our Nature? What is Right and What Is Wrong about the Seville Statement on Violence,' *Human Nature* 30, 149–154.
Geddes, Barbara. 1999. 'What do We Know About Democratization After Twenty Years?,' *Annual Review of Political Science* 2, 115–144.
Geddes, Barbara. 2018. 'Why Dictators Use Semi-Competitive Elections and Encourage the Use of Semi-Independent Courts: A Comment on Thornhill and Smirnova's "Litigation and Political Transformation",' *Theory and Society* 47, no. 5, 595–601.
Geddes, Barbara, Wright, Joseph, and Erica Frantz. 2018. *How Dictatorships Work. Power Personalization, and Collapse*. Cambridge: Cambridge University Press.
Gandhi, Jennifer. 2008. *Political Institutions Under Dictatorship*. Cambridge: Cambridge University Press.

Glaser, Charles L. 1997. 'The Security Dilemma Revisited,' *World Politics* 50, no. 1, 171–201.
Goldthorpe, John H. 2007. *On Sociology. Volume One: Critique and Program*. Cambridge: Cambridge University Press.
Goldthorpe, John H. 2016. *Sociology as a Population Science*. Cambridge: Cambridge University Press.
Grigoryan, Arman. 2020. 'Selective Wilsonianism: Material Interests and the West's Support for Democracy,' *International Security* 44, no. 4, 158–200.
Gwartney, James D., Stroup, Richard L., Sobel, Russell S., and David A. MacPherson. 2011. *Microeconomics: Private and Public Choice*. Ohio: South-Western Cengage Learning.
Gwartney, James, Lawson, Robert, Hall, Joshua, and Ryan Murphy. 2018. *Economic Freedom of the World. 2018 Annual Report*. Fraser Institute. Accessible via: https://www.fraserinstitute.org/studies/economic-freedom/.
Haggard, Stephan, and Robert R. Kaufman. 1995. *The Political Economy of Democratic Transitions*. Princeton: Princeton University Press.
Haggard, Stephan, and Robert R. Kaufman. 2015. *Dictators and Democrats. Masses, Elites and Regime Change*. Princeton: Princeton University Press.
Hainmueller, Jens, and Daniel J. Hopkins. 2014. 'Public Attitudes Toward Immigration,' *Annual Review of Political Science* 17, 225–249.
Hardin, Garett. 1968. 'The Tragedy of the Commons,' *Science* 162, no. 3859, 1243–1248.
Healy, Andrew, and Neil Malhotra. 2013. 'Retrospective Voting Reconsidered,' *Annual Review of Political Science* 16, 285–306.
Hedström, Peter. 2005. *Dissecting the Social: On the Principles of Analytical Sociology*. Cambridge: Cambridge University Press.
Hegre, Havard. 2009. 'Trade Dependence or Size Dependence?' *Conflict Management and Peace Science* 26, no. 1, 26–45.
Heid, Benedikt, Langer, Julian, and Mario Larch. 2012. 'Income and Democracy: Evidence from System GMM Estimates,' *Economics Letters* 116, 166–169.
Hoffman, Elizabeth, McCabe, Kevin, Shachat, Keith, and Vernon Smith. 1994. 'Preferences, Property Rights, and Anonymity in Bargaining Games,' *Games and Economic Behavior* 7, no. 3, 346–380.
Holcombe, Randall G. 2016. *Advance Introduction to Public Choice*. Massachusetts: Edward Elgar Publishing.
Hou, Yue. 2019. *The Private Sector in Public Office: Selective Property Rights in China*. Cambridge: Cambridge University Press.
Hsieh, Chang-Tai, and Peter J. Klenow. 2009. 'Misallocation and Manufacturing TFP in China and India,' *The Quarterly Journal of Economic* 124, no. 4, 1403–1448.
Huang, Jikun, Otsuka, Keijiro, and Scott Rozelle. 2008. 'Agriculture in China's Development: Past Disappointments, Recent Successes, and Future Challenges' in Loren Brandt and Thomas G. Rawski (eds), *China's Great Transformation*. Cambridge: Cambridge University Press, 467–505.
Hung, Ho-fung. 2016. *The China Boom. Why China Will Not Rule the World*. New York: Columbia University Press.
Ipsos MORI. 2016a. 'The Perils of Perception and the EU.' Accessible via: https://www.ipsos.com/ipsos-mori/en-uk/perils-perception-and-eu/.
Ipsos MORI. 2016b. 'Perceptions are Not Reality: What the World Gets Wrong.' Accessible via: https://www.ipsos.com/ipsos-mori/en-uk/perceptions-are-not-reality-what-world-gets-wrong/.
Ipsos MORI. 2018a. 'Public Wrong on Key Facts Around Brexit and Impact of EU Membership.' Accessible via: https://www.ipsos.com/ipsos-mori/en-uk/public-wrong-key-facts-around-brexit-and-impact-eu-membership/.

Ipsos MORI. 2018b. 'The Perils of Perception 2018.' Accessible via: https://www.ipsos.com/ipsos-mori/en-uk/perils-perception-2018/.

Jervis, Robert. 1976. *Perception and Misperception in International Politics*. Princeton: Princeton University Press.

Jost, John T. 2017. 'Ideological Asymmetries and the Essence of Political Psychology,' *Political Psychology* 38, no. 2, 167–208.

Kadivar, Mohammad Ali, Usmani, Adaner, and Benjamin H. Bradlow. 2019. 'The Long March: Deep Democracy in Cross-National Perspective,' *Social Forces* 98, no. 3, 1311–1338.

Kahan, Dan M. 2013. 'Ideology, Motivated Reasoning, and Cognitive Reflection,' *Judgment and Decision Making* 8, no. 4, 407–424.

Kahan, Dan M., Landrum, Asheley, Carpenter, Katie, Helft, Laura, and Kathleen Hall Jamieson. 2017. 'Science Curiosity and Political Information Processing,' *Political Psychology* 38, no. 1, 179–199.

Kahan, Dan M., Peters, Ellen, Dawson, Erica Cantrell, and Paul Slovic. 2017. 'Motivated Numeracy and Enlightened Self-Government,' *Behavioural Public Policy* 1, no. 1, 54–86.

Kahneman, Daniel. 2011. *Thinking, Fast and Slow*. New York: Farrar, Straus and Giroux.

Karatnycky, Adrian, and Peter Ackerman. 2005. 'How Freedom Is Won: From Civic Resistance to Durable Democracy,' *International Journal of Not-for-Profit Law* 7, no. 3.

Kelly, Robert L. 2013. 'From the Peaceful to the Warlike: Ethnographic and Archaeological Insights into Hunter-Gatherer Warfare and Homicide,' in Douglas P. Fry (ed.), *War, Peace, and Human Nature: The Convergence of Evolutionary and Cultural Views*. Oxford: Oxford University Press, 151–167.

Kendall-Taylor, Andrea, and Erica Frantz. 2014. 'How Autocracies Fall,' *The Washington Quarterly* 37, no. 1, 35–47.

Keohane, Robert O. 1986. 'Theory of World Politics: Structural Realism and Beyond,' in Robert O. Keohane (ed.), *Neorealism and Its Critics*. New York: Columbia University Press, 190–197.

Kiewiet, D. Roderick, and Michael S. Lewis-Beck. 2011. 'No Man is an Island: Self-Interest, The Public Interest, and Sociotropic Voting,' *Critical Review. A Journal of Politics and Society* 23, no. 3, 303–319.

Kim, Nam Kyu, and Alex Kroeger. 2017. 'Rewarding the Introduction of Multiparty Elections,' *European Journal of Political Economy* 49, 164–181.

Kinsella, David. 2005. 'No Rest for the Democratic Peace,' *The American Political Science Review* 99, no. 3, 453–457.

Kiser, Edgar, and Michael Hechter. 1998. 'The Debate on Historical Sociology: Rational Choice Theory and Its Critics,' *American Journal of Sociology* 104, no. 3, 785–816.

Kiser, Edgar. 2006. 'Mann's Microfoundations: Addressing the Neo-Weberian Dilemmas,' in J. A. Hall and R. Schroeder (eds), *An Anatomy of Power. The Social Theory of Michael Mann*. Cambridge: Cambridge University Press, 56–70.

Kostka, Genia. 2019. 'China's Social Credit Systems and Public Opinion: Explaining High Levels of Approval,' *New Media & Society* 21, no. 7, 1–29.

Kroenig, Matthew. 2020a. *The Return of Great Power Rivalry: Democracy Versus Autocracy from the Ancient World to the U.S. and China*. Oxford: Oxford University Press.

Kroenig, Matthew. 2020b. 'Why the U.S. Will Outcompete China,' *The Atlantic*. Accessible via: https://www.theatlantic.com/ideas/archive/2020/04/why-china-ill-equipped-great-power-rivalry/609364/.

Kuran, Timur. 1997. *Private Truths, Public Lies: The Social Consequences of Preference Falsification*. Harvard: Harvard University Press.

Laband, David, and John Sophocleus. 1988. 'The Social Cost of Rent-Seeking: First Estimates,' *Public Choice* 58, 269–275.

Lafrance, Xavier, and Charles Post (eds). 2019. *Case Studies in the Origins of Capitalism.* Cham: Palgrave Macmillan.
Lake, David A., and Matthew A. Baum. 2001. 'The Invisible Hand of Democracy: Political Control and the Provision of Public Service,' *Comparative Political Studies* 34, no. 6, 587–621.
Le Grand, Julian. 1991. 'The Theory of Government Failure,' *British Journal of Political Science* 21, no. 4, 423–442.
Leng, Sidney. 2019. 'China's GDP Growth Could Be Half of Reported Number, Says US Economist at Prominent Chinese University,' *South China Morning Post.* Accessible via: https://tinyurl.com/y26yogp7/.
Levitsky, Steven, and Lucan A. Way. 2010. *Competitive Authoritarianism: Hybrid Regimes After the Cold War.* Cambridge: Cambridge University Press.
Levitt, Steven D., and John A. List. 2007. 'What Do Laboratory Experiments Measuring Social Preferences Reveal About the Real World?' *Journal of Economic Perspectives* 21, no. 2, 153–174.
Lewis-Beck, Michael S. 2000. 'Economic Determinants of Electoral Outcomes,' *Annual Review of Political Science* 3, 183–219.
Li Donni, Paolo, and Maria Marino. 2020. 'The Role of Collective Action for the Emergence and Consolidation of Democracy,' *Journal of Institutional Economics*, 1–32.
Lipset, Seymour Martin. 1959. 'Some Social Requisites of Democracy: Economic Development and Political Legitimacy,' *American Political Science Review* 53, no. 1, 69–105.
List, John A. 2006. 'The Behavioralist Meets the Market: Measuring Social Preferences and Reputation Effects in Actual Transactions,' *Journal of Political Economy* 114, no. 1, 1–3.
Lührmann, Anna, Maerz, Seraphine, Grahn, Sandra, Gastaldi, Lisa, Hellmeier, Sebastian, Alizada, Nazifa, Hindle, Garry, and Staffan I. Lindberg. 2020. *V-Dem Democracy Report 2020. Autocratization Surges–Resistance Grows.* Gothenburg: V-Dem Institute, University of Gothenburg.
MacLean, Nancy. 2017. *Democracy in Chains: The Deep History of the Radical Right's Stealth Plan for America.* New York: Random House, 2017.
Mansfield, Edward D., and Diana C. Mutz. 2009. 'Support for Free Trade: Self-Interest, Sociotropic Politics, and Out-Group Anxiety,' *International Organization* 63, no. 3, 425–457.
Mann, Michael. 1986. *The Sources of Social Power, Volume 1: A History from the Beginning to 1760 AD.* Cambridge: Cambridge University Press.
Maoz, Zeev, Johnson, Paul L., Kaplan, Jasper, Ogunkoya, Fiona, and Aaron P. Shreve. 2019. 'The Dyadic Militarized Interstate Disputes (MIDs) Dataset Version 3.0: Logic, Characteristics, and Comparisons to Alternative Datasets,' *Journal of Conflict Resolution* 63, no. 3, 811–835.
Maoz, Zeev. 1997. 'The Controversy over the Democratic Peace: Rearguard Action or Cracks in the Wall?' *International Security* 22, no. 1, 162–198.
Maoz, Zeev. 1998. 'Realist and Cultural Critiques of the Democratic Peace: A Theoretical and Empirical Re-Assessment,' *International Interactions* 24, no. 1, 38–44.
Margalit, Yotam M. 2012. 'Lost in Globalization: International Economic Integration and the Sources of Popular Discontent,' *International Studies Quarterly* 56, no. 3, 484–500.
Margalit, Yotam M. 2013. 'Explaining Social Policy Preferences: Evidence from the Great Recession,' *The American Political Science Review* 107, no. 1, 80–103.
Margalit, Yotam M. 2019. 'Political Responses to Economic Shocks,' *Annual Review of Political Science* no. 22, 277–295.
McLaughlin, Kathleen E. 2005. 'Chinese Protesting More as Social Problems Grow/Beijing May Find It Harder to Take Reins,' *SFGATE.* Accessible via: https://www.sfgate.com/politics/article/Chinese-protesting-more-as-social-problems-grow-2637039.php/.

Mearsheimer, John J. 1990. 'Back to the Future: Instability in Europe after the Cold War,' *International Security* 15, no. 1, 5–56.
Mearsheimer, John J. 2001. *The Tragedy of Great Power Politics*. New York: University of Chicago.
Mearsheimer, John J. 2010. 'Why Is Europe Peaceful Today?' *European Political Science* 9, 387–397.
Mearsheimer, John J. 2013. 'Structural Realism,' in Tim Dunne, Milja Kurki and Steve Smith (eds), *International Relations Theories: Disciple and Diversity*. Oxford: Oxford University Press, 77–93.
Mearsheimer, John J. 2018. *The Great Delusion: Liberal Dreams and International Realities*. New Haven: Yale University Press.
Mercier, Hugo. 2020. *Not Born Yesterday. The Science of Who We Trust and What We Believe*. Princeton: Princeton University Press.
Mifune, Nobuhiro, Hashimoto, Hirofumi, and Toshio Yamagishi. 2010. 'Altruism Toward In-group Members as a Reputation Mechanism,' *Evolution and Human Behavior* 31, no. 2, 109–117.
Moore, Barrington. 1966. *Social Origins of Dictatorship and Democracy: Lord and Peasant in the Making of the Modern World*. Boston: Beacon Press.
Moravcsik, Andrew. 1997. 'Taking Preferences Seriously: A Liberal Theory of International Politics,' *International Organization* 51, no. 4, 513–553.
Mousseau, Michael, Hegre, Havard, and John R. Oneal. 2003. 'How the Wealth of Nations Conditions the Liberal Peace,' *European Journal of International Relations* 9, no. 2, 277–314.
Mutz, Diana. 2018. 'Status Threat, Not Economic Hardship, Explains the 2016 Presidential Vote,' *Proceedings of the National Academy of Sciences of the United States of America* 115, no. 19, E4330–E4339.
NCCS. 2015. 'Charitable Giving in America: Some Facts and Figures.' Accesible via: https://nccs.urban.org/data-statistics/charitable-giving-america-some-facts-and-figures/.
Norris, Pippa. 2017. 'Is Western Democracy Backsliding? Diagnosing the Risks,' *Journal of Democracy* Web Exchange. Accessible via: https://www.hks.harvard.edu/publications/western-democracy-backsliding-diagnosing-risks.
North, Douglass C. 1990. *Institutions, Institutional Change, and Economic Performance*. Cambridge: Cambridge University Press.
North, Douglass C., Wallis, John J., and Barry R. Weingast. 2009. *Violence and Social Orders. A Conceptual Framework for Interpreting Recorded Human History*. Cambridge: Cambridge University Press.
Olson, Mancur. 1965. *The Logic of Collective Action*. Cambridge: Harvard University Press.
Oneal, John R., and Bruce M. Russett. 2005. 'Rule of Three, Let It Be. When More Really is Better,' *Conflict Management and Peace Science* 22, no. 4, 293–310.
Opp, Karl-Dieter. 2017. 'When Do People Follow Norms and When Do They Pursue Their Interests? Implications of Dual-Process Models and Rational Choice Theory, Tested for Protest Participation,' in Benn Jann and Wojtek Przepiorka (eds), *Social Dilemmas, Institutions and the Evolution of Cooperation*. Berlin: de Gruyter, 119–141.
Oswald, Margit E., and Stefan Grosjean. 2004. 'Confirmation Bias,' in Rüdiger F. Pohl (ed.), *Cognitive Illusions. A Handbook on Fallacies and Biases in Thinking, Judgement and Memory*. New York: Psychology Press.
Owens, Lindsay A., and David S. Pedulla. 2014. 'Material Welfare and Changing Political Preferences: The Case of Support for Redistributive Social Policies,' *Social Forces* 92, no. 3, 1087–1113.
Persson, Anna, Rothstein, Bo, and Jan Teorell. 2012. 'Why Anticorruption Reforms Fail–Systemic Corruption as a Collective Action Problem,' *Governance* 26, no. 3, 449–471.

Phillips, John A., and Charles Wetherell. 1995. 'The Great Reform Act of 1832 and the Political Modernization of England,' *The American Historical Review* 100, no. 2, 411–436.
Pinker, Steven. 2012. *The Better Angels of Our Nature: Why Violence Has Declined.* New York: Penguin.
Pinker, Steven. 2018. *Enlightenment Now: The Case for Reason, Science, Humanism, and Progress.* New York: Viking.
Posner, Richard A. 2013. 'The Concept of Regulatory Capture: A Short, Inglorious History,' in Daniel Carpenter and David A. Moss (eds), *Preventing Regulatory Capture: Special Interest Influence and How to Limit It.* New York: Cambridge University Press, 49–56.
Przeworski, Adam, and Fernando Limongi. 1997. 'Modernization: Theories and Facts,' *World Politics* 49, no. 2, 155–183.
Przeworski, Adam. 2005. 'Democracy as an Equilibrium,' *Public Choice* 123, no. ¾, 253–273.
Przeworski, Adam, Alvarez, Michael R., Alvarez, Michael E., Cheibub, Jose Antonio, and Frenando Limongi. 2000. *Democracy and Development: Political Institutions and Well-Being in the World, 1950–1999.* Cambridge: Cambridge University Press.
Rand, David G., and Martin A. Nowak. 2013. 'Human Cooperation,' *Trends in Cognitive Sciences* 17, no. 8, 413–425.
Ray, James Lee, and Allan Dafoe. 2017. 'Democratic Peace versus Contractualism,' *Conflict Management and Peace Science* 35, no. 2, 193–203.
Recording. 2019. A Recording of the 3rd Regular Session of the Health Committee in Slovenia. Accessible via: https://4d.rtvslo.si/arhiv/seje-odbora-za-zdravstvo/174623919/.
Reiter, Dan, and Allan C. Stam. 2002. *Democracies at War.* Princeton: Princeton University Press.
Reiter, Dan. 2012. 'Democracy, Deception, and Entry into War,' *Security Studies* 21, no. 4, 594–623.
Reiter, Dan. 2017. 'Is Democracy a Cause of Peace?' in *Oxford Research Encyclopedia of Politics.* Available via: https://oxfordre.com/politics/view/10.1093/acrefore/9780190228637.001.0001/acrefore-9780190228637-e-287/.
Rho, Sungmin, and Michael Tomz. 2017. 'Why Don't Trade Preferenes Reflect Economic Self-Interest?' *International Organization* 71, no. S1, S85–S108.
Rindermann, Heiner, Becker, David, and Thomas R. Coyle. 2017. 'Survey of Expert Opinion on Intelligence: The Flynn Effect and the Future of Intelligence,' *Personality and Individual Differences* 106, 242–247.
Roessler, Martin. 2019. 'Political Regimes and Publicly Provided Goods: Why Democracy Needs Development,' *Public Choice* 180, 301–331.
Rosen, Jill. 2018. 'American's Don't Know Much About State Government, Survey Finds,' Johns Hopkins University. Accessible via: https://hub.jhu.edu/2018/12/14/americans-dont-understand-state-government/.
Roser, Max. 2013. 'Democracy,' *OurWorldInData.* Accessible via: https://ourworldindata.org/democracy/.
Roser, Max, and Esteban Ortiz-Ospina. 2020. 'Income Inequality,' *OurWorldInData.* Accessible via: https://ourworldindata.org/income-inequality/.
Ross, Michael L. 2001. 'Does Oil Hinder Democracy?' *World Politics* 53, no. 3, 325–361.
Ross, Michael L. 2011. 'Will Oil Drown the Arab Spring?' *Foreign Affairs* 90, no. 5.
Ross, Michael L. 2013. *The Oil Curse. How Petroleum Wealth Shapes the Development of Nations.* Princeton: Princeton University Press.
Ross, Michael L. 2015. 'What Have We Learned about the Resource Curse?' *Annual Review of Political Science* 18, 239–259.
Rueschemeyer, Dietrich, Stephens, Evelyne H., and John D. Stephens. 1992. *Capitalist Development and Democracy.* Chicago: University of Chicago Press.

Russett, Bruce. 2009. 'Democracy, War, and Expansion through Historical Lenses,' *European Journal of International Relations* 15, no. 1, 9–36.
Russett, Bruce. 2010. 'Capitalism or Democracy? Not So Fast,' *International Interactions* 36, no. 2, 198–205.
Russett, Bruce. 2013. 'Liberalism,' in Tim Dunne, Milja Kurki, and Steve Smith (eds), *International Relations Theories: Disciple and Diversity*. Oxford: Oxford University Press, 94–113.
Rutar, Tibor. 2019. 'For an Integrative Theory of Social Behaviour: Theorising with and Beyond Rational Choice Theory,' *Journal for the Theory of Social Behaviour* 49, no. 3, 298–311.
Rutar, Tibor. 2020. '"Varieties of 'Rationality'" and the Question of their Continued Theoretical Relevance,' *Social Science Information* 59, no. 4.
Scott, James C. 1985. *Weapons of the Weak: Everyday Forms of Peasant Resistance*. New Haven: Yale University Press.
Singer, Peter. 1996. *Marx. A Very Short Introduction*. Oxford: Oxford University Press.
Snyder, Jack, and Erica D. Borghard. 2011. 'The Cost of Empty Threats: A Penny, Not a Pound,' *American Political Science Review* 105, no. 3, 437–456.
Somin, Ilya. 2013. *Democracy and Political Ignorance. Why Smaller Government Is Smarter*. Stanford: Stanford University Press.
Stasavage, David. 2020. *The Decline and Rise of Democracy: A Global History from Antiquity to Today*. Princeton: Princeton Unviersity Press.
Stigler, George J. 1971. 'The Theory of Economic Regulation,' *The Bell Journal of Economics and Management Science* 2, no. 1, 3–21.
Stiglitz, Joseph. 1998. 'Distinguished Lecture on Economics in Government: The Private Uses of Public Interests: Incentives and Institutions,' *Journal of Economic Perspectives* 12, no. 2, 3–22.
Svolik, Milan W. 2012. *The Politics of Authoritarian Rule*. New York: Cambridge University Press.
Tang, Shiping. 2008. 'Fear in International Politics: Two Positions,' *International Studies Review* 10, 451–471.
Therborn, Göran. 1979. 'The Rule of Capital and the Rise of Democracy,' *New Left Review* 103, 3–41.
Tilly, Charles. 1985. 'War Making and State Making as Organized Crime,' in Peter B. Evans, Dietrich Rueschemeyer and Theda Skocpol (eds), *Bringing the State Back*. Cambridge: Cambridge University Press, 169–191.
Tomz, Michael R., and Jessica L. P. Weeks. 2013. 'Public Opinion and the Democratic Peace,' *American Political Science Review* 107, no. 4, 849–865.
Treisman, Daniel. 2020a. 'Economic Development and Democracy: Predispositions and Triggers,' *Annual Review of Political Science* 23, 241–257.
Treisman, Daniel. 2020b. 'Democracy by Mistake: How the Errors of Autocrats Trigger Transitions to Freer Government,' *American Political Science Review* 114, no. 3, 792–810.
Udehn, Lars. 1995. *The Limits of Public Choice. A Sociological Critique of the Economic Theory of Politics*. London: Routledge.
Usmani, Adaner. 2018. 'Democracy and Class Struggle,' *American Journal of Sociology* 124, no. 3, 664–704.
van Noort, Sam. 2019. 'The Structural Economic Roots of Liberal Democracy,' Working Paper. Accessible via: https://tinyurl.com/yye6p6me/.
Waltz, Kenneth N. 2000. 'Structural Realism after the Cold War,' *International Security* 25, no. 1, 10–11.
Williamson, Jeffrey. 2009. 'Latin American Inequality Since 1491,' VOX CEPR Policy Portal. Accessible via: https://voxeu.org/article/latin-american-inequality-1491/.
Winston, Clifford. 2006. *Government Failure versus Market Failure: Microeconomics Policy Research and Government Performance*. Washington: Brookings.

Wintrobe, Ronald. 1998. *The Political Economy of Dictatorship*. New York: Cambridge University Press.
World Bank. 2020. Accessible via: https://data.worldbank.org/indicator/NY.GDP.PCAP.KD.ZG?locations=CN/.
Xiaojun, Li. 2012. 'China's Geoeconomic Strategy: China as a Trading Superpower,' in Nicholas Kitchen (ed.), *SR012. IDEAS Reports – Special Reports*. London: The London School of Economics and Political Science.
Xin, Zhou. 2018. 'The Question Mark Hanging Over China's 400 Million-Strong Middle Class,' *South China Morning Post*. Accessible via: https://www.scmp.com/economy/china-economy/article/2168177/question-mark-hanging-over-chinas-400-million-strong-middle/.
Yudkin, Daniel, Hawkins, Stephen, and Tim Dixon. 2019. *The Perception Gap: How False Impressions are Pulling Americans Apart*. New York: More in Common.
Zafirovski, Milan Z. 1999. 'Public Choice Theory for Political Sociology,' *International Journal of Politics, Culture, and Society* 12, no. 3, 465–502.
Zaho, Jianzi. 2019. 'Chinese State-Owned Companies, Misallocation and the Reform Policy,' *Chinese Political Science Review* 4, 28–51.

INDEX

Acemoglu, Daron 22, 24, 29–30, 52–53
activists 8–9, 130
Africa 32, 34, 41, 42, 98; Algeria 36, 132; Benin 41; Liberia 32; Morocco 125; Senegal 44; Sudan 132; Tanzania 32; Uganda 32
aggregation 67–69, 78, 133
Ahmadinejad, Mahmoud 36
Algeria 36, 132
altruism 9, 91, 96–97, 105; of politicians 98, 101
Amin, Idi 32
anarchy 117–118, 121
Ancient Athens 2
Antigua and Barbuda 45
Arab Spring 31, 33, 34, 50, 124, 133
Argentina 45, 47–48
Armenia 132
Arrow, Kenneth 10
Asia: Hong Kong 132; *see also* China
al-Assad, Bashar 33
asymmetric information 87
atomism, methodological 11
Austria-Hungary 125
authoritarian regimes: in Africa 34; in China 19; downfall of 32; in Eastern Europe 34; hard and soft 42–44; historical 2; and human rights 55; in Iran 32; in Latin America 34; in the Middle East 35–36; popular resistance in 35; rejection of 9; repression by 32–33, 39, 42; reversion to 42; in Russia 19, 32; threat of elite coups in 37–38

autocratic regimes: in China 3, 52; compared to democracies 110–114, 123, 132, 134; illiberal 1–2, 3; and incentives for peace 113, 114; liberalization of 17; popular resistance to 25, 35; public interest in 103; regression to 48; in Russia 3; sanctions against 41–42; social welfare in 96 in Uganda 32
availability heuristic 70

Bahrain 34
Balkan wars 125
behaviour: influences on 69–70; political 18, 135; of politicians 98; pro-social 97; reciprocal 97; rent-seeking 18–19; and social context 14; socially pernicious 12–13; socially responsible 91; unconscious 15; of voters 135
behavioural economics 69, 97
Belarus 132
Benin 41
Berlin wall 35
biases 15; cognitive 72, 74, 75–76; confirmation bias 71–72; political 18, 74; of retrospective voting 18; tribal 73
Black, Duncan 10
Black Mirror episodes 50
Boix, Carles 24, 98
Bokassa, Jean-Bédel 32
Bolivia 132
Boudon, Raymond 11
Brazil 47, 63, 124
Brennan, Jason 80

Britain: economic development in 30; international trade 125; politics in 29–30; referendum to leave EU 60–61, 63, 64, 76–77; suffrage in 30
Buchanan, James 10, 96

Canada 61
capitalism 19; compared to socialism 84–85; and democracy 46, 109–116, 131; emergence of 26; and incentives 12; industrial/post-industrial 28–29; liberal-democratic 19, 133; liberal-democratic vs. authoritarian state 19; in Russia 104; spread and consolidation of 133; state-led 19, 54, 104; urban workers under 29–30; victory of 131
capitalist peace theory 19, 110, 114–116, 127; realist critique of 124–126
censorship 54
Central Africa 32; see also Africa
Chartist movement 30
Chile 44, 47, 124
China: authoritarian/autocratic regime in 3, 19, 52; democratization in 49–54; dictatorship in 132; economic development in 132; entrepreneurs in 52, 132; foreign investment in 50; and the household responsibility system 48–50; labor and social unrest in 50; modernization in 50; privatization in 50; pro-democratic protests in 50, 51; prospects of democracy in 17; social control in 17; Social Credit System (SCS) 50–51; urban boom in 52–53
Choi, Seung-Whan 127
clientelism 8, 135
cognitive ability 62, 73–74; see also intelligence
cognitive insufficiency 18, 62–63
Cold War 41, 124
Coleman, James 11
collective action 25, 37
confirmation bias 71–72
conflict resolution, non-violent 114, 123–124
constructivism 109
Converse, Philip 61
corruption 8, 19, 52, 98–100, 105, 135
cost efficiency 85–86
Costa Rica 47
credible signalling 111, 113, 115–116, 123
Crescenzi, Mark 127
critical theory 16
cultural evolution 15
curiosity 18, 73–75

Dafoe, Allan 127
Dai Guofang 52–53
de Mesquita, Bruce Bueno 88, 101, 102–103
decision-making 2, 15, 68; about values 57–58; democratic 57–59; political 27, 29; rational 17; strategic 38; and voter behaviour 135
defensive realism 118–122, 125
democracy: activist view of 8–9, 130; breakdown of 44–46, 54; and capitalism 109–116, 131; correlation with peace 108–114, 123, 126, 135–136; correlation with wealth 21–23, 45, 96, 105; credible signalling in 111, 113, 115–116, 123; and economic development 11; emergence of 25; historical peculiarity of 1–7; inequalities in 28; international effects of 19, 135–136; low-quality regimes 41; non-liberal 38; norms of 7, 113–114; opponents of 132; percentage of democratic countries 3, 5; popular power constraints in 111; prevalence of (by year) 2; puzzle/riddle of 17, 24–25, 44; realistic view of 130; rise and fall of 134; romanticist view of 8, 130; score in the U.S. 4; share of democratic countries in the world 5; shift in attitudes about 5; state-led 134; utopian view of 8, 130
democratic peace 109, 112–113
democratic peace theory 9, 19, 110, 111–114, 123, 127–128, 136; realist critique of 122–124; spuriousness of 127
democratic recession 3, 5, 7
democratic transitions 17, 24–26, 37, 54, 134; from above 36–44, 134; from below 24–25, 27, 29, 36–37, 42, 134; elite-induced 36–42, 54; in Poland 43–44
democratization: and capitalism 26–27; chaotic 46–48; in China 49–54; delayed 46; effect of exogenous shocks on 17, 30–35, 37, 54; forces leading to 22; international pressures for 41–42; in Latin America 46–48; and the middle class 27; and power-sharing 37–39; theories of 7; third wave of 41
demonstration effect 34–35
development: and democracy 17; see also economic development
Diamond, Larry 3
dictators: dilemma of 39–40; sharing of power by 37–39
dictatorships: geopolitical perks to 132; reversion to 48–49; U.S. support for 41; warfare started by 132

Index

diffused costs 19
dogmatism 69, 72–73; and curiosity 73–75
Downs, Anthony 10
Dunning, David 72
Dunning-Kruger effect 18, 72

Eastern Europe 34–35; Armenia 132; Balkan wars in 125; Belarus 132; Hungary 35, 63; Romania 32; Serbia 125; *see also* Russia; Soviet Union
echo chambers 75–76
economic development: in Britain 30; in China 132; and economic inequality 28; industrial 23; long-term 53–54; modern 26, 54; and popular rule 21–23; and the resource curse 35–36; and retrospective voting 76–77; in rich democracies 48
Economic Freedom of the World (EFW) index 45–46
economic inequality 28, 46
economic interdependence 116, 124–126
economic reform 53, 132
economic theory, neoclassical 86
economics: behavioural 69, 97; influence on voting 80; institutional 51; vs. politics 124
economics imperialism 10
economy: capitalist 54, 115; downturn in 32–33; political 10; post-industrial 115; reform in China 53–54; separation of politics from 26–27
efficiency 89–92, 94, 106; price 85–86
Egypt 31, 34, 124
El Salvador 47
"End of History, The" (Fukuyama) 19, 130–133
Enlightenment ideals 7, 69
entrepreneurs 10, 27, 84–86, 88, 93–95, 106–107n4; in China 52, 132
Europe: Austria-Hungary 125; France 12, 46, 60, 61, 117, 119, 125; Germany 17, 46, 60, 119, 125, 126; Italy 46, 60, 125; Poland 35, 42–44; *see also* Britain
evolutionary psychology 15, 69, 70, 97
exogenous shocks: and the 'demonstration effect' 34–35; effect on democratization 17, 30–35, 37, 54; reducing means of acquiescence 32–34; weakening capacities for state repression 31–32

fallacies 88; political 69, 75
false consciousness 33
Ferraz, Claudio 99
Finan, Frederico 99
Flynn effect 62
France 12, 46, 60, 61, 117, 119, 125

freedom: average global rate of 4; average rate of in the world 6; modernization and 25–30; political 26–27
free-market welfare states 131–132
Fukuyama, Francis 19, 130–133
functionalism, structural 16

Gambetta, Diego 11
game theory 11, 14
Gat, Azar 127
Gedded, Barbara 33
geopolitics 127, 132
Germanic tribes 2
Germany 17, 46, 60, 119, 125, 126
Gigerenzer, Gerd 68
Goldthorpe, John 11
Gorbachev, Mikhail 35, 44
government failure 18–19, 85, 88–89, 101, 105, 135; areas and causes of 89–93; in democracies 102; in dictatorships 104; and the public interest 102–103; and regulatory capture 92–95; theory of 89; unintended 106; in the U.S. 92
government(s): and economic growth 77; efficiency of 106; hybrid regimes 38, 40–41, 44; and market failure 88–89; popular power constraints on 122; and the primacy of survival 117–118; rationality of 118; support from 76, 80; uncertain intentions of 117; war-making capacity of 117; *see also* authoritarian regimes; autocratic regimes; corruption; democracy; dictatorships
Great Britain *see* Britain
Guatemala 47, 124

Hamas 124
hegemonic/bipolar peace theory 19
heuristics 15, 97; availability heuristic 70; ecologically rational 68; smart 68–69
Holcombe, Randall 105–106
Hong Kong 132
Hungary 35, 63
Huron Indians 2
Hussein, Saddam 32
hybrid regimes 38, 40–41, 44

ideological asymmetry thesis 72–73
ignorance: meta- 72; political 135; rational 63–65, 75; of voters 58–59, 63–65, 75–76, 105
imperialism, economics 10
incentives 15; bad 13; to change economic behaviour 54; determined by institutions and social circumstances 12; economic

28; and economic development 26; for peace 112–114; for politicians 91, 93, 104–105, 123; politicians' response to 98–100; positive 106; power of 11–12; for socially responsible behaviour 91; structural 90; for voters 96
individualism: methodological 11, 96; normative 14
industrial economic development *see* economic development
industrialization 46–48
in-group loyalty 71
intelligence: increase in 62; and political bias 18; *see also* cognitive ability
interactionism, symbolic 16
international pressures 41–42
international relations (IR) 109; absence of certainty in 120; and defensive/offensive realism 118–122; norms of 124; and war 111
international relations (IR) theory 19, 110; liberal vs. realist 19
international trade 125–126
invisible hand 10, 101
Iran 32, 36, 124, 132
Iraq 32, 59–60
Iroquois Indians 2
irrationality: irrational 66; political 67–69, 73; rational 65–69, 75; of voters 135
Israel 31, 124
Italy 46, 60, 125

Kadera, Kelly 127
Kahan, Dan 18
Kahneman, Daniel 68

Latin America: Argentina 45, 47–48; authoritarian regimes in 34; Bolivia 132; Brazil 47, 63, 124; chaotic democratization in 46–48; Chile 44, 47, 124; Costa Rica 47; democracy in 17; economic inequality in 46; El Salvador 47; Guatemala 47, 124; industrialization in 46–48; Nicaragua 44; Venezuela 47
Le Grand, Julian 89, 91
Leopold II 102
Levitsky, Steven 42
liberalism 109–111, 124, 126
Liberia 32
Libya 34
Limongi, Fernando 45
Lipset, Martin Seymour 21, 22

Mann, Michael 10
Margalit, Yotam 80

market failure 85–86, 106; due to asymmetric information 87; due to externalities 86–87; due to public nature of the good 87; due to selfishness of actors 88; government response to 88–92; intentional 93; in the U.S. 92
Marx, Karl 10–11
Marxism 24, 33
Mearsheimer, John 120–124, 126
Mercier, Hugo 33
methodological atomism 11
methodological individualism 11, 96
middle class: in Argentina 47; emergence of 27
Middle East 33, 36; Arab Spring in 31, 33, 34, 50, 124, 133; Bahrain 34; Egypt 31, 34, 124; Iran 32, 36, 124, 132; Iraq 32, 59–60; Israel 31, 124; Libya 34; Saudi Arabia 36; Syria 33, 34
Misperception Index 61
modernization: in China 50; economic 54; and freedom 25–30
modernization theory 17, 21–22, 37, 45–46, 54; evidence for 23; microfoundations for 22; and the resource curse 35–36
monopolies 86, 89–90
Morgenstern, Oscar 14
Morocco 125
Mubarak, Hosni 31
multiparty elections 38, 41, 43–44; as information-gathering device 40; in Poland 44
Muslim Brotherhood 124
Mutz, Diana 79

Nazi ideology 16–17
neoclassical economic theory 86
news media 18, 76, 79
Nicaragua 44
nirvana fallacy 84
nominal selectorate 103
non-democracies 106; compared to democracies 19; and the power of the elite 24; U.S. wars against 122
non-market alternatives 89–90, 91
North America: Canada 61; *see also* United States
North Atlantic Treaty Organization (NATO) 42, 126
n-person social dilemma 13

October Revolution 13
offensive realism 118–122, 125
oil regimes 35–36

Olson, Mancur 10
Oneal, John 127

peasantry, becoming urban workers 29–30
perception gap 18, 76, 79
Philippines 32
philosophy of science 14
Pinker, Steven 9
Poland 35, 42–44
political actors *see* politicians
political economy 10
politicians: incentives for 91, 93, 104–105, 123; motivations of 9–10, 135; response to incentives 98–100; self-interest of 89–90, 98, 101, 105, 106
politics: in Britain 29–30; corruption in 98–99; vs. economics 124; geo- 127, 132; and the need for power 101; and the need for supporters 101–102; and rational choice theory 95–96; of self-help 118; separation from the economy 26–27
popular disobedience 25
popular protests 24, 32, 51, 53
popular resistance 32, 35, 37, 43, 44, 47, 51
positivism 14
Posner, Richard 88
power-sharing 37–39
price efficiency 85–86; *see also* efficiency
principal-agent problems 40
privatization 50, 58
pro-democracy protests 25, 132
prospect theory 15
Przeworski, Adam 45
psychology: evolutionary 15, 69, 70, 97; political 72; social 69, 70, 97; tribal 18, 70–71
public choice: limitations of 95–101
public choice analysis 18–19
public choice theory 10, 95, 98, 100
public good(s) 8, 49, 104–105; non-excludable 87; non-rival 87
Public Goods Game 96–97
Putin, Vladimir 104

rational choice theory 10–11, 13, 100; critiques of 14; and government actors 118; limitations of 15; and politics 95–96; reasons for using 15–17
rational ignorance 18, 63–65
rational irrationality 18, 65–69
rationality: breakdown of 17; epistemic 65; instrumental 65
Ray, James 127
real selectorate 103

realism 109, 110–111; critique of capitalist peace theory 124–126; critique of democratic peace theory 122–124; defensive/offensive 118–122, 125; and international relations 117–122; sub-theories of 121
realist peace theory 126–127
Reform Act of 1832 (Britain) 29–30
regulatory capture 92–95, 102; concentrated benefits and diffused costs 95; strong/weak 93
Reiter, Dan 108, 128
rent-seeking 93–95, 104–105, 106, 135
resource curse 35–36
Robinson, James 22, 24, 29–30, 52–53
Romania 32
romanticists 8, 130
Ross, Michael 36
Rueschemeyer, Dietrich 24
Russett, Bruce 127
Russia 3, 19, 32, 104; *see also* Soviet Union

Sanders, Bernie 131
Saudi Arabia 36
science, positivist philosophy of 14
selectorate theory 19
self-interest 11–12, 13, 15, 16, 41; of bureaucrats 89–90; of economic actors 101; of entrepreneurs 85; of politicians 89–90, 98, 101, 105, 106; of voters 80–81, 96, 101–102
Senegal 44
Serbia 125
Shah of Iran 32
short-sightedness effect 89, 91–92
slavery/slaves 2, 58
Social Credit System (SCS) (China) 50–51
social dilemmas 11, 81, 96; n-person 13
social media 18, 61, 66, 76
social phenomena 11, 106
social psychology 69, 70, 97
socialism 84–85, 131
sociology 13, 14, 96
Solidarity movement 35, 44
Somin, Ilya 59
Soviet Union 41–42, 60, 103, 119, 126; *see also* Cold War; Russia
Stasavage, David 2
state-owned companies (SEOs) 52–53
Stiglitz, Joseph 93
structural functionalism 16
subsidies 89–90, 91, 102
Sudan 132
Sun Liping 50

symbolic interactionism 16
Syria 33, 34

Tanzania 32
taxes 89, 91
theory of collective action problems 10
Therborn, Göran 24
Tilly, Charles 10
Township Village Enterprises (TVEs) 53
tragedy of the commons 13
tribal psychology 18, 70–71
tribalism 70–72, 74–76
Trump, Donald 79
Tsarism 32
Tullock, Gordon 10, 96
Tversky, Amos 68

Udehn, Lars 96
Uganda 32
Ultimatum Game 96–97
United States: and the Cold War 41, 60, 124; democracy score in 4; government failure in 92; power projection capabilities of 127; response to regional instability 42
universal suffrage 2, 30, 98–99
urban workers 29–30
utopians 8, 130
values, decisions about 57–58
Venezuela 47
von Neumann, John 14
voters: becoming informed/educated 18, 58, 100; behaviour of 135; biased 81–82; economic perceptions of 77; egocentric 78–79; ignorance about the other side 75–76; ignorance of 58–59, 105; as the nominal selectorate 103; political illiteracy of 59–62, 135; rational ignorance of 63–65; rational irrationality of 65–69; representative values of 78; self-interest of 80–81, 96, 101–102; uninformed status of 18, 81–82
voting: altruistic 80–81, 100; paradox of 100; 'pocketbook' 78, 80; retrospective 18, 76–77, 91–92; sociotropic 78–81, 96

Waltz, Kenneth 121, 126
warfare 108, 111; and economic interdependence 116; lesser benefits of 115; opportunity costs of 116; public opinion regarding 111–112, 123; World War I 119, 125–126; World War II 119, 126
Way, Lucan 42
wealth inequality 28, 46
Weber, Max 10–11
Welfare Economics, First Fundamental Theorem of 87
welfare states 60, 131–132
winning coalition 103, 106
women's rights 2
worker emancipation 27

Yemen 34

Zambia 41

Printed in the United States
by Baker & Taylor Publisher Services